# The Journey Of A Lifetime



Larry L Booker

LIGHTHOUSE PUBLICATIONS

# The Journey Of A Lifetime
by Larry Booker



Published in the United States of America.
Printed in the United States of America.



ISBN 0-9717329-1-4
U.S. $12.95 / CAN $18.95

Cover and book design by Matt Jones of 7Dcreative.com
Back cover illustration by Mary Yoder

For publications and tapes please contact:

Lighthouse Publications
PO Box 520
Rialto, CA 92377
Phone: 909-820-2393
Fax: 909-820-6264
www.inlandlighthouse.com
sales@inlandlighthouse.com

## Dedication

To my Mother and Father,
Who loved me anyway.

To Bill,
God Bless You
So much!

# Table of Contents

# Foreword

Every individual has a story. Upon these pages is recorded one such amazing story: that of Larry Booker, the often willing victim of the depraved depths of sin that wracked our society during his formative years, and the recipient of the marvelous grace of God. The first night he walked into church, it would have been a toss up to decide whether he was a denizen of Haight Ashbury or a refugee from Barnum and Bailey. But beneath the world-pressured exterior was a heart that beat with a desire to walk with God.

I initially had no idea of the life story you are about to read. Had I realized what a messed up example of humanity had just showed up, I would have probably been quite hesitant about my ability to do much in this situation. I was 27, had all the answers and had been ministering to various 'hippies' and college age youth for several months. Fortunately, what came to pass was not dependent on my ability. God did the work. And only He could have done it.

I have watched the move of God in Larry Booker's life from that first uplifted hand and request to be baptized through years of development, honing and polishing to the point where he now pastors a fine, growing church and is in demand as a speaker for camps and special services across North America and in foreign lands. I must stand in awe and say, "To God be the glory, great things He has done."

Larry Booker was never a 'beginning' preacher. From the earliest times, the anointing of God rested upon what were obviously well-researched messages. I am sure that part of the reason for that is his deep and abiding love for God and His written Word. Another foundation of the anointing is his sincere desire to please God. Then there is the very basic fact that he has, through all that might be termed success as a minister, continued to be a man of prayer and of praise. I have watched him from his new birth and can readily declare that, of the hundreds of people I have worked with over the decades, none has matched his desire for the things of God. This has also produced in him an abiding humility and sense of compassion for others.

Over the years Brother Booker has identified himself as my "son in the Gospel." Although I tend to stand a little straighter when I hear that, I just happened to be the man on location when God moved to bring him to new birth through the water of baptism and the Spirit of the Holy Ghost infilling. What is precious to me is that he is my brother in the Lord and, of utmost value, my friend.

TO GOD BE THE GLORY! GREAT THINGS HE HATH DONE!

Roy L. Moss

Roy L. Moss, Pastor
Truth Tabernacle
United Pentecostal Church
Bartlesville, Oklahoma

# 1

## The Girl

I knew that it was going to be a long, long day. My head was killing me, I was in a horrible mood, and on top of all that, my leg was still aching. I stared out of the window of the pick-up trying not to look at Buzz. I had not wanted to come in the first place, and did so only to please my mother.

I'd known this day was coming but still couldn't believe it was here. It was the first time since grandpa had been placed in the nursing home that we had been back to the farm; that is, if you could call it a farm. Grandpa's place was more of a hodge-podge of junkyard, garden, alfalfa patch and boy's dream. While part of me wanted to see it, most of me dreaded it. Regardless, here we were, barreling down the highway (if you can call 57 m.p.h. 'barreling') to the old haunt.

It wouldn't have been nearly so bad if Buzz and I had started out the day on better footing. It was not that I disliked my stepfather; the truth was I did like him—in fact I loved him. Of course I never told him, or for that matter very often called him "Dad." Most of the time I just couldn't understand him, nor, I guess, could he understand me. This was one of those times. Surely the term "generation gap" had been coined for us… especially this day.

In the stony silence between us, my mind drifted back to when Buzz first came into our lives.

I was about six or maybe seven when Buzz started visiting Mom. Though he never acted the clown, he was a jovial, nice-looking man who was very kind to my brother and I. The most important thing to me, however, was that he had a nice car. The car was a big deal, since we'd never owned one. Not that it would have made any difference if we'd had one; Mom couldn't drive anyway.

But, as I said, Buzz was good to us and back then, when I really needed it, he always paid attention to me. If I had something to say (which I always did), he would hear me out and even ask me questions—which I was always more than happy to answer (this no doubt being where I earned my childhood nickname 'Gabby'). That *anyone* would pay attention to me, let alone buy me a Hershey bar, or every now and then even let me have a *whole* bottle of Pepsi Cola to myself, was just too much! If I ever forgot that Buzz was, after all, a really good guy, I'd be a world-class ingrate. This was the man who single handedly saved my mother, my brother and myself from dire poverty… and God only knows what else.

I was about ten when Buzz and Mom were married. That's when we moved from Canon City to a township called Rye that lies at the foot of the Greenhorn mountain range. We actually moved into a house—not just an apartment—and some men came and put *new* carpet on our living room floor. Later that day two other men came and put a brand new couch on it. And the *very same day*, others came and put a table and chairs in a room where we were supposed to eat—and it wasn't even the kitchen! I'll never forget that experience, nor Mom and I crying in each other's arms.

It meant everything to be able to go to school and talk about *my* dad and what neat places *he* took *me* to and what *my* Dad had bought *me* for Christmas. To bring home a report card full of 'A's and have *my* Dad brag on me. At the end of that school year, he actually gave my brother and I one dollar for each 'A' that we received on the last quarter's report card. I had *five whole dollars*, and it lasted me for almost half the summer! Finally, for the first time in our lives… everything was wonderful.

I think things began to change when we had to move back to Pueblo. Buzz worked at the steel mill and the drive back and forth was a long one and I guess too expensive. So we moved.

We moved into a smaller log home on a major street called Western Avenue that was later renamed Pueblo Boulevard. We lived about a hundred yards south of another large street called Thatcher. Though I was born in Pueblo and lived there off and on through the years, I was once again in a different home, in a different city, and in a new school. All of these changes meant new friends, which in my case eventually meant—trouble.

***

Now I was eighteen, felt like thirty, and headed back to Florence and to what was left of my grandpa's place—and hating every minute of it. I simply did not want to be going there, especially with Buzz. I wanted to be partying with my friends, period. Now if *they* were *there*, we would have a time! Being eighteen, I could have bought the beer legally—even though I'd already been buying it for a couple of years because I looked older than I was. Rocco, no doubt would have some pot, Edmund or Loren would always have wine, and there was no telling what JoJo would have.

I'd show them all the places where I used to play, especially the one room stone house with a dirt floor up on the hill where I used to live. I'd show them the well where my brother and I would fetch five gallon buckets of water and have to carry them back up the hill, and the spot (though they'd never believe it) where I used to watch my mother cook supper in a Folgers coffee can. Then I'd drag them out back to the 'outhouse,' open the door, show them inside and tell 'em, "Have a seat!"

I wondered if the old junked cars that I used to play 'drive like a madman' in were still there? And if that old rope still hung in the tree where we used to swing out over the irrigation pond, scream out our lungs like Tarzan and let go? Well, maybe going back isn't going to be so bad after all… I just wish it didn't have to be with Buzz. And I wish I wasn't so sick and tired, and I wish I wasn't so… well I guess I'd have to say, depressed. I also wish that I didn't have this hangover… and I wish my leg would stop hurting.

We made our way out of Pueblo and passed the dirt road that led to the city dump. Through the years Buzz and I had taken many trips to that dump with fifty-five gallon drums that our family used as trashcans. The drums were crammed so full that you had to pull most of the stuff out with your hands—and it was a nasty bit of business. At least I thought it was, but Buzz said it was stupid to pay a garbage collector good money to do what we could do ourselves for nothing. Right.

Mom and Buzz both would croak if they knew that with a right turn on the dirt road at the top of the hill, you could go down into a draw completely hidden from all prying eyes. It was far from any listening ears, and was big enough and flat enough for me and my buddies to park most of our cars and have some evermore raucous parties. Sixteen dollars would buy an eight-gallon keg of Coors beer, and many, *many* a keg had met their match down in that draw.

To be honest, that's why I'm so sick today. Not because we had a 'woodsy' in the prairie last night, but because we had two kegs over at Alan's house. His mom was out of town on business, so we carried on our business there. I don't know what he is going to tell her about the aquarium, or about the cut on his back. Oh well, it seemed funny at the time.

What did not seem funny was Norma. The beer was the cause of my headache and Norma was the cause of my bad mood. I knew it was Saturday and that by Monday we'd have our squabble all patched up, but I was getting more tired of it each time. If she wanted someone else for a boyfriend, why didn't she just tell me and get it over with. The next time she gave Jack, or Cliff, or Rick too much attention… Oh well, I knew better than to even think about it right then.

It was only a forty minute drive from Pueblo to Florence, but that day the trip took forever. Buzz's snail-pace drove me up the wall. When he shook me awake early that morning and reminded me that we were going to Grandpa's place, I thought I'd die and groaned to prove it. "That's what you get for coming in so late and smelling like a brewery," he said in response. I mumbled a counter-response to myself: "It's going to be a long day."

After going through the prairies in 'Conestoga time,' we finally swung down into the valley where my aunt and uncle have their dairy. I saw it off to the right in the distance and imagined we'd be dropping by there on our way home, hopefully for dinner. My Aunt Arvie fixed great feasts that she called 'supper.' I'd have asked Buzz if that was the plan, but I didn't feel like risking a conversation.

I looked across the pastures at the milk cows and realized that we were driving by a significant chunk of my life. My brother and I had spent many a summer at the dairy, working like dogs and eating like pigs.

This was due to my mother always needing to work, usually as a waitress or cook. While school was in session, Phil and I could be home alone for the few hours before she got there. But when school let out for the summer, we had to go somewhere to be watched—and Aunt Arvie's place was the best.

We used to spend a lot of time at Grandma and Grandpa's place before Grandma died. I actually liked her home better than Arvie's (though it was not nearly as nice) because you didn't have to work near as hard and ate almost as good. Also, when at Grandma's, I didn't have to put up with Roger. Roger was Arvie's son and my cousin. He was three years older than me and tended to make my life miserable. But that was when I was a boy and before I learned how to fight. I mean really fight. I actually wish that Roger were still around (instead of being God only knows where) and would try and pick on me now. Well, maybe I'd get lucky and Nixon will send him to Vietnam. Anyway, when this day was finally over, I guessed I could at least expect a good meal.

I also hoped it wouldn't be dark when we got to Arvie's. I wanted to traipse over the farm and woods and recollect when I was a kid. It seemed eons ago when I ran through the woods by the Arkansas river, laughing and screaming in what I realize now were halcyon days. That we had been poor, so what? I didn't know it. All I knew was that I spent the summer working like a dog, eating like a pig and seeing my mother three or four times.

I realize now that we actually had a lot of time to play and a delightfully simple life—except for hay hauling time when we really did have to work like dogs. Other than that season, all we pretty much had to do was feed and milk the cows twice a day, and help keep the garden clear of weeds.

But now I was older and no longer worked on the farm. I drank, and drugged, and fought, and laughed, and screamed, and was considered the 'life of the party.' And… I *ached* for those clean, carefree, simple days, before life was made up of failing grades, truancies, gang fights, arrests, juvenile courts, probation, speeding tickets, car wrecks, hangovers, bad trips, nightmares, fights with Buzz, and watching Momma cry.

Another strange thing (at least to my friends) was that I learned to like different types of music, especially 'country' while at Arvie's. It was quite a shock to their system to hear me sing a country western song that I'd learned while milking cows. Arvie played it for background music because she said it "helps calm the cows." No doubt Charley Pride or Buck Owens *was* more calming than Grand Funk Railroad, REO Speedwagon or Black Sabbath. And a guy weeping in his beer over being jilted had to be easier on a cow's nerves than an earsplitting scream over getting some bad acid. But then, the longer I live I'm not so sure. Between Geri and Tina and Rhoda and now Norma, I was about ready to either sink into a tub of beer or let some bad acid just take me away and never ever come back… like it did Mike and looks like it did to Ronnie.

I still don't like to think about those guys; I guess they'll never be quite the same. Joe says that when your number comes up, it just comes up, and there's nothing you can do about it (at least that's the philosophy in Vietnam). As for me, I would rather die than end up like them. But who knows, at least they don't seem to be in any more pain, especially Mike. He just kind of walks the streets and sleeps where he can. I wonder how his parents feel? I know they must hate me and think that I had a lot to do with it… and… I guess I did. This I do know, if something didn't happen to Geri pretty soon, she was going off the deep end as well. And, as much as I hated to admit it, Tina also. In fact, I was more worried about Norma than both of them. Oh, I'd give anything if life could be simple again. Just work like a dog, eat like a pig and play in the woods.

***

We turned left off the highway and began to make our way up into the hills. I looked down off to the right to see the huge weed patch where Grandpa's alfalfa field used to grow. It's so hard to believe Grandpa's not here. I thought somehow he would farm on, play horseshoes, smoke his pipe, and cuss forever. He was just so tough. He'd only been gone a year or so, yet looking at the field you'd have thought it had been a century.

Grandma'd been dead for almost six years. She died a few years after Mom and Buzz married and it was a real sad time for all of us. Looking back it must have been exceptionally hard on Mom as she and grandma were so close. They were especially close, no doubt, because for a while, grandma was the only person in the world Mom seemed to have. After my real dad did us dirt, (I was just born and Phil was two) we had to move in with Grandma and Grandpa. Through the years—until Mom married Buzz—we would move in and out of their house depending on the situations Mom found herself in. As I said, she was most often a waitress, but occasionally worked as a cook. I'd always taken her cooking for granted, but now I can understand why some customers would leave if Beulah wasn't on shift. At any rate, we all missed Grandma and now we miss the old homestead as well. It was here that we'd come to find refuge when the storms grew too large. It was during one of these flights that we lived in the house up on the hill with the one room and dirt floor.

Buzz pulled up to the barbwire gate and I got out and unhitched it. It seemed so easy now, but I remember when it was everything I could do to either undo the fence or lock it up. You always had to pull or push on the gate pole with the shoulder and one arm, while using your other arm to finagle the circle of barbwire that made the latch. If you could pull it off without slashing your wrist or throat or having grandpa finally climb out of the truck, kick you in the behind and do it himself, you considered yourself as having had a good day.

At that remembrance, I felt another pang for Grandpa. He was a hard man and hard to get to know, but in his own way he really did love me, though it was hard for him to express anything like that. I liked to think that he was more fond of me more than the other grandkids because of the way he would tease me. *I know* Grandma liked me best because of the way she would always sit me down and say "Larry, you're a special boy… and I want you to grow up to be a special man… make sure you do what you're supposed to do… and don't let that temper of yours get you into trouble." I really don't know if I *was* her favorite, or if was the *only one* she talked to like that, but if I wasn't, I don't want to know about it. I do know she played the starring role in the nightmare that was ever with me.

In the dream, my brother Phil and I were standing in the opening of a large cave looking down into the distance to where it makes a bend. As we entered the mouth of the cave, Grandma, in her old gingham dress, came from around the distant bend slowly walking toward us. Phil ran to her and she grabbed him and hugged him close to her breast. I was trying to run but felt like my legs were slogging through knee-deep mud. As I finally began to get close to her, I could tell that her eyes were filled with pain and by the look on her face that she didn't want to see me. She refused to embrace me and worst of all, I knew the reason why. I had failed her miserably. My Grandmother, who was always so sweet, so clean, so kind… the one who ever believed in me and encouraged me to do good and be good, now wanted nothing to do with me because my life had become so vile, so dirty, and so wicked.

I'd wake up from the dream in a cold sweat and feel sure that she was in the room staring at me. I cried out for her and asked her to forgive me and promised her that I really was going to change… and hope that I could. It was not a good dream, and I could never shake it from my mind.

***

Buzz drove through the gate and up to the rusty tin garage that leaned sharply to the left. Though it had been leaning for years, this is the first time I realized how bad it really looked. Almost all of the junk that had been piled in it was gone, and there's no telling who took it, or even why they'd want it. I suppose some of it had antique value, maybe even sentimental value, but then, I didn't know very much about either.

I do know that when it came to the stuff in the house there had been quite a scramble by some of the family members. All the mementoes that had been garnered by both Grandpa and Grandma through the years hadn't lasted very long. There were some raw feelings about how some of the family had swept in to get the best stuff. Not that there had been much of anything of any real monetary value, it was mostly just stuff that would mean something to the people that knew them. Actually, I don't blame them, but I must say that I was proud of my mother because she refused to get involved in all of that. She eventually came around in her quiet way and picked up a few things left by some of the others. But then, that is my mother.

Beulah Louise McBeth Booker is a wonderful woman and I'm more than lucky to have her for my mother. I don't deserve her and hated what I put her through these last few years—the most recent fiasco being exceptionally painful.

I had been in jail for thirty-six hours and she didn't known where I was and I hadn't bothered to call. I used the one call I was allowed to make to call 'time and temperature' and gave the information to my arresting officers. They didn't seem to appreciate it (though one officer did glance at his watch). Anyway, Mom and Buzz didn't know where I was until Aunt Arvie called saying she'd seen my picture and heard my name on the ten o'clock evening news.

That was the drug bust that should have sent me up the river, and would have had it not been for Mr. Biddle, our public defender. He loathed the Narcotics officers who had arrested us—Officers Leayva and Koncilia—and managed to squeak us by with misdemeanors. Larry Weder, and Mick Baker, along with Joe Arguello and myself were allowed to cop pleas to 'use of marijuana' so the DA could have four convictions instead of just the two felonies that he had on Joe and me. It was after all—as our attorney pointed out—an election year.

The police had found an aluminum Kodak can with over fifty tabs of LSD in Joe's car and over an ounce of marijuana on me. Well, they didn't actually find it on me, but on top of a chicken wire fence that I'd ran into while fleeing from Officer Leayva. He had been firing his gun after I'd shoved him to the ground while getting out of Joe's car. It had not been a smooth arrest.

They should have also found a Kodak can full of uncut Vietnamese Heroin, but I honestly believe that God blinded their eyes when they searched me—and it was almost a total strip search.

After finally being placed in a cell with a camera in it, I snuggled up close to the door where the camera couldn't see me, undid the Kodak lid and sprinkled the heroin onto the floor. I proceeded to grind it with a twisting, sliding dance with my feet until it could no longer be detected with the naked eye. I then wiped the can out with my shirttail and crushed it beneath my boot. After a minute or so, I told the officer stationed outside that I needed to use the bathroom. He followed me into the restroom but thankfully not into the stall. Then, just as I'd done with some evidence while in Kindergarten, I flushed the can down the stool—only to have it float back to the surface! I held my breath, hoped the officer wouldn't check on why I needed to flush twice… flushed once more… and up it came again. I replaced the can on my person and we walked back to the cell.

On the way back, I couldn't resist asking the officer if he'd went into the restroom with me because of Rocky. Rocky was one of my best friends who'd been arrested one night not long before and had also asked to go to the bathroom. That time, the officer didn't go into the restroom with him, and, though it was on the third floor, Rocky crawled out the window, jumped down onto an air conditioner unit that was on the second floor and then dropped to the ground and escaped. My officer didn't offer a word by way of an answer.

When they placed me in a cell upstairs, I finally flushed the Kodak can away and breathed a sigh of relief. The amazing thing about the whole episode was, that I knew God had mercy on me, and helped me out of it, even though I'd refused to ask Him—as I had every other time. On this occasion, as I lay on my cell bed, all I said to Him was: "God, it's me again… Larry… and you know what… I'm not even going to ask you to help me this time. Every time I've ever gotten into a mess, I've begged you for mercy and made promises that I broke as soon as the heat was off. So I'll tell you what, God… I'm not even going to waste your time. This time you can just let me sink." And yet… if I *ever* got out of a bad, *bad* jam, it was this one.

So, my Mom and Buzz found out where I was, by Aunt Arvie's phone call. The most painful thing was that this debacle happened so soon after the debacle that took place a few months before, when I was still seventeen. I'd been in city jail for thirty-six hours on that occasion as well, but at least they *knew* where I was. In fact, Buzz had decided to let me cool my jets for a while—and I can't say that I blamed him. He finally came to get me after the police called him a second time and told them they *wanted me out of there… now*!

Apparently, when they put me in a second floor cell for public drunkenness, I had pointed the nozzle of the shower out onto the floor, turned on the hot water and passed out on the bed. After flooding that floor of the jail—and doing thousands of dollars of damage to the ceiling of the first floor—they decided I'd better go home before the desk sergeant lost control and did something regrettable to me. I guess he was more than a little surprised, soaked and somewhat injured (especially his pride) when some water-laden ceiling tiles fell on his head.

I must say that it was one of the few occasions that Buzz ever defended me. He probably did so because the police chief was hinting that my parents might be held responsible for the damage I'd done. Buzz sat there for a long time, looking first at the chief, then at the ceiling and its drenched, drooping tiles and finally at me. Then he began speaking slowly and deliberately, "You do know, of course, since Larry is only seventeen, that you did officially place him in 'protective custody.' He was so drunk that he didn't know what he was doing. Being so drunk, he could have passed out in the water and even drowned. Under the circumstances, it probably wouldn't be a good idea to make me go and get a lawyer." At this the chief sighed, closed the folder he had been glancing at and told us that I was free to go. He mentioned that I would no doubt be hearing from my probation officer. Small wonder the police tended not to like me. Well, anyway, that's old news.

***

Buzz opened the tailgate on the back of the truck and pulled out his metal detector. If he was ever going to find something old and interesting this would be the place. Every now and then he asked me—no, he told me—to move some crate or box or whatever, so he could keep checking out the ground at an uninterrupted clip. What a way to spend a Saturday.

Three hours later, I was bored stiff. My right leg was aching and stiff, and without the hangover I'd have been hungry also. I really wanted to just lie down and go to sleep. I could remember a day when these activities would have somewhat excited me, but this was certainly not one of them. I sat down on a tree stump by the road and hoped that Buzz would forget my existence for a while.

If my leg didn't get better pretty soon, I was going to see if Norma's dad would take another look at it. He told me that it would be okay, but that I needed to take it easy for a few days. It had already been a week… but then I couldn't say I'd been 'taking it easy' either. "Gregg is so stupid," I muttered, rubbed my leg some more, and began to think that I could be pretty stupid as well.

The 'leg incident' had happened a week ago when me and several of the guys had been slumming down at the Grub Steak. The 'Grub' was a hamburger joint situated between a Texaco gas station and an Arapahoe food market at the corner of Prairie

Avenue and Jones. Between it and the grocery store was a parking lot that created the perfect arrangement for a hangout. So, that's where the kids from South High did most of their 'hanging out.' The Grub Steak was a great place to fight, get drunk, buy or sell drugs, or meet and plan *where to go* and fight, get drunk, or buy or sell drugs. We'd also been known to burn the rubber off our tires, flirt with girls, play tackle football, and get arrested there.

Across the street was a '7-11' type store that tended to change names every year or so. If we wanted anything from a candy bar to more beer, we would go there, buy or steal it, and come back for more partying. Sometimes, if too many of us went over at once, we tended to stop the traffic on Prairie Avenue. If only one of us was drunk or rambunctious enough, he could stop traffic all by himself. One time me and a bunch of our guys went out into the middle of Prairie Avenue, a very busy thoroughfare, and had our picture taken. It was quite a picture. I was sitting down in the front in my favorite railroad coat with my arms spread out as if presenting some of the gang to the world. We were not in very good 'condition' when the photo was taken, but tried to 'get it together' for posterity.

Last Saturday night we were at the Grub Steak, milling about, laughing, screaming and listening to the music. Three or four cars whose radios were tuned to the same local Rock station, KDZA, provided the music. The car windows would be left down or the doors open so we would never have to 'miss a beat.'

We were milling about, doing our thing when all of a sudden Richard—whom Rocco had surnamed 'Scab' because of a bout of staff infection he'd had back in the ninth grade—began screaming, cussing and holding the side of his face as if he'd been hit. As it turned out he had been hit—by a semi-rotten tomato. Ronnie Garza had apparently looked into the trash bin in back of the Arapahoe Food store and found a bunch of produce that had been thrown out. He lifted out an exceedingly ripe tomato and hurled it into the crowd that was about thirty yards away—nailing Richard in the side of the face. Thus the war began.

Within minutes the combined Grub Steak/Arapahoe parking lot was the scene of one of the mangiest 'slop fights' ever perpetrated. From brown heads of lettuce, to rotting tomatos, to apples, and oranges, to even a pineapple or two (now *they* really *did* hurt), a torrent of garbage filled the air and asphalt.

About this time, Greg Gilmore came pulling onto the parking lot. When he saw what was happening, instead of stopping, he gunned his car, which was a 1956 Ford 'soup-em-up' and was soon slipping and sliding on the swill. We found ourselves running, dodging, throwing, and rolling until we were all pretty well layered with muck. Greg drove his greasy way across the lot and turned his car around for another charge. Suddenly I received inspiration that the gray, revving, behemoth of a car resembled a bull, pawing at the ground, in preparation for another attack at the 'matador,' whose role I was more than glad to assume.

I pulled off my railroad coat and began to stretch it out and wave it like a red cape. Gregg immediately caught on and began revving his engine even more (no one ever said that my friends didn't have good minds, just that we didn't use them correctly). His engine now roaring, he began to peel his way through the slop and into the 'bullring.' He was picking up speed amazingly well and coming directly at me, while I waved the cape and yelled, "Toro! Eh, El Toro, Toro!" My footing slipped a little, but still I managed to step off to the left and brush his right fender with my coat as he plowed by, allowing the cape to drag along the car to the rear bumper. The only glitch in this rather smooth maneuver was Greg's antenna, which came out of it a little bent. Also, some of the guys chose to pepper the bull with a newly retrieved batch of slop from the dumpster—some of which went through the open windows and apparently going into Greg's left ear. He cursed as he passed the Grub Steak and went down the alley, apparently to go clean both his ear and front windshield. The reeking mob cheered the entire action as vehemently as any fans in Madrid. I bowed, swung my coat around my head and called for yet another beer. What I received was a half a head of cabbage to the back of my head.

We returned to the splatter, slinging and screeching when I heard two sounds at once. One was of someone screaming my name and the other was the roar of an approaching engine. I turned to see Greg's car barreling straight at me. Greg was at the wheel and he had the look of a laughing lunatic. I quickly tried to move to my left, while he tried jerking his front tires to the right, but both of us had made serious miscalculations. Mine were that I was drunk, couldn't react quickly enough, and continued to slip on slop. Greg's mistake was hitting the brakes. The asphalt had become so slick that the turning of the wheel and hitting of the brakes meant next to nothing. Fortunately, we both did *just enough* to save my life. The car hit me and hurled me into the air—in fact, quite a ways up into the air—but thankfully it hit only my right leg.

The newspaper reporter stated that I went "twenty feet straight up into the air." I don't know how high I actually went, but I do know that when John Garza tried to catch me—as I returned to earth—all he got for his valiant effort was my boot print in his face.

The police were called (by the same gas station attendant that gave his story to the newspaper), but by the time they arrived we were all long gone. Though it was a 'hit and run' situation there were no arrests made as the police could not find the victim or perpetrator. I (the victim) suffered painfully that night and went the next day to Norma's and had her father check me out.

Norma's father was a medical doctor of the highest repute in Pueblo, who for some reason liked me. We gave him some story about my falling off of one of the cliffs at Monkey Mountain (a huge man-made mountain at the city park), and he checked me out thoroughly. He dubiously accepted my story, informed me that nothing was broken—just barely—suggested that I stay off it as much as possible and get some whirlpool treatments. Right. He also gave me some pills for the pain—an instruction that I followed too thoroughly.

The Arapahoe food store, the Grub Steak and the police were pretty upset over the garbage that covered the parking lot. (After that night we never did find more than a couple of pieces of produce in the trash bins and never could figure out what they were doing with it.) As for the Grub Steak, in all the years that we hung out there, I don't remember buying more than one or two hamburgers from them, nor did any of my friends. (Why do that when you could buy four bean burrito's at Taco Bell for a dollar?) This lack of decent patronage is, no doubt, why the Grub Steak eventually became a used car lot.

***

So here I sat, a week later, with an aching leg and head (though the head problem was due to a more recent folly). Buzz had begun working an open area between some of the buildings—or shacks, depending on your definition—while I continued to sit on the stump hoping my misery would go away. After a while I lifted my octagon-shaped glasses to my forehead with one hand and with the other began to rub my eyes, which felt as if there was burning grit in them. I bent over, rested my elbows on my knees and held my head in my hands—wishing I had a cigarette.

It was then that I heard the screech, the squeal, the shriek of a dog from somewhere behind me. On a better day I would have called it barking, but today it was like chalk screeching on a chalkboard and set the only nerve I had left on edge. I turned towards the approaching storm to see a small collie straining at a leash held by... *The Girl.*

How can I describe her? She was laughing as hard as the dog was screeching, and stumbling forward as he pulled her along in a straight line towards me. Her hair was a brownish blonde (though more blonde than brown) and hung down to her shoulders. Threads of her locks glinted in the sunlight as it weaved its way through the jumbling dance it was performing, and her eyes, even at this distance, seemed azure blue. She was about five foot six or seven—I was already on my feet and calculating—and wore white loafers with a turquoise pleated skirt that whipped like a flag on a windy day. Her blouse was a light pink that matched her cheeks and I guessed her to be about sixteen or seventeen. I based her age by the excited demeanor she wore, but knew that she could be as old as nineteen or even twenty.

She was not what you'd call beautiful, and was in fact more

'comely' than even pretty. But she had a definite alluring appeal that was hard to define. In spite of myself, I felt my heart clutch as she bounced towards me… and it took me a moment to realize why. It was her smile.

She had a smile and laugh that could grip a heart and squeeze it. It was clean and sweet and lovely and lively.

"Stop, Scotty, stop!" she entreated the wonderful creature that was dragging her straight to me. I prayed that Scotty wasn't obedient, and I had nothing to fear. He finally complied when he began to sniff my boots and pants.

For a boy once known as 'Gabby' I found myself strangely speechless. I just stood open-mouthed, looking stupid and staring at *the girl*. She couldn't seem to stop laughing and placed her free hand over her mouth in an effort to stifle it down to a giggle. "I'm sorry," she said in a childlike voice, "But he must like you. From the minute he saw you he just took off, running and barking."

"Believe me, the honor is all mine," I should have said, but instead came out with: "Is… is he your dog?" This had to be one of the more stupid questions I'd ever asked.

"Yes, this is my Scotty… but he's really not a Scotty, he's a Border… Border…"

"Collie," I finished.

"Yes!" She giggled. "A Border Collie and he's eight years old!

I just stared at her, and she stared at me and giggled. And I just stared at her. After a while she asked, "Do you have a dog?"

"Do I what?"

"Do you have a dog?"

Uh… umm, no, I don't." I said, wishing that I did have a dog. Any kind of dog would do just now.

"That's too bad. Dogs are neat and Scotty's my best friend," she said a with tilt of her head and with her mouth and her eyes and her smile.

"Do you… do you live around here?" I sputtered, hoping to goodness she wasn't here on vacation from Minnesota.

"Yes, we live up on the hill in that gray house," she said turning and pointing with her free hand. I looked momentarily up to the house that I knew so well, and then stared at the back of her hair. She turned and looked directly into my eyes, smiled again, giggled, but this time didn't bother to put her hand to her mouth. Her teeth were as pretty as her smile.

"Who's we?" I asked.

"Whose what?" she said, looking at me oddly.

"You said, '*we*' live in the gray house. Who is '*we*?' Who lives there with you?"

"Oh... well, me and my Mommy and Daddy... and Scotty!"

"Oh...well that's nice," I replied and continued to stare.

"You really should get a dog so you could have a friend," she said.

"I have lots of friends," but immediately added, "But none of them are as nice as Scotty," knowing that I had just stated a profound truth.

"Really? You have lots of friends?" she said with her eyes open even wider.

"Well, yes, of course," I said, a tad uncomfortably and not sure why. So I went on to say; "You sound as if Scotty is your only friend. I mean, really, a girl as pretty as you no doubt has scads of friends!"

She looked at me, finally smiled and replied, "I'd like it if you were my friend." I felt as though my heart had just fallen into my feet. Maybe it had, because Scotty took up a renewed interest in sniffing them.

"I... I would love to be your friend," I stammered. "Uh... what's your name?" I finally decided to ask—not that it mattered.

"Molly" she said. "What's yours?"

"Larry... Larry Booker"

She smiled.

"What's your last name?" I asked.

"Marcus. My name is Molly Mae Marcus," she said smiling.

"Do you spell your middle name M-A-Y or M-A-E?" I asked, not really caring but stalling for time.

"Well, sometimes I spell it with an Y and sometimes I spell it with an E."

"What?" I said, taken aback.

"Well now, let's see;" she said as she bent down to the ground, picked up a stick and began to write M-O-L-L-Y… M-A… Y in the dirt. Then she stood up with a gleaming face and said, "With a Y. Today it's Molly Mae with a Y."

At that point I couldn't have cared less if she spelled it with a D, but I had to ask her why she did it that way.

"Because, now it's springtime… and I like MAY," then looking around a little sheepishly she said, "But really… it's an E."

I had never heard it on that wise, but God knows that I'd heard things a whole lot stranger. Besides, I was looking into her eyes and drowning in the childlike innocence they possessed. Already I knew that I had never before met anyone like her.

Had I met her in Pueblo, she no doubt would have approached me with a saunter, chewing a wad of gum or smoking a cigarette, in skin-tight blue jeans, sandals, a T-shirt bearing a smart-alec slogan and probably would have sic'd her dog on me. She may even have tried to pick a fist fight, like Joyce had done with me a few weeks ago. Not that *this girl* wouldn't have been attractive even at that, but to be honest, I realized at that moment how burnt out I was on 'knockouts' and the mind games they were into. If Molly Mae Marcus was just half as sweet as she appeared to be—my heart could possibly be gone forever.

"Molly Mae is a really beautiful name," Gabby said starting to get his tongue and rhythm back.

"Really?" she said, and began to glow as if I'd just put a crown of jewels upon her head.

"Oh yes, and it is as beautiful a name as you… the girl who owns it," I said warming to my stride.

In an instant I knew I had said something amiss for she actually took a step back, and pulled on Scotty's leash. Though she wasn't frowning, she was no longer smiling either.

"Is there… is there something wrong? Did I say something wrong?" I asked unconsciously clenching my hands.

"No… no… it's just that Daddy says I need to be careful of people who say too nice of things to me."

"Really?" I answered somewhat surprised. "I mean, all I said was that it's a pretty name for a pretty girl."

Though she didn't say anything, she did finally give me a small smile and loosened up somewhat on Scotty's leash.

"Is your dad afraid that someone might, uh… get fresh with you?"

She looked quizzically at me and said, "What do you mean by …fresh?"

"What?"

"What do you mean by 'get fresh with you?' "

"Well, fresh means that someone is, like… flirting with you."

"What's flirting?"

"Are you serious?" I asked, incredulous, "You really don't know what flirting is?"

I saw pain in Molly's eyes as she asked, "Are you making fun of me?"

When I saw that she actually meant it, I had to keep myself from stepping towards to her, and trying to somehow sooth away the hurt.

"Molly, of course I'm not making fun of you. I wouldn't do that. Though I hardly know you, I… I would never hurt you."

"Ok then… what is flirting?" she said, smiling again as though what had just happened was the brief passing of a small cloud.

Having again lost my stride, I began to ponder, "How in the world do I explain what I have been doing without giving myself away in the process."

"Well… flirting is like… when a boy or a girl wants to… well, catch the attention of someone from the opposite… uh, opposite… Well, it's like if a boy… no… I mean, if a girl wants a boy to know that she is interested in him, she will like, drop little hints, or smile, or maybe she'll wink at him, or something, to kind of let him know that she likes him."

"I do like you. That's why I smile at you," then she went on casually, "I smile at everybody I like."

"Well, yes, I am sure of that. It's just that if you *really* like somebody, I mean, like, you … you know… a boyfriend, kind of type of deal, then you give him a kind of, uh…uh… a *special* smile," said Gabby, struggling very badly.

"What do you mean a *special* smile?"

I was beginning to think, this is either the most innocent girl that I've ever met, or she is into mind games deeper than any of the girls that I was currently sick of.

"Okay… a *special smile* is kind of 'coy,' it's kind of…of… oh I don't know Molly, it's just special… it lets the person your smiling at *know* that you want to be their girlfriend… or boyfriend." Well, there it was. I then smiled at her very broadly, even leaning over a little in her direction.

"What do you mean by girlfriend?"

I swallowed my smile and gaped at her.

"Well?" she said.

"Molly… a girlfriend is a girlfriend to a boy when they have a special understanding that they are… 'going together.' That is, well… they mean a lot to each other. It's more than just being friends. They are really *special* friends… close… very *close* friends that you know, maybe even… *love each other*." I wasn't sure at that moment who was trying to suck who into what.

"I love my Mommy and Daddy… and I love Scotty," she said with her eyes bright. Then a shadow came over her face and she said "And I really loved my sister. But she's gone now."

I didn't really want to talk about her sister just then, but at the same time I didn't want to come on too fast and have this apparition disappear before my eyes. So I asked, "Did your sister move away?"

"My Momma says she went to be with the angels, but my Daddy won't say anything."

I looked at Molly, swallowed and said, "What happened?"

"What do you mean?" she asked.

"I mean… what happened that made your sister go be with the angels?"

"Mommy says Daddy and me and Katlin was in a car wreck."

"Katlin was your sister?"

"Yes, and she was ten and I was twelve."

"You mean she was ten years old when she went to be with the angels?"

"Yes… and she was my friend. That was before I had Scotty."

"Did you say that you were in the wreck?"

"Well Momma says I was, but I really don't remember."

"Were you hurt?"

"I must have been because I was in the hospital a long time. Daddy was too but he got out before I did."

"So he was hurt in the wreck as well?"

"Yes, but he's okay now."

"I see... well, and you're okay now ... so that's good, that's very good," I said.

"Do you have a sister?" Molly asked.

"No, I only have a brother. His name is Phil."

"Does he have a dog?"

"No. Phil is two years older than I am. We haven't had a dog since we were little, and lived in Canon City," I answered, but really wanted to get back to the subject of flirting and girlfriends and boyfriends.

It was at that point that Buzz's voice finally broke through to my consciousness. "Larry! Will you get over here!" he was yelling. What utterly horrible timing.

"Look," I said to Molly, "That's my dad, and well, I guess he needs my help. Could you stay here just a minute and... hey, you can come with me... he probably just wants me to help him move something. It'll just be a minute..."

"Okay," she said, and we began our trek, Scotty leading the way to where Buzz's metal detector had apparently led him.

He was standing over a huge cast iron pot that was face down in the dirt. I couldn't believe it when I saw it. "Buzz," I said, "I used to take baths in that pot. I've watched Grandma make lye soap and wash clothes in it many a time."

"Really?" he said looking up at me and back down to the pot. "That was a long time ago," he said. Then he looked at Molly and Scotty and back to me. "Who's this?" he said.

"This is Molly... Molly Marcus, she lives up on the hill across the street from the house where Uncle Johnny and Aunt Evie used to live." Buzz stood looking at Molly and she stood smiling at him for what seemed a long time.

Though Buzz and I didn't agree on a lot of things, I respected him as being a very intelligent man and knew that he was already into deep evaluation of this situation. The only thing that broke his concentration was when Scotty began his sniffing of him in earnest. Buzz pushed him aside with one hand while he stuck out the other and said, "Hello, Molly, it's good to meet you."

"Hello" she said, and while, shaking his hand, asked, "What are you doing?"

"Oh, this is a metal detector and I'm looking for old coins and artifacts."

"Old coins and what?" she asked.

"Artifacts… uh… relics… metal objects, anything that might be of value."

"Oh," she said, and smiled. Buzz smiled back and then looked at me. I smiled at him and then at her and then I really smiled at Scotty as he renewed his sniffing. Then the dog turned from Buzz and jumped up, putting his paws and weight on my leg… my right one, and the yelp I uttered scared him and Molly both.

***

For some reason, Scotty's jumping on me took my mind back to when I was a very little boy. We lived over on West Corona in an apartment that we rented from a lady named Addy. I did have a dog then… but no dad. That was when Buzz first began to come by and visit. Our dog, 'Butch,' (well…it was technically Addy's) was a black and white 'something or other.' One evening as we were outside sitting on the patio swing, Buzz began playing with him and both seemed to enjoy it immensely. However much Buzz and Butch enjoyed it —I was ecstatic. Here was this nice man, and this nice dog playing, while Mom and Phil and I laughed. For a moment it actually felt like… like a family, with a mom and a dad and a dog and everything!

A few days later, Buzz pulled up in his neat car (a 1954 blue and white Ford) on the gravel parking lot in back of the apartments and began talking to mom. I wanted to make Buzz happy and maybe have another good time watching him play with Butch, so I let the dog out of the gate and we ran together to Buzz's car. Butch must have recognized Buzz, because he jumped up and put his paws on the door and began scratching like he wanted inside. I thought Buzz would be thrilled, but instead he yelled at us and knocked Butch away from his window. The dog and I both took off running, having no idea of what we'd done wrong.

A little later, Mom came inside and explained to me the reason Buzz was so upset. He had just picked his car up from the body shop that afternoon and—it had just received a new paint job. I still didn't catch the full import, and wouldn't until after I owned my first car. Funny how a little thing like that will get stuck in a memory.

***

At any rate, I jerked back with a yelp and limped backwards a step or two (as for my leg, the dog couldn't have hit a more sensitive spot). I immediately pasted on a smile and said, "It's okay, it's okay, I'll be okay." Molly was trying to rein in the dog while looking me over to make sure I was all right. As for Scotty, his interest in me quickly passed and was now yanking at his leash in another direction. Buzz also went back to scanning the ground and, thankfully, did not ask me to expedite his work by moving any more stuff out of the way.

Wanting to get Molly's mind off my leg (as well as my own), I asked her, "Why do you keep Scotty on a leash? Why not just let him go? It's not as if he's gonna hurt anything."

"I can't let him go. If I do, he'll most likely jump in the pond."

"So what? What's that going to hurt?"

"Well," she said somewhat sheepishly, "My dad's afraid that if he does, I might jump in after him."

"Why's he afraid that you'd do something like that?"

"Because I've done it before."

"You jumped in the pond after your dog?" I said incredulously.

"I was scared for him!" she answered defensively.

"What difference does it make it he jumps in the water, what's it going to hurt? Why should you get wet, and even risk your life, just because your dog likes the water?"

"Well, he sprays me with water anyway when he gets out, and the water is so dirty that I guess I just don't want either of us to look filthy. And, I don't know why but… I just worry that maybe Scotty won't make it out of the water."

I tried to absorb this statement, rolled it around in my mind two or three times, stretched it, turned it and pondered it from several angles—and still couldn't make sense of it. In fact, it was so senseless that I thought it was somehow… cute. Even Scotty had stopped and was looking up at Molly—but I'm sure that was coincidental…

I don't know if this line of questioning made her nervous, but Molly suddenly said, "Larry, I have to go home now. I've been gone a while and my parents will start worrying about me."

"Are you sure?" I asked. "I haven't heard anybody calling for you."

"No, but if I stay gone very much longer they will. My dad doesn't like it if I'm gone too long."

"Is it okay if I walk you up the hill?"

"I think that'd be okay."

"What kind of girl was this?" I thought as we began our trek to her house. I thought I had met and been interested in just about every type girl available, but I'd never encountered anyone like this before. She was such a strange mixture. I didn't see how she could fit in the world, as I knew it. Obviously, she was a physically blossomed young woman, but one who must have been raised in an extremely sheltered environment. But what a breath of unbelievably fresh air she was! No agendas, no mind games, no tricks, no guile. I was—to put it simply—floored. How I longed for this. How I craved purity and emotional simplicity. Where a guy could just be himself and not have to put on 'airs.' Where a guy could actually be sweet and kind—and not be laughed at, or taken advantage of. In a word, I was sick of going out with girls that the better you treated them, the less they liked you, and the bigger jerk you were, the more they loved you. Maybe, just maybe, a guy like me, a mess like Larry Booker, could actually change with a sweet girl like this in his life. Maybe, just maybe, Molly Mae Marcus was the answer I'd been longing for.

"Molly," I suddenly asked, "How old are you?"

"Eighteen... almost nineteen... no wait, I am nineteen, but will be twenty in December."

I thought to myself, "Is this girl really this simple and sweet?" I stopped walking, took her by the hand and turned her towards me.

"Molly... are you in high school?"

"Yes."

"What grade?"

"I'm in the eleventh grade... why?"

So that was it... Molly must be in actuality a little slow mentally... probably failed a year, maybe even two.

Then she continued, "If it wasn't for the accident, I would have already graduated... but like I said I was sick a long time."

"Of course," I said to myself, "She's not dumb, she's just backwards because of crucial time spent recovering from a car wreck!" I allowed a big smile to cross my face, let go of her hand and began once again walking her towards home.

As we drew near to Molly's house, I began to wonder if I should introduce myself to her parents or not. The decision was taken out of my hands when Molly's father stepped out of the house and onto the porch.

"Daddy, oh daddy!" Molly called out to him, "I want you to meet Larry. He's a very nice boy."

Her dad walked out to the edge of the porch completely ignoring his daughter and said to me, "Who are you and where'd you come from?"

Part of me—a big part—wanted to come back with something like: "I'm your worst nightmare and future son-in-law," which no doubt would have had quite an impact but probably wouldn't have secured an invitation to come back any time soon. Therefore I simply said, "I'm Larry Booker... Joe McBeth's grandson. My father and I came up here so he could run a metal detector around and see what he could find… and we're from Pueblo."

He didn't seem especially impressed, but then, I couldn't blame him. I was, in fact, a pretty sorry sight. My blond hair was parted in the middle and hung down past my chin. My sweatshirt bore a picture of a teeth-baring wolf with a "*Born to be Wild*" slogan beneath. My bell-bottom jeans (my favorites) were not much more than a conglomeration of patches sewn together hanging down to the ground over a pair of scruffy cowboy boots. I perceived that Mr. Marcus feared what I had in mind concerning Molly for he stared at me as he would a burglar at midnight.

"And it's very good to meet you, Mr. Marcus," I said trying to reassure the accusations his eyes were asserting.

He started to say something, stopped, started again, stopped, finally cleared his throat and said, "Yes, well… uh… good to meet you, uh…"

"Larry... Larry Booker."

"Yes. I know your Grandfather. He's a good man… down underneath… in his heart, where it counts."

I thought that was a pretty terse, but accurate, assessment of my grandfather and was about to respond when I heard the horn honk and knew that Buzz must be ready to go.

"I have to go now, Molly. It was really wonderful to meet you," I said, not wanting to leave at all.

She faced me and said, "Goodbye, Larry. I hope I can see you again before long. I really do want to be your friend." The late afternoon sunshine was her face and eyes and smile and I once again felt my heart fall into my boots. I guess her dad felt it too for he was all but shoving me towards the gate.

"I'll come back, Molly, I'll be back as soon as I can!" I gushed, feeling the hand of Mr. Marcus on my back. I thought that maybe he would like to meet Buzz but, alas, it was not to be. He turned and beat a hasty retreat into the house, taking Molly with him. I stood there for a moment and watched the door close behind them. Its closing seemed like an omen that was meant to separate more than just our physical presences. I shrugged my shoulders and turned to go.

I almost tripped over Scotty who had decided to sniff my boots one last time. I was instantly in a good mood, reached down and scratched him behind the ear and made my way out the gate. As I closed it behind me I looked once again to the door hoping for a glimpse of the girl. I started to turn away but something caught my eye and I looked towards the upstairs window. There stood Molly waving at me excitedly and smiling her beautiful smile. I waved back like a school kid until I saw her being pulled away from the window. Whether it was her mom or dad doing the pulling I could not tell. What strange people I thought. Molly would probably be glad to get away from them.

Whistling, I walked down the hill, climbed into the waiting truck, rolled down the window and strained my neck to see if I could get one more glimpse of her. Eventually, I turned back, leaned my head back and let out a sigh.

***

As we headed towards Aunt Arvie's, Buzz's snail-paced driving bothered me not in the least. In fact I rather enjoyed it, since I knew that it would give me time to think before we arrived.

Was it really possible for me to know innocence again? This entire afternoon brought back to mind an incident of my early childhood that took place when I was in Kindergarten. Back so, so long ago when I was… well… innocent.

School had just begun one morning when I saw one of the little girls give our teacher a pack of candy cigarettes that she knew wasn't allowed in class. The teacher patted her on the head, told her what a good little girl she was and placed them on the desk. She said she would keep them for her until school finished that day.

I never thought much about them until we came to the time of day where we skipped in a large circle around the room. I don't remember how long we skipped, but I do remember that as I passed by the teacher's desk the candy cigarettes caught my eyes. To the best of my knowledge, I'd never actually had this type of candy and had never stolen anything in my life. I also knew that what I was thinking about doing was wrong. But with each skipping pass I began to desire them more and more. Finally, skipping by, I snagged them with more than my eyes and thrust them deep into my little pocket and kept on skipping. Every moment or so, I ventured a look round about to see if I'd been observed. Apparently, I had gotten away with it.

By and by, when we'd all laid down on our own towels, supposedly to take a nap, I slipped them out of my pocket and began acting like I was a really cool dude and 'smoked one.'

Presently I had the feeling that I was being watched. I slowly turned my head and there peering at me through many table and chair legs, with very big eyes, was Bruce and Pat. Bruce and Pat were two neighbor kids that lived across the alley from us and down just a little. They were twins (a brother and a sister) that didn't look like twins. They were staring incredulously at me, as if not believing what their eyes were telling them. I was caught. Thinking quickly, I slipped two more 'cigarettes' out and began by gesture to offer them to my would be accusers. They shook their heads in the negative with eyes so wide that you'd have thought that Lucifer himself was offering them an apple.

I kept trying to bribe them (it was amazing how quickly I was learning the ropes I'd never touched before) but they wouldn't budge. Failing to corrupt them, I quickly devoured all the evidence (not being allowed any savoring luxury at all) and wadded the box up into a little ball and put it in my under shorts. As soon as the teacher told us we could get up, I folded my towel and asked if I could go to the bathroom. Once I got there, I flushed the last of the evidence down the commode, (it still amazes me that this was the exact same trick I used many years later to dispose of the Kodak can that had held heroin).

School dismissed, and I was just about out the door when I heard my name being called. I turned to see my teacher standing with the little cigarette-less girl who was now in tears. Next to them both were ... Bruce and Pat. The teacher was motioning for me to come over with her finger. I looked around me and placed my finger on my chest and said, "Me? You want me?" My teacher nodded and waved me over vigorously.

"Larry, did you happen to see Cathy's little box of candy cigarettes?"

"No!" I said, lying through my teeth and shaking my head heartily.

"You did too! You did too!" Bruce and Pat chimed in with great enthusiasm.

Before it was over, I was crying—and denying. The little girl cried even more. The teacher was very frustrated and promised to bring her some more candy cigarettes first thing in the morning. Bruce and Pat continued to glare at me while I stood there with my pockets turned inside out and looking stupid.

I will never forget my walk home that afternoon. I had never in my life remembered feeling so bad and so dirty. My little heart was so very heavy and I felt terrible. It was the first time in my life that I ever truly knew that I'd done something terribly wrong. I felt guilt, horrible, powerful guilt. And somehow from that day on I never felt 'innocent' again. It was shortly after this experience, that I had the dream. That horrible nightmare of being trapped in the room… forever.

Maybe Molly could restore that sense of innocence for me. Maybe this sweet, innocent girl could somehow make me feel clean once again.

***

Buzz and I slowly made our way to my Aunt Arvie's. I now knew that once I got there, I wouldn't want to leave but would want to stay as close to Grandpa's place as possible. But how could I? It was my senior year (such as it was) and I would—hopefully—graduate in a few months. Maybe then…

That's it! I would see if Arvie would let me come back for just one more summer! I would get a job, maybe somewhere in Florence, or even Canon City and then I could spend time with Molly. Good, sweet, simple Molly. I would move out of Pueblo, get away from my friends, who, as sure as the world, were killing me. Rather, we were in the slow but sure process of killing each other. I'd let Norma go her way, which she had probably wanted to do for a while anyway, and I'd see how it went with Molly. Molly is the kind of girl a guy could settle down with. I wouldn't need to booze or drug it anymore, and, to be honest, I was sick of it all anyway. I was sick of the drinking and drugging, I was sick of being on probation, and being thrown in jail. I was sick of fist fights, gang fights and fighting with Buzz. I was sick of everything. But thankfully, it looked like it all was about to change.

These and a thousand other thoughts flooded my mind, and somehow they all kept coming back to the role that Molly would play in my life. My mother would *absolutely* love her. Though Mom has always been good to keep most of her opinions to herself, I know that my girlfriends had been anything but a joy to her heart, even Norma and especially Geri. The beautiful thing is that I won't miss either of them—not if Molly is there. I wonder what my friends will say when they hear that Larry Booker has gone straight. It will take them a long time to believe that I'm not just off into some new mind trip. Others will no doubt feel sorry for Molly, thinking that it will only last until Larry gets bored. What they will probably never realize is that I'm bored now. I am thoroughly sick of this sick world, and as close as I have been to my friends, I just don't want their world anymore. I can't take it. I just can't take it anymore…

But I've got to get on the good side of Molly's parents. When meeting Mr. Marcus, he made me feel like a snake trying to crawl in under the door. Oh well, it'll happen. I know that Mr. Marcus and I could never do much talking about hunting or fishing, since I know virtually nothing about it. But…

My reverie was interrupted by our arrival at Aunt Arvie's. I could tell by the cattle still in the holding pen that they were not yet finished with the evening milking. It had been quite a while since I'd been here and I wanted to relive what it was like to milk cows again. It seemed that my dreams during the drive had rejuvenated me and I was actually more eager to go to the barn than to the dinner table.

I jumped out of the truck before Buzz was finished parking, ran into the milk tank room and saw Arvie through the viewing window in the milking room. She was bent over, and had just placed a set of milkers onto a cow. I quietly opened the door and snuck up behind her while the radio played the song 'Little Green Apples' by Roger Miller. My friends would have died. I filled the lungs within my Steppenwolf sweatshirt, and began to sing into the ear of my totally unprepared aunt. She must have jumped a foot in the air before she turned and tried to hit me. Aunt Arvie is only five feet two and it was easy enough to 'dance' her somewhat reluctant body around the floor. Her free hand beat on my chest while I ignored her and continued to sing.

I don't know how comforting this was to the cattle, but you cannot begin to imagine the effect it had on Arvie... and me. Not only was it a shock for her to see me, but also this was first occasion in a long time that we had actually laughed together. More than all of my aunts, Arvie and I were the closest. This was only natural as she, more than anyone but my mother, had helped raise me. And this dear woman, more than any of the others, was hurt by what I had become.

Finally she said, "Well, it's good to see your face on something besides the ten o'clock news."

"And it's good to see you! You look wonderful and I've missed you and what's for dinner?"

"Oh Larry," she said while trying to take a slight slap at me, "What's going to become of you?"

"You know, I may just end up surprising you. Now, refresh me on how all this is done so I can help finish milking... while you go start dinner."

"Boy, you *must* be hungry," she said as Buzz and Uncle Bob came in. Bob looked at us both, saw the smile on our faces and said, "This is a switch, I thought when Arvie saw you she'd take club to ya."

"Well, the day's not over yet, but I think we'll make it," I said and set about to milk cows. My friends simply would not believe this.

We finished the milking and cleaned up while Arvie prepared one of her banner dinners. Though I had not worked nearly like a dog, I did proceed to eat like a pig. I had not yet brought up the possibilities of my coming to spend the summer with them, as I thought it best to get Arvie out of earshot of Buzz—let alone uncle Bob. Though I knew Buzz wanted what was best for me, I didn't want to run the risk of hurting his feelings. I also thought it best to talk to my mother before he did. So I figured I'd bide my time until Arvie and I had a chance to talk alone.

I was finishing up on seconds, having thoroughly enjoying the first round, when Buzz and Uncle Bob got up and went out to the truck to view some of the coins, keys and what-nots he'd found at Grandpa's. When the door had closed I said to Arvie, "I met a neat girl today."

"Really?" said Arvie. "Who? And for that matter, where'd you meet her?"

"Well, there's a family named Marcus that lives up on the hill in the house across from where Uncle Johnny and Aunt Evie used to live."

"Yea, I know the Marcus family. Cleveland Marcus is the dad's name. I think they used to live down in Florence closer to town. They were in a bad car wreck a few years ago."

"Yeah, that's what Molly said. Tell me about the car wreck."

"I don't know much to tell, 'cept that it was a nightmare for everybody… especially for the mom and dad. What a waste, what a sad, sad waste—for both of the girls. What'd you say her name was?"

It's hard to explain what I was beginning to feel, but it was as if a cold steel hand was slowly beginning to wrap itself about my entrails. "Her name is Molly… Molly Mae, and what do you mean, 'a waste' for *both* girls, and, *especially for the parents*?"

"Well, I can only imagine how her mom and especially her dad must feel, what with one girl being killed and the other, that… Molly, being so, so… messed up. It's really a very sad, tragic thing."

I had put both my fork and knife down on the table, and felt my mouth go dry. "Arvie, what do you mean? What are you talking about?"

"Well, you know... her mind... I mean couldn't you tell? She was not really hurt in the wreck... physically that is... but she was in the hospital for a long, long time. The doctors were worried, and it wasn't until she had actually been out of the hospital for a year or so that they knew for sure."

"Knew what?" I said, with an inexplicable anger, and sickening dread climbing upwards into my heart.

"Her mind... Larry. Couldn't you tell that something's wrong with her mind? Molly has the mentality of a six year old... and they say that she always will."

There was an immediate stillness in the room, which Arvie could not have fathomed. After taking some unsteady breaths to somehow quell the detonation, I slowly rose from the table and stared down at the scraps that were left on my plate. I raised my eyes but saw nothing. Without a word I lay down my napkin, turned, and walked out the door

I went through the woods towards the river to where I used spend what I now knew were the only halcyon days of my life. I came to the water's edge and looked across the rapids to the deep pool on the other side... where I'd almost drowned many years before. I don't know how long I stood there, but it took the cold water seeping into my boots to rouse me to the fact that I was in it. I looked at my feet a long time... then turned and walked back up the bank. I sat down on a stump and rested my elbows on my knees with my head in my hands. At that moment I would have given anything in the world to hear Scotty barking behind me. But he didn't, and I knew that I would never—could never—hear him again. I began to cry. In a few moments I found myself in a heap on the ground as the pain sobbed itself into the earth.

Eventually, I found my way back to the truck and we rode home in silence. Buzz tried to ignite a couple of conversations but they died on his lips in my deadness.

When we arrived home mom was already in bed and he told me not to worry about unloading the truck, we could take care of it in the morning.

I walked downstairs to my room and again felt the pain in my right leg. I sat on the edge of my bed, pulled off my boots and socks and crawled under the covers.

I noticed a handwritten note on the nightstand by the lamp. It was from my mother saying that Geri, Norma, Rocco, and Loren had called. Sadly, I knew that I would be with all of them tomorrow.

I turned off the light, and lay looking at the ceiling for a long, long time until, at last, mercifully, my tears and my dreams were pulled beneath the surface and drowned in exhaustion.

It had indeed been a very long day.

# 2

## The Journey

"Shut the stupid door!" I screamed.

"It won't shut I told you!" Rocco screamed back while JoJo laughed so hard that he was in tears.

The brakes of the Plymouth squealed as I gingerly tried to pull over the car for the fourth time since we'd left Pueblo. It is only a hundred and twenty miles from Pueblo to Denver, but at this rate it was taking forever. I got out from behind the steering wheel, walked back to the trunk, fumbled around with the keys and finally got it open. "This is so stupid," I fumed. Inside the car I could hear JoJo and Rocco laugh and howl. I saw the tire iron and for a moment thought about using it on them but decided it wouldn't help. I did finally see something that could… a cardboard box. Ripping out two sides of it, I slammed the trunk and went over to Rocco's side of the car.

I pulled open the unlatchable door, and slammed it a couple of times to see if it really had become impossible to shut or if Rocco was just playing more mind games. Apparently it was the Plymouth's turn toy with me. I began folding the cardboard over the edges of the door trying to wedge the stupid thing shut. After several futile attempts, I got the rest of the box out of the trunk, wedged it in even more and eventually got the ignorant thing to stay closed. I looked down at the rear right tire and knew that I was going to have to put some more air into it before very long, as well as buy some gas. The Plymouth was a gas hog if I'd ever seen one. If it weren't for the odometer being broke, I'd check and see just how many miles per gallon it really got. Oh well, what can you expect from a car won in a penny-ante poker game that had gotten out of hand.

"Don't lean on the stupid door, Rocco, or you're going to be hamburger on the highway," I yelled through his window... though I knew he couldn't hear me.

I got behind the steering wheel, turned down the radio that JoJo had cranked full blast, and pulled back onto the Interstate. This was really shaping up to be a lousy trip and a lousy summer, I thought. But then it was turning out to be a lousy life.

We were on our way to Boulder—about thirty miles northwest of Denver, but were planning on spending the night at Tom and Marcy's. My hope was that the Plymouth would make it on to Boulder where I planned to unload it. It was mid-summer and I was finally out of high school.

Thank God, at least I'd graduated. I'd already had one dream in which I opened my diploma to find it blank...like the one that Frank and Jimmy and Geri, my old girlfriend, had received. Frank assured us that just a few more classes at summer school and he'd get a real one. The fake diploma was just so his family could see him walk across the platform and receive it from the principal that we all hated. So far, Frank had taken no steps to enroll in the necessary classes, but he kept assuring his parents that he would. Poor people.

But I did get a diploma, and it was real. I know because I kept checking it out to make sure—especially after I'd had the dream that it was blank. Granted, my grade point average was pretty low, a D minus, but how does the saying go... "An inch is as good as a mile." At least that's what I kept telling Mom and Buzz.

Somehow, when I was young, (before I hit the seventh grade and became omniscient) my good grades must have spoiled my parents. How they figured I could keep that up forever I don't know. Anyway, they did learn to lower their expectations and eventually came to the place that they were thankful for anything... even a 'D' and a rather less than stellar, but at least graduated, son.

Although, one time, in my senior year, I had almost made them happy. I finally decided at the beginning of the school year to go out for football. Coach Pankinan had been hounding me since I was a sophomore, and so I thought, "I'll give it one more shot." I'd played defensive tackle in the ninth grade and I must say, did pretty well. But that was before the bad trip… the bad drug trip that I had in the middle of my ninth grade year. After that experience I just wasn't good for much of anything. What was funny about the experience—funny is really *not* the word—was the way it had played into the dream I had when I was in kindergarten (not long after I stole the little girl's candy cigarettes).

At the time of the dream my name was Larry Lee McBeth. Mom had not yet married Buzz and when I had the dream, Mom, Phil and I were living in the upstairs apartment that we rented from Addy. Addy was a character. She was as tough as a boot and more than once took it upon herself to spank me. She wasn't even family, for goodness sake! She was my mother's landlady! But I think Mom let her do it because she knew that if we couldn't live there we might have to go back to Grandma's again. It's also possible that Mom may have thought that I needed it. I *know* Addy thought I did.

At any rate, it was while we were living in that apartment that I had the dream. In it, I was standing in the corner of a dark room and for some reason was very frightened. A young man with dark hair approached me and screamed into my face "GO!" As I stared down at him, I grew even more frightened and ran into another corner of the room, as if I was trying to hide. Then a young red haired man with bright freckles ran up to me and screamed "GO WHERE?!" Upon hearing that, I ran to the next corner of the room, did the same trying-to-act-like-you're-not-there-routine while yet another young man, that resembled the first but whose hair was much longer, ran to me and yelled, "GO WITH WHOM?" I ran yet again to the last corner of the room only to be met by one more stranger who had a can in his hand and said, "Pass it to Booker." I didn't even know what a 'Booker' was. In that terror-filled moment, I felt doomed to run from one corner to of that room to the next… evermore.

I woke up crying, soon realized that I was in my own room in my own bunk. It had been some kind of a horrible dream. After wondering what it was all about, I fell back to sleep and as six-year olds do, woke up in a new world. In a day or two, I forgot about the dream.

It was not until the early spring of my ninth grade year, after a fairly successful football season, that I remembered the dream, and when and where I'd had it. My friends Loren, Bernard (also known as 'Pinky' due to his red hair and freckles), Richard, his brother Edmund and I had broken into a home on a Friday night. It was a newly built house that had yet to be moved into, and from Friday night until Sunday night we did absolutely nothing but inhale the fumes of several different kinds of chemical substances all of which are destructive and dangerous. When I say, that's all we did, I mean, that's *all* we did. I don't even remember eating or sleeping during that time, though I'm sure we must have done some of both.

It was probably around nine o'clock Sunday night when I told my buddies that I was going to 'blow my mind' and that I didn't want anybody messing with me. As I went into one of the corners of the room to begin my folly I had no idea how close I really would come to 'blowing my mind.' I don't know how long I gave myself over to the substance, but eventually I was absolutely and completely 'out of it.' Not knowing who or where I was, I stood in the corner of the room like a frightened, trapped animal. It was then that Richard (also known as Scab) ran up to me and yelled into my face, "GO!" Like an automaton I ran to the next corner, trying to somehow hide from my fate. Then red-headed, freckle-faced Bernard ran up to me and screamed, "GO WHERE?" I sped to the next corner, where Edmund yelled in my face, "GO WITH WHOM?" Whereupon Loren walked up to me with a can in his hand and said "Pass it to Booker." It was then—gripped with fear so thick that I could literally taste it in the back of my throat—that I believed I was consigned for eternity to run the course of the room. And so I began to run. My friends later told me that my scream was that of the damned.

When I came to, I found myself outside the house lying on my back on the lawn. Richard, Edmund, Bernard and Loren were on their knees looking down at me. I stared up at them wondering who they were and what they wanted with me.

"Larry, are you okay?" one of them said.

I just stared. I couldn't answer. I didn't know *who* I was, let alone if I was okay. Furthermore, I couldn't seem to make the connection between my thoughts and any physical function. "I must be paralyzed," I thought.

"Larry… Larry, talk to me," the red haired boy was saying. But I did not know who Larry was, nor could I talk—I could only feel and taste the fear.

I don't know how long the process took, but eventually it drifted back to me piecemeal that these were my friends, what their names were, who I was and that I'd better go home. Whatever had happened, I'd had enough for one night. While I don't remember saying good-night, I do remember the walk home. I kept putting one foot in front of the other while looking up at the sky. The half moon was just above the mountains and the drifting clouds brought it in and out of sight. It would have been beautiful except for the stars. The stars seemed… accusatory. They looked down at me as if I had shattered their peacefulness and they would now spend eternity in an effort to get even with me. Their tiny beams of light were like tiny pin-pricks boring into me and like eyes inspecting me. I made myself stop looking up and determined to look to the ground only. In doing so I found that I'd passed my street by several blocks, and was not even sure where I was.

Then a new fear gripped me. I would never find my way home. The stars would get their revenge by never giving way to daylight. It was so clear to me now. I was not doomed to the house and its endless running from corner to corner, but to the streets, and nighttime and the accusing stars, forever. So I walked faster, and then began to run to find the light, in order to find the sun. I had to find the sun… I just had to find the sun! It had to be here somewhere… and then finally I spotted something familiar. Two trees with their trunks painted white with big red dots. This was Rocco's house! His mother had allowed him and his sister to paint the trunks of the two trees in their front yard so their friends could find the house easier. I knew that they lived just two streets away from me. But which way did I need to go?

I stood on the corner looking both ways and just couldn't make my mind work. "Oh, God, please let the sun come up!" I said out loud. "Then I'll know which way to go." Finally I turned to the left but hadn't gone very far when I saw the elementary school. I knew that was not the right way so I reversed my steps and walked past Rocco's street and made myself pay close attention. I passed one street and came to the street sign and looked up to read, HOLLYBROOK. "This is it," I said so relieved that my voice began to break. At that point, I said, "C'mon Larry, get a grip." And so, I set my face and began walking up the street to my home.

When I'd reached the house I stayed outside a long time. Bending over with my hands on my knees I kept taking deep breaths. I knew that I had to get my mind in order. What was it I'd told my parents we were doing this weekend? I had given them some story about where we all were going to be… but now I couldn't marshal my memory. Maybe I'd get lucky and they'd be asleep and I wouldn't have to worry about it for tonight. I walked around to the back of the house so I could enter and go straight down the stairs to my room in the basement. Looking in the back window I could see that Buzz was watching T.V., but didn't see Mom's feet on the footstool. That meant that she was probably already in bed and hopefully Buzz would be so engrossed he wouldn't ask questions. Normally I could field most any question, regardless of how high I was, but tonight was a different case altogether. I really didn't know if I had it in me to keep myself together. If I started to unravel I was sure I couldn't stop and would shatter in front of Buzz. "Please, God, just let me make it to my bedroom," I prayed.

I slowly began to turn the doorknob… it was locked. No! It can't be… not tonight! I had to actually step away from the door in order to catch my breath. Did I have a key? No, of course not… if I'd had a key I would've lost it somewhere. I knew it and my parents knew it and that's why they never gave me a key. But why did they lock the door tonight of all nights? This is so stupid!

Now what am I going to do... I'm going to have to knock... I am going to have to get Buzz's attention... I am going to have to talk to him. Get a grip, Larry.

Before knocking I turned on the water faucet on the back patio and splashed cold water on my face. I thought it might help to clear my mind and prepare me for whatever questions Buzz might ask.

I screwed up my courage and began to tap on the back window. Buzz showed no recognition so I took a breath and began tapping louder. This time I could tell he heard me for I saw him glance in the direction of the back door, but his eyes returned immediately to the television screen. What is this, I thought, is he going to play games with me? I tapped loudly knowing that even my Mom might hear me now, but still he showed no inclination in my direction. For what is was worth, the anger that was beginning to rise in me was also clearing my mind of some of its confusion. I was about to get into some heavy banging when I saw his feet more or less kick the footstool out of the way and he began to get to his feet. I could also see that his lips were uttering some choice words, no doubt about me.

He unlocked and yanked open the door. "Where have you been?" he grumbled.

But before I could answer—whatever I would have answered—he had already turned and was making his way back to the chair and the television. I mumbled something as I made my way down the stairs. Apparently, there was something on television more interesting.

Once in my room I sat on the edge of the bed for a long time. After a while I realized that if my light was off the chance of someone coming down to ask me questions, was pretty slim. Quickly, I undressed, got under the covers and turned off the light. The streetlight outside gave a faint glow to my room as I stared at the ceiling trying to make sense out of my still whirling mind. Eventually I fell asleep.

Then I had the dream. The dream that I'd had when so very young came again, just as it had became reality in the room with my friends. Once more I was condemned to run the circuit of the room forever. It was as real as when I experienced it in that empty house. And it was every bit as terrifying. The only thing, and I mean *only* thing that entered into my mind that could possibly help me was… God. So I cried out to him for help.

"OH GOD! Please get me out of this! If you do I swear to you that I will never whiff fumes or hauto again!"

Then, suddenly, I realized that I was safe in my own home, downstairs in my room. I was not in the infernal, eternal room, nor was I six years old in Addy's apartment. I was fifteen years old and I was in the ninth grade at Pitt's Junior High. I lay there breathing hard, trying to make myself stop shaking.

After a while, somehow, I fell back to sleep. But it was short respite as I once again experienced the nightmare, just as I'd had it when I was six, and as I'd experienced it only hours before. And again I cried out to God for help and promised him that if he'd get me out of this, I'd never… smoke cigarettes. Once the promise crossed my lips, I again came to myself, realized that I was downstairs in my room and in my bed. Once again I somehow fell asleep.

The dream returned with the same vengeance and impact as before and I responded with a plea to God that if He would get me out of this horror I would never smoke marijuana. I awoke, realizing that I was downstairs in my room and in my bed, with my covers thrashed about me.

But I fell asleep, suffered the nightmare, offered yet a new promise that if delivered, I would never drink alcohol, and awoke to find myself in my room, in my bed.

This hellish dream and my desperate promises went on and on, over and over again throughout that night. I made promise after promise to God of things that I would never do. Speed, cocaine, LSD, heroin, you name it. If I'd heard of it, I promised that I'd never do it. Finally, the last time the dream occurred, in my dread I said, "God… if you'll get me out of this I promise you that I will never, ever shoot up anything into my arms!" I came to, downstairs, on my bed. This time when I fell asleep, I slept for whatever was left of that desolate night.

It was my mother that gently awakened me. "Larry… Larry,

wake up, it's time for school." I was facing the wall when I opened my eyes but dared not roll over. I knew I had to lie there and try to sort out once again who and what I was supposed to be. Already I was breathing hard as an unnamed fear rose in my throat. As Mom began to softly shake me, I said, "It's okay Mom, I'm awake… I'll be up in a minute."

"Well, you should have been up thirty minutes ago. What time did you get home from Tao's?"

That was it! I had told them I was going to be spending the weekend at Tao's house. Tao's father was a well-known, respected bone doctor in Pueblo, and my parents didn't worry much if they thought I was going there.

"I don't really know what time it was… but Buzz was still up watching television," I said rolling over.

"Well, anyway, get up and get dressed. I'll make you something that you can eat on the way to school. I'll get Philip to wait a little longer so he can give you a ride," she said, and was off.

Phil and I rode together in silence. He was my older brother by two and a half years and was a senior at South High School while I was ninth grader at Pitts Junior High. When we were little we had been close, but the years and the dynamics of school and our own sets of friends had pretty well separated us. I didn't dislike him—nor did he dislike me—we were just on two very different wavelengths. Phil was a good guy who always got the best of grades and never gave Mom and Buzz or his teachers much trouble. I say 'much' because, for whatever reason, there were days when he and Buzz just did not jive at all. Not that Buzz and I were always hunky-dory, but I knew how to 'work him' when I really wanted something out of him. But Phil didn't, and if he didn't get what he wanted, or needed, he and Buzz could clash big time. And both of them—well all three of us—had pretty ferocious tempers. The only really sweet one was Mom.

Phil let me off in front of Pitt's—well named I thought—and I could tell by the squeal of his tires—before I had completely shut the door—that he was not happy that I had made him late.

I turned to face the school, took a deep breath and walked

inside. Looking past my reflection on the front glass doors, I could see a group of guys huddled together looking at me. I reached the door and it was opened from inside by Loren. "Larry, are you okay?" he said. "You really freaked out last night!"

I can't explain what his question and the stares of my buddies did to me. It was like the stars checking me out all over again. Had Loren said, "Hey, Larry, I thought you needed to know, you forgot to dress and have nothing on but your underwear," I couldn't have been more mortified or petrified. My mind was struggling to get a grasp on reality let alone my emotions, which were racing almost as fast as my heart. I could hardly breathe. All I managed to produce in response was a curt nod as I hurried past them. This was totally out of character for me and they and I both knew it. I was saved by the bell which sounded as I rushed away. My friends must have thought that I didn't want to be late to class and was therefore avoiding a conversation. But then, that was also out of character.

I managed to turn my head in their direction, squeeze out the briefest of smiles and keep walking away. They must have made their way to their own classes, but I didn't know for sure as I couldn't bring myself to look back. I just kept moving forward down the hall to... where? Where was I going? I didn't even know where I was supposed to go. "Oh God," I muttered, "I've stripped my gears a lot worse than I thought."

I did not stop until I reached the end of the hall, opened the door and kept on going. I'd exited the east wing of the school, crossed the area between the school to the street and was halfway across it before I began to get myself together. I stopped on the street corner, leaned up against the stop sign and began taking slow deep breaths. "Larry Booker, you are a paranoid." I said out loud, "An absolute freaking paranoid."

I'd seen it in others, especially in Sam Gardenas. I used to watch him in class, especially P.E. as his eyes furtively roved in every direction to see if someone was looking at him. He seemed to me like a hunted animal, or haunted boy who was ever looking over his shoulder in a dirge of constant fear.

"So, now it's my turn. It's finally happened to me." I said aloud. "I am now an utter paranoid, and this is what it feels like to really lose it." I thought I was going to be sick.

It was everything I could do to make myself let go of the sign and begin to make my way across the street back to the school. "What am I afraid of?" I kept asking myself and then, "Get a hold of yourself, Larry boy, or they're going to come and take you away!" I forced my legs and feet to make their way up the steps, and my mind to figure out where I was supposed to be going. "It's your first class period you idiot! Think… *think*… where are you supposed to go?"

The hall was empty. Everyone was already in class, and it seemed lonely and endless. "My locker," I whispered, "I'll go to my locker and work it out from there." I went down the hall, across to the west wing and stopped just before Mr. Akers math class. "Three-oh-two," I said, "locker three-oh-two." I stood facing it and actually remembered my locker combination without a second thought. How stupid to remember something like that and yet not even remember what class I'm in!

I looked at the books on the shelf above the coat hanger. They were an American history book and math book and I remembered that those classes were at the end of the day. I bent over and began rummaging through the stuff at the bottom of the locker. When I saw the book entitled "Metal-working, Designs and Pattern," I groaned. "Of course, Mr. Brown's class. He'll fry me, he will absolutely fry me." I dreaded being late to his class on a good day, let alone now that my brain was shredded. Worst of all, I couldn't even think up a good excuse, in fact I couldn't even think up a bad one. On a good day I might enjoy fencing with Mr. Brown—if he were in a half-way decent mood. But on a day like this… "Oh God, help me… what day is this? Monday… Monday… What about Mondays? Get a hold of yourself, Larry… Oh, yes! Mondays are always bad days for Mr. Brown." This was not good.

I gathered my books and walked back down the hall to the door of his classroom. I knew that I was not up to facing him and was about to turn and leave when I decided to chance a look inside. Mr. Brown was sitting at the workbench where the drill presses were with the students gathered around him. He must be holding court, I thought. Sometimes the students would get him off on a subject that they knew interested him, in order to kill time and get out of work. Apparently they had pulled it off again, and I could tell by the animated motions of his hands and arms that he was off to an impassioned start. My hope was that they'd got to him before he'd had a chance to take attendance. I slipped in, placed my books under my desk and quietly began to make my way across the room behind him.

"I'm telling you I wouldn't be surprised if before it's over, big portions of Detroit and Los Angeles are burnt to the ground," Mr. Brown was remonstrating. "And that'll just be the beginning, you wait till Louisville gets..."

"What's he talking about?" I whispered into the ear of a fellow classmate.

"The King assassination," he whispered back, "He was on a roll before we were in our seats."

"Violence is never justified, and whoever performs these acts of violence is as wrong as whoever killed Dr. King..." Mr. Brown continued, occasionally glancing at Michael Tannehil, one of the few black guys in our class. "But at the same time, what are these people supposed to do? People can only take so much. Think with me boys, is our government really doing..." As messed up as I was, I could see that Mr. Brown was worked up and well into another harangue on what he felt were 'injustices of the 'system.'

While not one to keep up with the news closely, I knew everyone was shaken last Thursday when Martin Luther King, Jr. was killed. The school was abuzz over it on Friday. Some of the kids were sick about it and some said he got what he deserved. But then that's the way of life; it's full of opinions, good and bad, smart and stupid. What my buddies and I had been doing had kept me in the dark concerning the most recent developments. Maybe, before it was over, what we'd been doing would put me in the nuthouse. Now that I think about it, the assassination may have been what Buzz was watching on television, but it could have just as easily been a western.

As interesting as Mr. Brown's monologues were, he was making at least some of us uncomfortable. Even Mike, who'd been looking at his shoes, lifted his eyes every now and then to glare at Mr. Brown. Even though we were all 'young and impressionable' and considered part of the upcoming 'radical generation,' I was personally uncomfortable with… anarchy—even though I had a lot of it in my life—if that's what he was advocating. I wanted to say something to stop him or at least change the subject, but in my condition I knew that no good would come from any intervention on my part. It was at that point in my thought process that I heard my name being called.

"Mr. Booker, do you hear me? What do you think, Mr. Booker?" Mr. Brown was saying and staring at me forebodingly.

All I could do was stare back at him.

"Can't you hear me? Has the cat got your tongue for once in your life?" Mr. Brown persisted.

In times past I would have relished both the verbal confrontation, the test of wits, and the waste of work time—but today it threw me into a panic. I could already feel the sweat running down my armpits, and my stomach was queasy.

"I, I don't know…" I managed to stammer.

"What do you mean, you don't know?" Mr. Brown said, way too quietly.

"I… I mean… what did you say, I mean what did you ask?" I said, feeling as if I was suffocating.

Mr. Brown, as well as the class, looked at me rather oddly, with their heads tilted as if they were all trying to figure me out.

"My goodness, it appears you may have killed Mr. King yourself, you look so…so… guilty," he said with a slight smile on his lips.

For a brief moment my heart stood still and I had to force myself not to scream; "NO! NO! I didn't do it. I promise!" But I gulped and stood and stared. Even Mike looked at me with an all-to-odd expression. I was beginning to realize how messed up my mind in fact really was.

Abruptly Mr. Brown cleared his throat and said, "O.K.,

everybody go to your projects and get started. I'll be around in a little bit to check out how it's going." As he spoke he was rising from his work stool and moving almost imperceptibly towards me. The boys began to make their way to their places as he sidled up next to me, took me gently by the arm and in as much as his gruff voice could, whispered up into my ear, "Larry, are you alright?" I stared down at him, and again could not make myself talk.

"Larry," he said even quieter, "You haven't done anything… stupid have you… I mean… to yourself?"

"I, I don't know what you mean?" I finally uttered, beginning to tremble.

Mr. Brown must have felt it in my arm for he began to walk me over to the sink and said, "Why don't you wash your face and go sit down at your desk for awhile."

Readily, but clumsily, I complied while noticing that the other guys were pretty much viewing this out of the corner of their eyes. When I sat down, I folded my arms on my desk and laid my head on them in an effort to hide. Mr. Brown's voice was markedly louder as he made his way around the room as if he was trying to draw the attention away from me—a gesture that I appreciated immensely.

After what seemed like hours, the bell rang and the guys began to make their way out. I lifted my head and began to move when I felt Mr. Brown's hand on my shoulder.

He was seated at a desk across from me, and looking at me very intently.

"Larry, I want to know… are you okay?"

"Yes sir. I, I'm okay… I, I just didn't get much sleep last night, that's all." Mr. Brown sat there looking into my eyes and I found that I couldn't look at his.

"Larry, I want to talk to you for a minute."

He got up from the desk, went to the door, shut it, and locked it, then pulled down the shade over the window. He returned to the desk that was too small for his bulky frame and sat down again. This time he sat a little closer and leaned towards me. His green eyes were very serious and I noticed tiny beads of sweat scattered throughout the tufts of his white hair.

"Larry, I want you to listen to me. Believe it or not, I like you and care about what happens to you. I know some of you think I'm out in the woods mentally, and maybe I am. To be honest, I don't know what to think half the time. But I know that it is very important that you boys learn *how to think*! I'm telling you that we are in a monumental time in this nation. It is convulsing... maybe to pieces, and nobody knows where it's all going to end up. People are talking, singing and screaming revolution. And before it's over it might just happen, but ... who knows. This I do know Larry, you've been given a very good mind—though you don't seem to use much of it, and, I don't want to see you destroy what's left of it, or yourself. Whatever it is you've done to yourself, it's written all over your face and actions."

I just sat there, looking at my hands.

"And I know that you and your cohorts think I'm just an old, stupid, bumbling man, and that I'm half senile because you can get me off track so I'll ramble away your work time. I know this is Metals Working class, but you're not going to grow up and make candle sconces for a living, and neither are any one of these boys. I know it, you know it, the administration knows it, and if your parents would ever think they'd know it too. So when you and your cronies start me down one of my little stray paths, don't think I'm an idiot. Listen to what I'm talking about... I'm trying to make you think, Larry! I don't know where all of these events are heading, but I do know it's far from over and the repercussions are going to be felt for a long time. It kills me to see this nation coming apart, and it kills me to see you coming apart. Don't throw your life away for God's sake! He's given you a beautiful mind and whatever you're doing to it I'm begging you to stop. Stop... before it's too late."

At that point we both heard the next class knocking on the door. Mr. Brown heaved himself up from the chair, went to his desk, wrote something on a pad of paper, tore the page loose and handed it to me. It was to Mr. Gonzales, the teacher of my next class. It was a short note explaining that it was not my fault for being late; rather it was Mr. Brown's. I had no idea that he knew what my next class was and who the teacher was. As I arose and headed towards the door Mr. Brown stopped me.

"Larry, don't forget your books."

I looked down at them, picked them up and started to turn. "And Larry," he said, "Don't be late to my class anymore." But he did not smile. In fact he looked very sad and older than I'd ever seen him before.

"I'm sorry Mr. Brown, I... I'll try to do better," I said and walked out the door.

***

I somehow made it through that day, and week and even through the rest of the school year. But I was never quite the same after that fateful weekend.

For one thing, I was through with sports. All the desire and drive in that direction had drained out of me. I wish I could say that I made Mr. Brown proud of me, and that I kept the promises that I'd made to God... but I didn't—though for a couple of weeks I did actually try. I did not smoke, drink or do anything during those days. When my friends would tell me that they would pick me up at such and such a time I would make excuses and tell them I couldn't go. They would look at me as if I were strange but go their raucous way. The next day I would hear all about their latest escapade.

So, I would sit at home and watch T.V. with my parents. One night we even watched a Billy Graham crusade together. When they saw my response to Mr. Graham's plea, to "Accept the Lord as your personal savior"—my parents knew something was up. Though they themselves made no move, from that night on my mother would ask me, "Are you going to be home tonight?" When I'd say "yes," she would take great pains to fix a good supper. And Mom's good suppers, are *really good* suppers. I think it was her way of trying to extend the waves of peace as long as possible.

The foremost reason I would not go anywhere was because of the promises that I'd made to God that nightmare night. My terrors had been so great, my prayers so fervent and my coming back to reality so wonderful, that I really did not want to break those promises. At least that's how I felt for the first two weeks.

Then it began to dawn on me that my drinking buddies were just that, "*drinking buddies*." If I was not going to drink—or drug with them, we were no longer buddies. My nights therefore were now spent at home, bored to death. Even at school I found myself being relegated to the back burner of conversation and company. I had estranged myself from 'decent' company, a long time before, and the only world I knew was the wild one and the only friends I had were the crazy ones. So I found myself sitting at home, bored out of my mind with nothing to do but watch T.V.—or do homework—although I hadn't actually gone as far as to attempt much of that. I mean, after all, I never promised God that I'd do my homework.

My slide from goodness began at the beginning of the third week. In math class I leaned over to Rocco and said, "Is anything going down tonight?" He smiled and said, "Hey, is old Lare coming back to the land of the living?"

"I might… what's going on?"

"Were going over to Loren's… his sister scored some pot."

I went cold inside. I didn't want to do anymore drugs, but I didn't want to sit at home anymore either. So, I made my first compromise. I came to the conclusion that if I could just sit around with a can of beer in my hand, taking an occasional sip, I would still be included in the group. I would only be breaking one of the promises, not to drink, and even then it would only be one can.

"You know Rocco, to be honest with you, I really don't want to do anymore of that stuff… and I mean it. I think I just want to stick with drinking a little. I… I don't want to end up like Charlie."

Charlie was a guy about five years older than us but who was a good friend of Bernard's. His father was a cop, but you'd never know it by Charlie's actions. He was really messed up on drugs and was all the time in and out of jail or some hospital. And he was mean, especially when he was drinking, and even when he was sober—which was rare. Bernard told us he had actually seen Charlie tell his father to get out of his own easy chair so that he could sit down. And watched as his policeman father did it. But Charlie was in prison now and I didn't want to end up like him—and—I didn't want to break my promises.

Even so, that night I went to Loren's. His parents were out of town for a couple of days and it was left up to one of his older sisters—just in her early twenties to watch over things. I'd made sure that I had a six-pack of Coors, but only intended to drink one can. While Rocco, Loren, JoJo and Richard smoked their pot, I sat off to the side and sipped my beer. "Well," I thought, "at least I'm not home bored stiff." After awhile I finished my beer, and absently fetched another. I finished the second in a short period of time, and before I knew it the six-pack was empty. To my credit I did not smoke any pot that night. Not that I could have: they were out of the stuff before I was through with the beer.

Nevertheless, for the next couple of weeks that was my method of operation. I'd drink and they'd smoke. But more and more I found myself on the outside looking in. I was no longer the life of the party, the quick-witted prankster, the center of attention. I was becoming to them 'just a boozer,' and a 'brew sucker' at that.

One night in the back room of the Piñon Truck Stop where Richard and Edmund worked for their uncle, I finally succumbed to the pressure. I told God, "Now, God, I'm going to break this promise, but I'm really not going to break it completely, because… I'm not going to inhale." Well, so much for that.

I kept smoking pot (and inhaling) as over the next few weeks my friends began to graduate into other drugs, such as speed and then a hallucinogenic called mescaline. When mescaline came on the scene I found that I didn't have to break a promise to take it. I had never heard of it when I made all those promises to God. In but a short time however, the source of mescaline dried up and my friends started taking LSD and singing "Lucy in the Sky with Diamonds." So… I told God that all I would do was take one-fourth of a tab—never dreaming that before it was over

I'd be eating it almost like candy. The slide was quick, sure...and exceptionally slippery.

At the end of that painfully momentous ninth grade year, I walked into Mr. Brown's class one Friday morning to find him sitting unusually quiet. As my classmates came in they also picked up on his strange mood, and quietly began to sit down. His forehead was resting on the tips of his fingers, his elbow on his desk. Without looking at us he said, "Go to your benches and work on your projects."

With less chitchat than usual we set about our tasks. Mr. Brown continued to sit with his head in his hands for the remainder of the class saying virtually nothing unless asked.

When class was over and we began to file our way out I heard him call my name. I went to where he was and he motioned me to sit down. Over the last two months I had been able to pick back up on our old repertoire of banter, but, sometimes I still had a hard time looking at him—or anyone else—in the eye. "You know, Larry," he began, "I told you several weeks ago that this nation was coming apart at the seams, and that basically I didn't want to see you come apart with it. I guess now you see a little bit better what I was talking about."

I stared at him, trying to piece together his meaning and trying to remember if I'd done something that I hadn't got in trouble for yet. After a moment he could tell by the look on my face that I wasn't connecting the dots. He leaned towards me and said, "You *do know* what I'm talking about don't you?"

"No sir, I guess I don't."

"Good grief, boy, don't you read the papers?! Don't you watch T.V. or listen to the #%$&! radio?"

"I, I haven't yet today—what's up?"

Mr. Brown stared at me as if I was from another planet, shook his head and mumbled, "And these are tomorrow's leaders...God help us all. Larry... Bobby Kennedy was killed last night in Los Angeles." He then put his head back into his hands and mumbled, "God only knows where all of this is going to lead..."

I thought I now understood why Miss Engstrom—the English teacher—was crying as she came out of the school office. But I really couldn't relate to her or Mr. Brown's trauma. While I was shocked about Bobby Kennedy, I couldn't see that it meant the end of the world. Maybe it was the times that they had come through, or more likely I was just too young, dumb and spaced out to realize the full import of all the things that were happening. Later, when Hendrix, Joplin and Morrison died, I did feel that the world was coming apart. But a presidential candidate, even JFK's brother, just didn't grab me. Then again, that just wasn't my world. This I did know, Mr. Brown's fears unnerved me almost as much as the drugs were unnerving me.

Howbeit, certain things did have the ability to get next to me. One of the occurrences that did rattle me—at least temporarily—were the dreams I had that I knew were warnings from God—such as the one with the scorpions.

In that particular dream I was standing at the edge of a small lake at my Aunt Ida and Uncle Frank's place, southeast of Pueblo. I was looking towards the east, viewing the sunset as the clouds began to swirl majestically and form a huge, utterly stunning palace. It consisted of a glorious multi-hue in shades of orange and gold. I gazed in awe at this most lovely place—which I knew represented Heaven. I also knew that I wanted to go there more than anything else in the world. As I stood spellbound, I began to notice off in the distance to the northeast, small dark storm clouds beginning to gather and roll towards me. As the dark clouds grew closer the ones that formed the Palace began to break up and dissipate. The dark billowing clouds replaced the golden ones and soon formed a sinister, foreboding castle. It had become ominous and evil to behold… somewhat like my life. I knew that the dark castle represented Hell, and that I was going there—not to the other wonderful place.

Suddenly, in the dream, I was no longer at the edge of the lake but inside Aunt Ida's house. In her home there were no doors or windows or furniture, just the floor, the walls and the ceiling. I was looking for a way out, when the room began to slowly fill with water. I didn't know where the water came from, but it was murky, swirling, and seething in turmoil. It moved upwards from my ankles, to my knees, to my waist and then to my chest. There was no way out of the house and I finally had to tread water to stay afloat. As I did, I floated ever closer to the ceiling. I was horror stricken and knew that I was going to drown if something didn't happen. Then my terror intensified as I noticed that on the ceiling were literally dozens of scorpions and they were all converging towards the spot where my lips would soon be. When my face was but a few inches from the ceiling, I began to thrash about in sheer terror. Dozens of the scorpions were right before my eyes, crawling over the tops of each other in order to get to me. I let out a scream and awoke to a deathly, still room.

I lay on the bed as still as death except for my heavy breathing, drenched in sweat with my covers completely kicked off of me. Then from the darkness I distinctly heard a voice speak to me and say; "Larry…you are drowning in your sin."

I was too scared to move. I knew—I did not imagine it—I knew, that someone was in the room with me. Eventually I made my eyes move to my left, then slightly turned my head and began to look around. In the dim light from the street I could see no one. As I slowly felt the presence leave, I said, "Jesus, please have mercy on me." Then it was over. Everything, that is, but my heavy breathing and fear.

Other times there were dreams that were equally unnerving (such as my grandmother rejecting me). Yes, these things as well as what was happening in 1968 unnerved me.

It was not as if I was totally bereft of any positive spiritual influence, just pretty close to it. There was the time, as I said, shortly after I'd flipped out in the ninth grade, when my parents and I were watching the Billy Graham evangelistic crusade on television. When he began to call for a decision for Christ, I actually got down on my knees, laid over the footstool in front of the television, and began to ask Jesus to please forgive me of my sins and let me become a Christian. Mom and Buzz were stunned. That's when they knew something was really up with me. My mother was never comfortable with these types of things but would say nothing, while Buzz always had some smart remark to make about religion—especially 'organized religion.' This night however—at least while I prayed—he said nothing. I would be less than honest to say that I felt nothing. In fact I did feel a lot better—for about two or three days. But before long, I slid from my brush with God and the changes it had spurred and retreated back into my dark world.

Then too, in spite of how my friends and I carried on, we would often attend Mass. Though I was not Catholic, most of my friends were, so it wasn't too hard to get them to go…as long as their hangover or drug stupor would allow it.

I'll never forget the Christmas Eve when we all partied in ties and jackets, because at midnight we were going to church. We were all pretty excited because after the service the priests were going to serve rum and orange juice and cake in the big hall.

During the rather dull service, my friend, John Garza started getting a little mouthy, so I told him to "Shut up," and, "Don't act like a fool in Church!" John didn't take very kindly to my words and neither did the people around us (they were not spoken in hushed terms) but rather than get into a brawl then and there he got up in a huff and left.

After the service we all went around to the dining hall and lined up with the fellow parishioners to get our ration of rum. Presently I noticed some of them storming out the door saying in effect that they wouldn't stay around a church like this. After about the fifth or sixth such exit, I grabbed one of the exitors and said, "Hey, what's going on? Where's everybody off to?" He none too politely, shook off my hand and said, "Some low down *blankety-blank, blank-blank* stole the *blankety-blank, blank* rum!"

I could not believe it and began muttering to myself and anyone else who cared to listen, "How sorry and low down could somebody be, to actually steal the church's booze! What's this world coming to when even the church's booze is not sacred?!" After a moment or two I felt John pulling at my sleeve saying, "C'mon Booker, let's go."

I said to him, "Hey, did you here what some no good, low down *blankety-blank, blank-blank* did? He stole the *blankety-blank, blank* rum!"

He looked away and said, "C'mon Let's just get out of here."

I was rehearsing once more my views on the decadence

of mankind, when John looked up at me and with a pained expression said, "C'mon, Larry, let's go... I... I've got the rum in the trunk."

"Oh," I said, and we left to go party.

All that night—what I remember of it—John would break down crying and say that he was doomed because the priest would never give him absolution for taking the rum. I would just pat him on the back, laugh and tell him not to worry, and that if he would go to the priest across town and confess, *that* priest would get a big kick out of it, would surely forgive him and that he might even get a blessing to boot.

That pretty much was the extent and depth of our religious service.

Because I was one by one breaking the promises that I'd made to God, my summers and next three years of high school were a blur of trouble and madness. Such as the times we would go out into the prairies and shoot cigarettes out of each other's mouths and beer cans off each other's heads with .22 caliber pistols and rifles. Or when we'd have Bernard drive down dirt roads in excess of one hundred miles per hour while some of us would sit on the hood of his car hanging on to the Pontiac Indian head. One time while doing so, a retread flew from off one of the rear tires and out towards the front of the car scraping and taking much of the paint off the drivers side. It also just barely missed decapitating Bill who had been hanging his head out the window.

***

And so, my disheveled life somehow continued on. Between the alcohol, drugs, arrests, probation, ditching school for sometimes two weeks at a time, fights between our 'gang' and the other high schools around Pueblo, and bad girlfriends, I had become a walking wreck that was now driving a wreck, with two spaced out friends going to Denver. Well... at least I had graduated.

And, oh yes, I did almost make my parents happy. I played football my senior year and had one university—Colorado, at Boulder—and one college—Adams State, at Alamosa—contact me about scholarships. But before the season was over, me and twelve other guys were kicked off the team. We were kicked off because we couldn't bring ourselves to cut our hair under one inch in length.

I actually still had a chance at a scholarship, but between my grades and especially after the drug bust with Joe (when my Aunt Arvie saw me on T.V.) those hopes went down the drain forever. Almost happy parents, once… in my senior year.

***

I pulled over north of Castle Rock to buy some gas, though the gauge showed that we still had half a tank. I had ran out last week thinking I had half a tank—the gauge didn't work—but then, that was but one of a long list of things about the car, and my life, that were dysfunctional. I drove up to the pumps and looked around at my fellow wrecks. "You guys got some money for gas?" I asked, knowing what the response would be. Rocco seemed to be sleeping and JoJo was staring off into space.

I knew that unless JoJo had scored on something pretty good lately he would have next to nothing by way of money. JoJo was raised in the Sacred Heart orphanage and pretty much had to scrounge about for anything he got, which was surprisingly sometimes quite a lot, especially if it had to do with dope. He was a walking pharmacy. But if anybody had some money, it would be Rocco.

We'd been buying and sending thousand lots of LSD to Vietnam for close to a year. We would buy them up on the Hill in Boulder (I was almost always with him) and send them to Joe Arguello in Saigon, having paid anywhere from 19 to 29 cents a tab for them. Joe, in turn, would sell them to fellow G.I.'s for $5.00 a hit, then use what money he didn't blow or save to buy uncut heroin, send it back to Rocco, where we'd use a little, cut down the rest, sell it, go back to Boulder and buy another thousand lot of acid. While running terrible risks, we saw very little of the profits. At least I didn't. But, in all honesty, Rocco probably didn't either as it all got spent on partying. At any rate—asleep or not—I intended to get some gas money out of the 'sleeping wreck.'

"Wake up!" I said shaking him. "Give me some money for gas."

"Ahhh, man! Why fool with a man's sleep for something as stupid as that?"

"Because gas stations seem to make you sleepy, and I know you'd rather wake up and fork out some money now than wake up and have to walk when we run out of gas." He turned to his right a little so I couldn't see his cash roll and pulled out three bucks.

"Cheapskate." I said.

"What! That's almost twelve gallons of gas! That ought to get us to all the way to Boulder and back!" he bleated.

"It might get a normal car there and back, but I got a feeling this thing ain't doing but about six or seven miles a gallon."

I put in sixteen gallons and paid the attendant $4.08. Then I thought I'd better check the oil and remembered to put air in the rear right tire. It took two quarts of oil so I had to pay another eighty-five cents. It's a good thing Mom had given me some money before I left. I sure hoped I could sell the car in Boulder and get some more.

We started to pull away when Rocco who apparently really *had* gone to sleep, leaned against the door with the cardboard latches. He screamed as he fell out, hit the ground and rolled to a stop. Though I'd only been going about fifteen miles per hour, I was accelerating pretty quickly. When I stopped, JoJo jumped out and started to run back to where Rocco was picking himself up off the ground and cursing a blue streak.

When we got the door wedged shut again, and Rocco seated on the other side, we took off again towards Denver. I was hoping we could make it to Marcy's in time for her to fix us some kind of dinner.

It took some kind of gall to even think of dropping in on Marcy and mooching a meal and a place to stay after what I'd done to her in the latter part of our junior year.

We'd been having a woodsy in the mountains up above the small town of Beulah when she and I had gotten into quite a row. Marcy had for some time been like a kid sister to me and we thought nothing of fighting like brothers and sisters. Though I cannot remember the subject of our disagreement, I do remember the intensity. Finally I told her "Well why don't you just hit me?" So she did. Though Marcy is only about five feet tall, she was a lot stronger than she looked, and when she hit me in the stomach I literally doubled over. It made me so mad that, when I recovered, I picked her up by the shoulders and walked her over to the edge of a cliff about ten feet from where were standing. I began to shake her like a rag doll over the precipice. The cliff was about twenty feet tall and as she fought, kicked and screamed, I lost my balance—which wasn't all that steady at the time anyway (after all… it was a woodsy) and we both fell over the precipice.

We landed on our backs, bent backwards over two large round rocks. I literally thought I was dead. I lay there thinking, "So this is how I die… I always wondered how I would go." After what seemed like forever, I felt myself take in a gulp of air. Pain like you can't believe shot through my body. Well, thank God, at least I knew I was still alive. In another moment or two I began to hear three things. First and most important was Marcy's pitiful moaning. Now I thanked God that she was still alive. Secondly I could hear the voices of friends yelling to us from the top of the cliff trying to ascertain if we were alive. Thirdly I could hear others thrashing through the brush on their way down to help us.

Then two more impressive items worked their way into my ears. The first was the sound of Marcy crying and the second was the sound of her cursing me soundly and colorfully.

After several very uncomfortable, slow-moving and painful days, I began to get back to normal. It wouldn't have hurt either one of us to go to the hospital, but neither she nor I was about to. To this day I am told the Marcy goes through spells of back pain that can sometimes be pretty awful.

And here I was, going to her house, unannounced, looking for a free meal. What kind of a glob of goo did my mother raise?

I glanced at my classy looking wristwatch in order to figure our arrival time. It read 11:15 a.m. "What!?" I said, "It can't be just 11:15." JoJo scratched, stretched, looked at his wristwatch and said, "It ain't 11:15 Larry, it's 1:45." I knew then that what I had feared was true. I'd won the watch in a poker game a few nights after I won the Plymouth, and it was just as messed up as the car. I took it off, hit it on the dash and it started ticking again. I put it back on and cursed my good luck at cards. All I won was junk.

***

The last time I'd traveled north on Interstate 25 was just a few of weeks ago. Tyrone, JoJo, Loren, Rocco and I had been dragging Pueblo's Main Street in Pueblo in a 56 Chevy station wagon that belonged to one of the guys at the orphanage. Tyrone got to talking about his girlfriend who lived up in Pierre, South Dakota. Her name was Theresa Bordeaux and was supposedly a beautiful Indian girl, the daughter of the Chief of the Sioux Nation. Tyrone kept going on about her so much and about how pretty she was that somebody finally said, "Hey, why don't we go see her! If she's such a knockout and her family's so neat let's go see them." So we did. We slipped two blocks over to I 25 north and headed out. We did not stop for clothes or food, but we did stop on the east side of town and got more drugs.

By way of memory, that night was pretty well lost to me, save for one main theme; my sorrow. Norma and I had finally broken up—if that's the term—and I took it much harder than I thought it would. After my experience with Molly Mae, I found myself almost clinging to Norma emotionally. I had hoped to somehow find in her a reason to change, and to do better. She and I both knew that if we kept up our lifestyle we were going to go destroy any hope of having a meaningful life.

Norma was not a bad girl; in fact in many ways she was a wonderful girl. Her father was one of the most renowned physicians in southern Colorado, who, again, for some reason, had taken a liking to me. On more than one occasion they had asked me to come to dinner and I had of course accepted. We then would sit over the baked zucchini, lamb chops—which I abhorred, but ate anyway—and discuss what I was going to do with my life.

I couldn't bring myself to say, "Well, one of these days I'm going to come into a really good line on some Iranian Hashish, buy it cheap and sell it high, keep some to smoke then retire to an island in the Pacific." So, I kept these thoughts to myself, watched Norma smile and listened to her father pontificate about the virtues of education and the tragedy of wasting a mind—let alone a life. The problem was that he actually made a lot of sense. But I was very uneasy, if not depressed, because I knew he was all but wasting his breath on the likes of me—and his own daughter. Both of Norma's sisters were very much driven and success oriented. Norma was the black sheep of the family who was dating a black sheep. No doubt these rather intense dinner parties were last-ditch efforts to stem the inexorable tide of losership in both of us.

Again, Norma was not a bad girl. She was actually very sweet, but she liked to party and drug so much that I didn't know if she could ever pull out of it on her own. And I knew that with all my partying and drugging we could never pull out of it together. But that's not why we broke up. The fact is, our relationship simply died... on her end. She just quit calling and quit returning my calls. As soon as the painful message got through to me, I was too proud to cling another minute. We lost contact, made no plans to be together and unless we happened to show up at the same party, we were finished.

That, coupled with the heartbreaking episode of Molly Mae, my whole dismal life and its prospects—especially now that I'd graduated—had left me horribly depressed. That night, as we traveled to meet Tyrone's girlfriend, and I sat in the back of the station wagon, stoned out, listening to 'Color My World' it came crashing in on me. Tears streamed down my cheeks and I felt like my heart was being crushed within my chest. I had not been this broken (thankfully I suffered in silence) since the night I knew that I could never see Molly Mae again. The night I realized it would be impossible for me to spend my life with her because I would eventually, unquestionably, break her innocent heart.

I was glad my friends were in the car. Their presence kept me from going to pieces. I just cried quietly to myself, thankful that it was dark. My next recollection of the trip to Pierre concerned what took place the next morning.

We had stopped God only knows where, and had simply passed out. When I came to, I opened my eyes and lay there trying to piece things together. It slowly came back to me: we had started this crazy trip on a whim and were on our way to somewhere in the Dakotas. My friends were asleep. JoJo was next to me in the back of the station wagon our heads by the tailgate. Thankfully, JoJo was a little guy—about five foot tall—so he didn't take up too much room. Rocco was at JoJo's feet while Loren was leaning against the right front door and Tyrone was on the other side passed out cold. I could see that it was just about to dawn, so I got up on one elbow and peeked over the edge of the tailgate to see where we were. The first thing that met my eyes were... dinosaurs. Big, very big, pink and blue and green and yellow dinosaurs were standing about thirty to forty yards away just off to the right. I lay back down with a groan and thought, "Oh, God, please help me, I have finally gone over the edge, and there's no coming back." I was trembling.

After a while, I reached over and began to shake JoJo. "JoJo... JoJo, wake up. Wake up JoJo," I whispered. Finally, he opened slits that turned out to be eyes, and began to run his tongue over what I knew from my own condition was a very dry, foul-tasting mouth.

"What?" he said with his eyes closed again.

"JoJo, I want you to look outside," I said quietly.

"Huh...do what?" he mumbled, his eyes starting to reappear.

"I want you to look outside, here, look out this window...above our heads."

I had to shake him some more but with a moan he began his struggle to one elbow and slowly raised his slits towards the window. I watched as his slits became a wide-open stare. He then blinked a couple of times, stared again for a long while and then he closed his eyes altogether. With a groan he lowered himself, laid his head back on his arm and said, "Larry… are, are they real? Cause if they are, man, we are in really, really bad trouble." He said this without ever opening his eyes. And I don't think he kept them closed from exhaustion, but rather, fear.

I didn't know how to answer him, so I propped myself up for another peek. They were still there. I lay back down to think.

Then I thought of something. After sliding over and down, past Rocco, I put my hand on the door handle and slowly opened it about eighteen inches or so. Then I slid quietly out the door and down onto the ground. I did not care that the ground was wet with dew as I crawled on my hands and knees towards the back of the car. Slowly I peered around the edge of the bumper. The dinosaurs were still there. I stayed still for a long time, waiting. I was waiting for the slightest movement. Had I seen so much as a twitch of a tail I would have ran like a madman (which I was close to being anyway) and left my friends to their fate. My screaming on the way out would have afforded them at least some warning.

After long inspection, I realized that these behemoths could not be real and thanked God. I stood to my feet. As I dried my hands on my pants I happened to look down and see JoJo. His eyes were once again peeking over the edge of the tailgate, looking first at the dinosaurs, then back at me, then back at them. Then we smiled at each other and winked.

We both had fun waking up our friends to the horror of this primeval world. The terror in their bloodshot eyes was worth the whole trip. By the time everything settled down we were reinvigorated, starving for breakfast, and ready for the rest of the journey. And we didn't have that far to go. We were at the 'Dinosaur Park' in Rapid City, South Dakota.

The Bordeaux family were better than Tyrone's claim. They received us into their home graciously, gave us board, fed us well. Theresa's mom even washed our clothes a couple of times while we were there. She would do it while we swam in the Oahe Lake that touches the town of Pierre. We were only there for four or five days but it really was a wonderful time. I was not only able to set aside my sorrow but, as we had ran out of drugs, was actually 'normal' for a few days. One morning in particular affected me deeply and I'll never forget it.

I had talked the guys into rising before daybreak in order to watch the sun rise over the city. Mrs. Bordeaux told us that sometimes in the summer the Missouri River Valley in which Pierre lay would be filled with a morning fog. If one would climb the hill to the north of the city, he could look down upon the top of the fog bank.

So on this particular morning we did just that. We had not been up half the night partying and it was actually fairly easy to get out of bed. So up the hill we trod.

Once on top, a light fog danced about our feet as we watched the sun come over the horizon. The sun caused the top of the cloudbank to shimmer in an orange gold haze. As my eyes went from the sun before me down the cloud-engulfed Missouri river towards the swallowed up town of Pierre, I saw something that made my heart stop.

Rising up through the cloudbank was the top of a church steeple. A large beautiful white cross—now turned gold—was the only thing to be seen, save for the cloud and the colors. Not only was it beautiful, it moved me in a way that neither I, nor my friends, would ever expect. It was solemnly stirring, and I came close to weeping as I stood finding myself unable to take my eyes off it. Except for the presence of my friends, I would have knelt and prayed. It was stupid that I didn't for, except for Loren, they were Catholic and were crossing themselves anyway. I never knew what this moment meant to them, for we never discussed it, but as I stood there I realized that something vitally important was missing in my life.

It wasn't as if I'd never attended church. When I was little, Addy, the tough landlady, made my brother and I go all the time. She attended a Foursquare church on Elizabeth Street on the North side in Pueblo. There are three things that stand out in my mind about our many journeys there. The first is that I hated it. The reasons for this was that, for one thing, I knew absolutely nothing about the Bible and when I'd go to Sunday school, I was scared to death that the teacher was going to ask me a question that it would be impossible for me to answer—which they sometimes did—and I'd feel like an absolute fool—which some of the kids thought I was. They didn't come right out and say it—probably because they knew I could wreak some vengeance—but when they would giggle and snicker at my ignorance, it was all the same.

I also hated it because I found the Church service agonizingly boring. It was so bad that I thought by simply sitting there, I was doubtless paying for all the bad stuff I had done that whole week—but that if I had to stay one minute longer I would surely die. It was no doubt during those services that thoughts of eternal punishment first began to plague me.

But again, there were two other things that stood out in my mind about that church.

One morning as I sat there nodding off, Addy punched me in the side and said, "Go on, go on up to the front… you won!" I had no idea what was going on, but I could tell that everyone was looking at me and smiling. I went up to the front like she told me to, and when I got there, the preacher gave me a bag of *gold coins*! I couldn't believe it! A bag of probably twelve or thirteen gold coins! Needless to say, I was very happy. I clutched the coins to my chest and simply wouldn't let go. I knew exactly what I was going to do with them. As soon as I got home, I was going to give all but two of the coins to my mother so she could pay off the bills that I'd heard her talking about, buy a whole refrigerator full of food and maybe even buy a car. I also intended to give one coin to my brother Philip—we got along pretty good back then—and keep one for myself.

I left the big church and went to our Sunday school class still clutching my treasure. Almost all of the kids asked me for a piece, but my adamant answer never varied; "No way!"

When it was over, I remember riding the Sunday school bus home that day. I don't know why we didn't ride home with Addy like we usually did, but then maybe it was a bus promotion or something. All I know is that on the way home, kids were still asking me for a piece and I was clutching it to my chest tighter than ever. When I was almost home, I looked down at my fortune and saw that the coins were all bent and warped and what was worse, the front of my shirt was smeared with brown stuff. It was not until that moment that I realized the coins were not real gold but were real chocolate. I couldn't believe it and was immediately sick with disappointment. Now I understood why all of the kids were asking me for a piece, though I couldn't believe their audacity. Mom would kill me if I went around asking people for money (anybody but her that is.) Anyway, though I was bitterly disappointed, I did manage to eat all the coins and lick my sticky fingers clean before I got off the bus.

The final thing that I remember about the church took place when I was a little older. One morning when the preacher, Pastor McClure, finished preaching, I felt compelled to walk down to the front like I saw some of the other grown-ups doing. I got up from my seat and went down. I knelt, folded my arms on the platform, placed my head down on them and in just a little while I began to cry… and I mean, *really cry*. I didn't even know why I was crying or what I was crying about. After a while I felt a hand on my back, and somebody said, "You'll be okay son. Jesus really does love you." That was it. Pretty soon I quit crying, got up, and went and sat down again. Though I didn't understand that moment, I never forgot it either.

As I stood on the hills that morning overlooking the fog bank that socked Pierre in, and stared at the cross, I knew that I was experiencing the exact same feeling I'd felt that morning as a little boy. I also knew that if I were to get down on my knees I would cry once more. But this time—I had an awful lot to cry about.

Though I did not pray that morning, I did that night. I went down to the river by myself and knelt on the bank. I didn't know how to pray, so I prayed a prayer that every now and then (since I'd had the scorpion nightmare) I'd pray. I buried my head between my knees, and slowly, fearfully began to say, "God… if in this lifetime…I end up doing more evil than good… would you please just kill me now and get it over with." I uttered this simple prayer in utmost sincerity, meaning every single word. So intense and sincere was I that I would completely tense up. I really did believe that God had no choice but to kill me. When no lightening split me asunder, I slowly got up and walked shakily back to the Bordeaux home.

***

Now, as the Plymouth made its agonized way into Denver over the same highway, I couldn't believe that it had been only a couple of weeks ago that we'd been in Pierre. I had thoroughly enjoyed the stay and would love to go again, but I didn't see that happening anytime in the near future. Just before we left, Theresa broke up with Tyrone and it was now his turn to be miserable. My heart went out to him; Theresa was even more beautiful than Tyrone had depicted. Well, Ty' old buddy, welcome to the lonely-hearts club band.

We finally made it to Denver and spent the night with Tom and Marcy, or at least what portion of the night was left after the party collapsed in drug-drunken fatigue. For the life of me, I don't know how Tom and Marcy got up in the morning and went to work, but when we finally rolled out about eleven they were gone. I told the guys that it wasn't right to leave the house in such a mess but they didn't listen. So we left.

I had to buy more gas in Louisville. I also put in more oil, put more air in the tire, put some water in the radiator, and had JoJo crawl under the car and hook the muffler back onto the exhaust pipe. One mixed blessing was that the radio broke also. After that pit stop, it only took us about thirty minutes to get to Boulder. We went straight to the University and Alan's dorm, hoping he was there or had left the door unlocked. It might get crowded and we would no doubt sleep on the floor, but Alan was always good to let us stay. Our plans, however, were to get an apartment in a few days and hopefully live in Boulder until winter—if not for good. Well, we would see what we would see.

# 3

# The Hill

Steve slept fitfully, his head leaning on his jacket that was rolled into a pillow against the window. His older sister Barbara was sleeping a little better because she was blessed to be leaning on his shoulder. As for Mark, it seemed that he never slept, let alone in the car, but thankfully he was on the other side of Barbara, and Timothy was next to him. Steve had a crick in his neck and really needed to move about but thought better of it for her sake. "Thank God this is a station wagon," thought Steve for the thousandth time, but still he wished it could have been a vehicle with a little more room.

His little sister Carol must have been thinking the same thing for she groggily said; "Dad, do they make any cars bigger than station wagons?" She was in the far back of the wagon with Becky and Elaine. Her father couldn't hear her, so she repeated the question. When her dad asked her what she was saying, Steve finally relayed it to him.

"Well, I imagine they do, but I don't see us driving one any time soon," Dad said as he tried to keep his eyes on the road, while glancing back in the rear view mirror to glimpse Carol's twelve year old face between Mark and Timothy's scrunched up shoulders. He also kept checking to make sure that the U-haul trailer was still behind them. Steve and his family were traveling from Fort Worth, Texas and, as was their annual custom, were headed towards a vacation in Colorado. Steve had four sisters and four brothers. This year his oldest brother, Roger, age twenty-two, had to stay home because of his work schedule. The responsibilities of life were beginning to take its toll, as this was the first family vacation he'd ever missed.

In 1971, a 1968 Mercury station wagon was a Godsend to any family of nine kids, and a vacation of this type without it would have been a nightmare. Even with the space, the U-haul that they pulled behind them was a necessity in order to carry the tent, clothes, food, bedding, fishing poles and tackle needed for an excursion of this dimension.

Steve was now eighteen years old, and was a 'favorite' of his neighbors, teachers, and most notably, his pastor. In fact, he was probably one of the few kids in Tech High School that ever received permission to play hooky and yet still received 'A's despite the fact. The reason he could do this was his special friendship with his Pastor.

Reverend Chester Walton Shew was a colorful character who pastored one of the largest Pentecostal churches in Fort Worth. He loved Steve and would often have him drive him to and from many of his preaching engagements held in other cities and states. Many a time on a Sunday night Pastor Shew would say to Steve's father, "Steve's coming home with Momma and I tonight. I need him to do some work around the place for me." When that would happen—which it did quite often—Steve's teachers readily conceded and made sure that his grades never suffered. They loved him and knew that in the long run, the boy's time spent with his pastor was as important as anything else he could do. This was public school in Fort Worth in the 1960's.

Steve's father was a minister who helped in his local Church. He and his wife had come to the Lord in 1950, three years before Steve was born. They loved God with all their hearts, and their church and Pastor as well. Clarence Mooney worked for the Comvair Corporation that later became General Dynamics. Although he had a good job, with a family that eventually reached nine children, there was never a 'surplus' of anything but God, church, preaching, worship and lots and lots of love.

The Mooney's were Apostolic Pentecostals, which meant they were open to receive everything God's Word said to them and in return, they meant to do all they could for Him. Everyone in the family had received the experience of the 'Holy Ghost,' and they thought little of dedicating their lives to His service rather than to the world's ways. Steve had been raised in a home filled with Bible and prayer and again…lots and lots of love. He had never in his life taken a drag off of a cigarette, sipped a beer, or even watched one immoral liaison, murder, theft, or beating on television. For the sake of their family, Clarence and Margie Mooney, from the beginning of their walk with God, had refused to bring any of these things into their home.

The family lived in a large house on Akers Street that was edged by a wooded area. Steve had heard many preachers tell of going out into the woods in their younger days to pray and seek the face of God. One evangelist in particular (Steve's hero) was known far and wide for his ability to pray for hours and hear from God. His name was Verbal Bean. Steve decided, as there were woods by him, he too would visit the woods to pray and listen to God. Though he did not know it at the time, the neighbors often listened to him and were moved deeply by the fact that a mere boy could seek after God so earnestly and faithfully.

One night while Steve was in the first grade, he had a dream that the Sunday school annex their church was in the process of building was finished and that he was standing in the corner of one of its larger rooms. His hands were raised in the air and as he worshipped God with all of his heart, he suddenly he began to "speak in other tongues as the Spirit gave him the utterance." He had seen himself receiving the gift of the Holy Ghost.

Several months later the building was finished and evangelist Verbal Bean came to hold the church a revival meeting. One night at the end of his sermon, Brother Bean asked everybody who wanted the Holy Ghost to come to the front of the church. Little Steve went, and although several received the Holy Ghost, he and a few others did not. After a while Brother Bean said, "Okay…now everyone who still wants the Holy Ghost but hasn't yet received it, follow me." Whereupon he lead a faithful band of seekers into the newly finished Sunday school annex.

Brother Bean said, "The scripture teaches us that, 'Ye shall seek me, and find me, when ye shall search for me with all your heart.' Now I want everyone of you to find yourselves a place to pray somewhere in this room, and then I want you to cry out to God with *everything within you* and say three times; Jesus, I love you with all of my heart and I want the Holy Ghost! Remember, you have to do it with *everything* within you!"

Steve went into a corner of the room, lifted his hands, and cried out to God with all of his heart; "Jesus I love you and I want the Holy Ghost!" He was only able to say it twice as before he could say it a third time, God gloriously came down and filled him with His Spirit. He spoke in other tongues (languages) for a long, long time. It was not until then that he remembered the dream and realized that it had just been fulfilled.

Through these experiences Steve learned the value and the power of prayer. Once, while in prayer when he was fourteen, he experienced what it was to have a vision. In the vision he saw a woman standing in an arched doorway weeping. Though he did not know what it meant, he knew that it was from God. A few days later he and his sister Becky were out knocking doors and inviting people to church. As they drove by one house, Steve yelled for them to stop. He recognized it as the doorway he had seen in his vision. When he and Becky knocked on the door, the woman he had seen in the vision opened the door crying. They began to talk to her and invite her to come to church. She told these two children that at the same moment they were knocking on her door, she had been in the front room crying and praying that God would send someone her way to show her how to be saved. She went with them to church the next Sunday, poured out her heart to God in repentance, was baptized in the name of Jesus Christ and received the gift of the Holy Ghost. Through these formative years Steve continually witnessed the value and power of prayer.

The world Steve grew up in was a world filled with the truth and guidance of God. Steve Mooney and his family loved God and knew that He loved them. The years passed and now the Mooney family was once again taking their annual summer vacation.

"Where are we going to stop tonight?" Joel asked his father.

"Well, I don't know son...we're going to have to stop and get gas somewhere pretty soon. Then I imagine we'll only go as far as William's Creek, set up camp and try and do some fishing."

"What's the name of the nearest town, Dad?" said Rebecca.

"I don't know. Mom... look it up on the map and see."

After fumbling around with the map, and finally turning it right side up, Margie Mooney said, "Hmm, let me see here... it looks like the nearest town is a place called... Boulder."

***

I guess I was awake, but for all I felt, I could be dead. Opening my eyes was like doing a bench press carrying too much weight. After a minute or two I did manage to get at least my left eyelid up and working. The first thing I beheld was a McDonald's hamburger wrapper laying upon a couple of long dead french fries about twelve inches from my face. Beyond the wrapper was an extremely scuffed brown loafer draped with an overworked sweat sock. Beyond the shoe, sticking up into the air, was a set of toes that badly needed their nails trimmed. "I wonder who that is?" I thought to myself. I began to roll over on my back but was hindered by what felt like another shoe. Though I really did not feel like sitting up just yet, I figured it would be the best and perhaps safest route. As I did, I thought the top of my head was going to explode and propped myself up with my left hand. I held my scalp on with my right hand and kept my eyes tightly closed. "Oh God...what have I done to myself?" I groaned inwardly.

When I finally opened both eyes, I realized that we were still in Alan's dorm and that I was about two feet from his couch. Except for Rocco's prone body being stretched over it, it looked a whole lot more inviting than the floor I was on. The shoe that I'd felt in my attempt to roll over I removed, examined, and realized that it was my own boot. The other one was still on my left foot, so thankfully, I wouldn't have to look for it. I turned my neck very slowly to view the damage and to spare my throbbing head and saw JoJo in the corner fast asleep with a pillow under his head and blanket wrapped tightly around him. "Lucky dog... how did you rate?" I wondered.

The bare foot belonged to… to… Tito. Yes, I think that was his name. We'd only met him day before yesterday and were already having a hard time getting rid of him. I think he was a friend—or said he was—of Tyrone's. Good grief, that didn't mean we had to take him to raise! He was like a leech, once he hooked on, you couldn't hardly get him off. And he made no bones about asking you for anything you had; from food, to money, to drugs, to a ride, to a place to stay, to ad-infinitum. Well, he was like a lot of other kids that had made their way to Boulder. No friends, estranged from their family—if they'd ever really had one—and at totally loose ends with life. Thankfully, at least for me, if worse came to worse—which it seemed might be likely—I could always go home to Mom and Buzz. Thank God for that. What was it my English teacher used to say; "Home is the place that, when you have to go there, they have to take you in." I think he was quoting… oh somebody, some poet I think. Well, anyway if I did have to go there, I knew they would have to take me in.

I also knew that seldom had a floor felt so hard or looked so dirty. Last night must have been something else. My mouth was rancid. I made myself get up and walk to the sink. I ran some water, splashed my face and got a drink at the same time. I dried myself with a T-shirt that was on the floor and looked into the bedroom where Alan and Tony slept. Their room was also a wreck but their beds were empty, they having apparently already left for class. Whereas the front room looked like it had been hit with a 8.5 earthquake on the Richter scale, their bedroom was a mere 7.0 by way of destruction. I can't even imagine what Alan's neighbors must have thought about last night, but then again, this *was* a dorm at Colorado University and here… most anything goes.

I remember the rather impromptu beginnings of the party, and I kind of remember the roar of it at its peak, but for the life of me I can't remember anything else, or… how I ended up on the floor. Not that I hadn't slept—or passed out—on the floor for the last five nights, but usually I can at least remember *some* of the details, and would wake up with either a blanket, pillow, my coat, or something, under my head. Waking up in this condition is… not good.

I went to the restroom and leaned against the wall for a while as I felt I might be sick. If I were, Alan wouldn't appreciate it if I had been too far from the commode. After a moment or two I noticed something move to my left. I slowly turned my head and saw that someone was sleeping in the bathtub. I leaned over to get a look at the face and could see that it was a girl—at least I think it was—but I did not for the life of me know who she was. She was probably a street person who had somehow sniffed out the party. She was small enough to fit fairly comfortably in the tub, though she was curled up somewhat. Her blue jeans were dirty and she was snuggled up in a denim jacket that was about three sizes too… 'Hey, that's my railroad coat!' I started to wake her up, decided against it, lingered around the commode and finally went into Alan's room. Both of the twin beds were a mess, but at least Alan's didn't have the remnants of potato chips all over it. So, I flopped down on his bed, covered up and went to sleep.

Two days later Alan's patience gave out and we began to seek in earnest for an apartment. Rocco had seen an ad in the paper that two guys in a three-bedroom apartment were seeking roommates in order to share expenses. We didn't know if they'd go for three of us moving in or not, but it wouldn't hurt to check it out. Rocco called them asked if three more renters was even a possibility. They said it might be but that we'd better come over and all of us would check each other out.

We parked the Plymouth down the street lest its appearance turn them off completely, and made our way to apartment complex. The name of the complex was Varsity Apartments, and it looked like a nice place with lots of pretty trees out in front. The apartments were three-story affairs and were set on nicely kept slopes of grass. We made our way up the stairs in the back and as we approached could hear nothing but, 'Grand Funk Railroad' playing from inside the apartment. I rang the bell. No answer. JoJo rang it again, and still no answer.

"There's no way they can hear us over the music," I yelled to Rocco, so he began beating on the door. After a bit we heard the music turned down and one of our future roommates opened the door. He was in his early-to-mid twenties, had blonde hair that immediately made one think of the Beach Boys. He was chewing gum and wearing a pair of cutoffs—period. "You the dudes looking for some space?" he said, never missing a beat on his gum. "Yeh, you the dude renting space?" answered Rocco. The beach boy mumbled something while nodding his head and waved us on in. We entered and knew immediately that if we could afford it, we were home. The walls had a few posters—Morrison, Santana, Sly and his Family, but other than that it looked like my mother could be living there. It was clean, neat and totally domesticated—except for the posters. Two of the bedrooms were upstairs and he said that we could have the one on the right. "There's no furniture in that room so if you want to make pallets and sleep on the floor there would be enough room for all of you. Or if one of you wanted to"—at this point he looked at JoJo and Rocco who were much shorter than my six-foot-six—"you could sleep on the couch, provided you don't make a huge mess and were up and out of the way by 8:30 every morning except Saturday and Sunday. On those days nobody is allowed to get up before noon. If they do they'd better keep quiet," he said, smiling.

"How much do you have to pay a month?" I asked.

"Two hundred and twenty-five and that covers utilities," he said and didn't even crack a smile.

"Two hundred and twenty-five!" all three of us said in shock, "Are you serious?"

"Hey man, this is Boulder, and this is a university bunch of blood sucking money fiends and that's what you got to pay. Why in the world do you think we'd even be interested in taking in the likes of guys like you?"

I had to admit he did have a point. We looked around and at each other. Then I said, "So it's two-twenty-five split five ways?"

"That's right, forty-five bucks each—due upon entry—and then due every thirty days—to the day." This time he smiled.

We told him that we needed to convene a conference and went into the empty bedroom upstairs. We immediately saw that it would be plenty big enough for three pallets and some boxes for the meager amount of clothes that we'd brought with us. As for our first payment, I knew that Rocco had his money... and then some, but I wasn't sure about JoJo As for me, I had $57.34 left.

"I can do it," I said, "but it's going to be tight until I can round something up or sell the Plymouth. What about you JoJo?"

He looked rather uncomfortable, but shook his head yes. Then he said, "But I can't have my part till probably tomorrow." Neither Rocco nor I wanted an explanation of that cryptic remark, so I said, "Well, I'm for doing it. You Rocco?"

"Yeah," he answered and then said, "JoJo, I'll lend you the money but you got to pay me back...tomorrow."

"I will... thanks Rocco," he said.

We went back downstairs, paid the beach boy the money and told him we'd be back sometime later that afternoon. When we asked about a key, all he said was; "Won't ever need it." We then left to get something to eat and pick up our stuff from Alan's.

On our way back to the C.U. dorms JoJo asked if we would mind letting him off on the Hill. He said that he needed to get his share of the money and would we mind grabbing his possessions from Alan's. We said that would be fine (as they would fit into a small paper bag anyway). We weren't sure what he had in mind by way of fundraising, but we knew that 'resourceful' was Jo Jo's middle name. When you've had to scramble your whole life for most everything... you just learn how it's done. So I swung the Plymouth towards that infamous area known as "The Hill."

***

The Hill. Would there ever be another place like it? It was a city within the city, with its own culture, codes and causes—or lack thereof—and the strangest collection of people gathered anywhere in America, if not in the world. Talk was, that the closest thing to it was Haight Ashbury in San Francisco. The Hill however was even more free from the hassle of the authorities. That figures when you consider the size of Frisco—and its police force—and the size of Boulder.

Mostly it was a conglomerate of youth from late teens to early twenties, but that was by no means all. There were men and women in their thirties, forties, fifties, and older. Even to characters like the 'Old Snake' who, while no one really knew how old he was, had to be in his late seventies or maybe even eighties. In a normal time and place, Old Snake would have been merely a hobo, but on the Hill, he was an icon of wisdom, insight, and dark sayings, not to speak of some pretty rank body odor. No doubt, until his wanderings brought him to Boulder, he really was just a hobo, but once there, he had found his niche. Like many other social outcasts he was just weird enough to fit right in with the rest of that strange entourage that made up the sub-culture of Boulder—the culture whose meeting place was… 'The Hill.'

Here they would gather to talk, argue, scream, laugh, play music, listen to music, panhandle, consume copious amounts of drugs, trip out, freak out, sell drugs, sell photos and paintings and flowers, old record albums, clothes, pottery, and… themselves. Sometimes there would be hundreds if not thousands of these aimless souls just wandering or sitting or running or driving about like ants on 'a Hill,' seemingly and in actuality, going nowhere… with no rhyme and no reason. The only thing that they all had in common was their drugs, their music and the fact that they had all dropped out of society, or were very close to it. They were shirt-less and shoe-less and bra-less and clue-less and as far as society was concerned, useless.

Added to that was the fact was that they came from everywhere. Colorado University drew youth mainly from across Colorado and the mid-west. But the Hill drew them from across America and even from around the world. Like the Gold rush days of California that drew a select breed of people from all areas and walks of life, their commonality being their lust for striking it rich, so it was on 'The Hill.' These 'hippies' also came from everywhere and from every lifestyle. The common thread between them not being 'gold lust' but a certain… 'craziness,' and a type of 'social insanity.' What they were looking for, I'm not certain they knew themselves. But this they did know, whatever it was they sought, they were not finding it in the 'norm' of society.

So here they came to… 'The Hill,' all having their own various levels of weird-ness. The most 'normal' would hardly fit anywhere else, unless it was a place like Haight Ashbury, Greenwich

Village, or Stockholm. In any other social climate than that and they would be misfits. Granted, you could find people just like them in any major city in America—especially in those days—but there they would cling to their own rather small circle, and move in a dark, sub-rosa world. Here, on the Hill, it was out in the open and in your face. It was nothing for several people at one time to walk down 13th Street, College Street, or Broadway like carnival barkers yelling out, "Acid… Purple Haze, Blue drop… got some Green Machine." Or, "Pot from Nam, Columbia, or PCP" Or, "Turkish Hash… anybody want to buy some Turkish Hashish?" Had you been at a ball game it would have sounded like, "Peanuts! Popcorn… get your Cotton Candy!"

How did they get away with it? Why didn't the police do something? Really, I don't know. But for one thing—how do you arrest a city? A roving, walking, talking, breathing, crazy anthill of wandering people doing their thing in broad daylight… and moonlight. How do you stop and frisk one person when you pretty well know that eighty percent of the others are all carrying something? And if you stop one you can fully expect the news to spread like a flash flood and you would quickly be converged upon by masses of indigents that simply aren't going to put up with being 'hassled.' Or if you pull a gun to get the crowd to 'back off' half of them are so stoned, or burnt out on life that they don't care if they live or die anyway. This was 'The Hill,' in Boulder Colorado, in my summer of 1971.

We let JoJo off at the corner of 13th and College and told him that we'd be back to pick him up around four p.m. As we drove off, I held up the rear view mirror and could see him facing the Hill with his hands on his hips, no doubt contemplating his first move. When I saw someone approach him—no doubt either begging for something or trying to sell something—I knew the move was on and the gears in JoJo's mind were whirling. You couldn't help but both love and admire the guy and his tenacity to survive.

It didn't take long to get our stuff, our clothes and paraphernalia, into the car once we had rounded them up from Alan's place. I found most everything that belonged to me… except my coat. Whoever it was in the bathtub that morning had taken it with them, and none of us ever found out who she was. The loss of the coat really did irk me as it held a special place in my heart. We had been through a lot together. Just the front of the coat alone was quite a conversation piece. You could tell at first glance that it had at one time been shredded and sewn back together. My mother had repaired it after a man with a strait-razor had sliced it to pieces—while I was wearing it. He was actually going for my juggler while I was dancing back and forth kicking him to pieces. We had got into a fight while driving down Court Street in Pueblo one night. I was in the back seat, passenger side of my brother's 57 Chevy and he was in the back seat, driver's side of a… I can't remember what kind of car. At any rate we had exchanged verbiage and then began exchanging blows. We finally pulled over and in the middle of Fourth Street, he and I went at it, me with my boots and he with his razor. His wife was with him—if you can imagine that—and was several months pregnant. My brother Phil was hooking it up with another passenger of the other car, while my buddy—a lunatic named Larry Weder—was trying to talk sweet nothings to the women in the enemy vehicle. Well, eventually we both came to the conclusion that I was not going to stop kicking and he wasn't going to stop slashing. So, we said good-bye and each group drove away looking for other adventures. That was just one of many reasons why I knew I would miss my coat… so many memories. Tito may have known the girl in the bathtub—if indeed she was a girl—but he never told us and anyway, he wasn't around anymore.

While Tony, Alan's roommate, found it in his heart to put up with us he didn't feel he owed the interloping Tito anything. When he came back from classes the afternoon after the party, he and a female classmate had made plans to go for a drive up into the mountains. Tito in his usual brash, intruding style invited himself along. At first I thought Tony was going to blow up, but then he stopped, smiled and said "Sure, Tito. I'd love to have you go."

Apparently Tony went on a lot further drive than he had

originally planned and even furnished Tito with a bottle of wine—Santa Fay Tokay—that cost him the vast sum of one dollar. He must have thought it a good investment, for at some point in the trip when Tony's female companion was at her most upset at having this drunken loud mouth mooch in the back seat, and at the point where Tito asked to be let out to go to the bathroom for the third time, Tony let him out—and drove off and left him.

We left Al a note telling him how much we really did appreciate his hospitality and once again how sorry we were about his refrigerator, and that we would stay in touch.

We stopped at a gas station and put in thirty cents worth of gas. Rocco asked if that was enough as he would be glad to buy another gallon of gas if I wanted.

"No, one gallon's enough. I'm going to try and unload this piece of junk tonight and besides that, the price of gas in Boulder really makes me mad." When I put the car into drive the transmission began to slip so I did let Rocco buy a two quarts of tranny fluid. We put it in gear and began to make our way back to the Hill to find JoJo

JoJo was not on the corner when we pulled up even though we were thirty minutes late. About the time that we had decided to go around the block, the back door flew open and cardboard went flying everywhere. JoJo from out of nowhere jumped in, held the door shut and said, "Let's go…now!" Not asking why but innately understanding, I sped away. As we rounded the corner, I turned to see JoJo looking out the back window to see if anyone was following. When he felt that all was clear, he turned and said, "Where in the world were you guys? You said four o'clock!"

"We got hung up at the gas station," Rocco answered.

"I been hiding behind a phone booth for twenty minutes!"

"I take it you got your rent money?" I said.

"Well, not yet… but I'll have it this time tomorrow." With that JoJo reached into his coat pocket and pulled out a wallet and what looked like a very nice wristwatch. He let the worthless door swing open a little and dropped the wallet to the pavement, having already extracted its worthwhile contents. I noticed

Rocco immediately felt for his bankroll as if to say, "Good grief! This slippery eel could get to me just as easy!"

"How much did you get?" I asked.

"Oh… let's just say that I got my lunch money for the month," JoJo said with a Cheshire cat grin on his face.

"If you got that much, pay me my forty-five now," Rocco said whirling in his seat.

"The deal was that I'd pay you tomorrow… and tomorrow you'll get paid," JoJo said smiling even more. While I really was not comfortable with this kind of escapade…what was one to do—work? With that we went back to our new apartment and roommates.

Upon arrival, I let the guys take our stuff to the room while I scrounged through the apartment dumpster for some more cardboard. Having repaired the door I went back to the dumpster and got another two boxes to serve as our chest of drawers in the apartment. I entered the front door to find JoJo and Rocco sitting at the dining table looking across the room at a man who was sitting on the couch.

"Who's he?" I asked.

"Says he's the new renter," answered Rocco.

"The what!?" I said.

"Renter…" said JoJo

Though he was sitting I could tell that he was obviously a fairly tall, thin, but muscular man. He had long graying hair that reached past his chest and a beard that did almost the same. His glasses were octagonal—like the ones I'd misplaced somewhere—and the eyes behind them were black and piercing. As we stared at him and he back at us I realized that if this was indeed a 'stare down contest' there was no question who was about to lose. It felt as if he were looking through us at something beyond that we could not see. Rocco must have felt it too for presently he turned in his chair and checked out the wall. Seeing nothing there but Jim Morrison's stare, he turned back and we continued our inspection of this strange stranger.

Clearing my throat I asked, "Where's…" At this point I realized that we never did get the real name of the 'Beach Boy' to whom we had given our money. "Where's Beach Boy… the blonde headed guy that lives here?"

The man on the couch answered nothing. He just continued his unblinking… unnerving stare. For a moment I thought, "Man I hope JoJo didn't pinch this guys' wallet, if he did, we're dead meat."

I cleared my throat once more and, lifting my voice a little, said… "Do you know where the guy is that lives here? The guy we gave money to… to stay here…to pay the rent…to live here… don't you see…" The words died in my lips, as there was absolutely no response other than the stare that made me feel like we had just entered the padded cell of a serial killer. Speaking much more softly now I said to JoJo and Rocco, "Let's take our stuff upstairs—and bolt the door behind us." I said this half tongue-in-cheek in order to lighten the atmosphere but it didn't help.

"I'm for it!" JoJo said and started grabbing and moving at the same time. As we all started to do the same, in a bit too loud of a voice, the sphinx said, "What are you doing? Where are you going?"

We froze. I finally said, "I…I thought we'd take our stuff upstairs to our room… where we live… and sleep and stuff…" We were watching him, no doubt, like a rabbit watches a fox.

It wasn't that we didn't know how to fight or were even adverse to it; God knows we had been in literally dozens of absolute chair breaking brawls. But it's one thing to get into a fight with someone who is simply looking for a good fight, but there was something menacing and pathological in the creature that sat before us. He reminded me of the rather small kid in our high school class that we called "Birdie." Nobody—and I mean nobody—messed with him. We all somehow knew that while Birdie probably couldn't fight his way out of a wet paper sack, and he really did resemble a small bird, he had a kind of weirdness that said, "It's okay… mess with me. I won't say or do a thing. But one night, very, very late, when you're not expecting it I am going to slide under the door into your room and with my rusty strait-razor slowly slit your throat from ear to ear and whistle the

'Pink Panther' while I do it."

We knew he could do it because one time a really arrogant, semi-big, semi-rich, sorry outfit named Andy Seber shoved Birdie's face into the drinking fountain while he was getting a drink. Birdie never said a word. He just stared. When Andrew asked him if he had a problem, Birdie just smiled his little smile and said, "No, no Mr. Seber… I don't have a problem at all." Then he just kind of melted into the crowd. The next morning when Andy went to get his car out of the very-much-locked garage he saw that all four tires had been slashed. There was a single white rose under the windshield wiper that had a typewritten message wrapped around the stem. When Andy Seber unwrapped it and read it, his bowels were all but loosed. It read,"*Next time Mr. Seber… it will be your throat…*"

When Andy finally got to school (his mother had to take him) the first thing he did was look up Birdie. He stormed up to him in the lunchroom where Birdie—as usual—was eating alone. He was furious but stopped cold when he looked down at him. Birdie was wearing a black shirt, pants and jacket—and of all things looked like a mortician—with a white rose stuck in the lapel. Birdie never even looked up at him…he just kept on eating, taking his time about it and looked up at Andy only as he swigged the last of his milk. Then he dabbed his lips with his napkin, belched and smiled. Andy, after clenching and unclenching his fist several times, finally turned, walked off and never said another word.

While it was never actually proved who slashed Andy's tires, everybody knew, and nobody ever gave Birdie any more problems. Everybody just kind of left him to himself and he drank at the water fountains of life untroubled. And I felt like this man who was sitting on the couch staring at us—like Birdie—needed to be left to himself.

"I am living here," he finally said, "I am paying for the right to live here. I made the arrangements with the rather vacuous young man who put the advertisement in the rather sub-standard local periodical known as the 'Daily Camera.'"

Well, there it was. Who knew but before it was over there would be a hundred people in here all paying forty-five a month to the Beach boy. Me and Rocco and JoJo looked at each other till I said, "C'mon" and nodded towards the room upstairs. Up we all went and put our stuff in the room and in the boxes. I noticed as JoJo shut the door that he checked it for a lock but found none.

"Well, what are we going to do about Herman Munster down there?" Rocco asked, "I'd rather put up with Tito than that guy."

"Me too," said JoJo emphatically.

"We'll just have to wait for the beach boy to return and see what's up," I said and, looking around, remembered that we were going to have to get some blankets and pillows from somewhere. "Maybe we should leave Beach Boy a note asking him about the mad man and go and get some bedding," I said.

"What if the mad man reads it? Rocco said.

"Yeah… you're right. I guess we'll just have to wait."

"Well, I'm more interested in buying a dead bolt than I am a pillow," said JoJo And though we didn't say it, we all agreed.

We went downstairs and saw that the new renter looked like he had not moved so much as a muscle. He didn't look like he had anything to say to us, and we certainly felt the same, so we just nodded his way and left. As we made our way down the steps of the sidewalk, the beach boy pulled up in a 66 Mustang convertible. Another young man was with him who, seen from behind, looked like another blonde Beach boy. When he turned towards us I couldn't believe it. "Jerry Cox!" I exclaimed, "Jerry, what on earth are you doing here?" The look on his face was as surprised as mine.

"Larry…Larry Booker! Is that you?"

Jerry had been a senior when I was a sophomore in high school. In those days when two years difference really meant something, Jerry was like a god to me, though I couldn't stand him. He was a football, wrestling and track star with a capital S. He could do it all, including drink everyone under the table and beat up most everyone on top of it. Of course because of the age and grade difference we didn't hang around together, but through the years he had developed a grudging admiration for my ability to take care of myself. Finally, as we showed up at some of the same parties, we got to know each other and actually, slowly, began to like each other. The thing that clenched it for us was the summer of my junior year when we all got in a fight at the State Fair with the "Carnies"—guys that worked and traveled with the carnival.

Every year there were three groups at the fair that somehow ended up in a fight. The 'Goat-ropers,' or Cowboys, the 'Carneys' and the 'Druggies, or Hippies.' The latter being my friends and I. Though Jerry drank and drugged, he was also a cowboy type guy that would sometimes enter rodeos. Well, that year—for reasons that are not real clear to me because of the condition I was in—the cowboys and the hippies teamed up against the carnies and ended up having one more mean brawl. For once Jerry and I were on the same side, did quite well together, and were genuine if not distant friends after that. We never did run around together, but the respect was there, and more than once since then we had watched out for each other's backside. Now here he was in Boulder of all places and running around with the beach boy.

"Are you the renters?" Jerry asked.

"I think so… are you the other rentee?" I asked.

"Yeah… man Larry, if I'd have known it was you we'd have told you the rent was four hundred instead of two hundred," he said laughing and hitting me on the shoulder. As Rocco, JoJo and I looked at the Beach boy he immediately said, "It's two hundred and *twenty-five* Jerry. Remember… two hundred and *twenty-five*." Jerry looked at him, never missed a beat and said, "Of course it's two twenty-five… what? What'd I say… two?"

I wasn't about to haggle over the rip-off of twenty-five bucks, since I was far more concerned about the psycho who was waiting inside. "Jerry, who's the nut case inside?"

"The who?" Jerry answered.

"The nut case…the whacko… the Charlie Manson that even now sits in your—make that *our* front room," I said. Jerry looked to the beach boy for some kind of explanation. Beach Boy had a puzzled look on his face that in a moment changed to an expression of shocked dread. "Oh no…" he said, "Did he come back, the tall guy… the Professor?"

"What's going on?" asked Jerry, "What Professor?"

"Well this weird guy came by this morning, said he used to be a professor at Harvard and that he wanted to rent from us. He said he'd be back but he didn't give me any money so I shrugged it off. I never thought I'd see him again. You know how some of these weird guys do," the beach boy's voice trailed off.

"Well were going to just have to let him know that it's a no-go and tell him to hit the road," Jerry expostulated. I felt a little better, but not completely. Until Charlie was gone, gone, and gone again I wasn't even sure I could sleep at night.

Presently we all turned and with determined faces walked up the steps and entered the apartment in a more or less single file arrangement with Jerry at the lead. We were not too far past the front door when the bumping into one another began like a string of cars that couldn't quite figure out why the lead car had suddenly put on his brakes. When we all came to a standstill Jerry was still front and center with us all jammed together. Then we all saw the cause for the pile up.

Charlie Manson was asleep, or at least he looked like he was, on the couch with nothing on but a very short scarlet kimono. He was flat on his back, his arms folded on his chest with his legs straight and his feet together. If you could slip him into a coffin—a long one—he was ready to go. Because he was rather tall, his head was propped up on one arm of the couch and his feet were sticking out over the other. His glasses were folded shut and lying on the armrest to the right of his face.

We stood there for a long time, no one speaking, just staring. After a time the professor slowly raised his head and opened his eyes—in that order—and glared at us with what looked like an indomitable hatred. Then he closed his eyes and laid his head back down… never moving another muscle in his body. Without opening his eyes he said, in a low but distinct voice, "There's a one hundred dollar bill and one dime on your pillow, Beach Boy. I've paid—up front—for three months. At two hundred dollars per month, divided by six inhabitants, it figures out to be $33.30 per month each... and I paid the dime."

At that moment everybody—except professor Charlie—looked at Beach Boy.

He continued, "If the Boy Scouts here decide that they are uncomfortable with my presence and decide to leave early, I'll up my share. Till then... stay out of my face." Without another word (he literally did not speak for the next 24 hours) he rolled over on his side with his face towards the back of the couch, curled up and apparently went to sleep. It was then we saw the dragon emblem on the back of the kimono.

As he lay there with his bare backside to us, I knew why I would probably never be into wearing short kimonos. I also knew that the Beach boy would not be waking the professor at 8:30 on weekday mornings either.

No one moved and after a moment of impressed silence, Jerry said, "Larry, do you remember that crazy kid in your class... you know the really quiet one with the funny name... the guy that nobody ever messed with?"

"Birdie," I said.

"Yeah... Birdie. Well I think we'd be wise to put the professor into the same category as Birdie."

"You know... I already have. And I'll tell you something else... we're putting a lock on our door."

"Yeah? Well...I don't blame you. And Sammy" (apparently Beach Boy's real name) "give each of these guys back $11.70... it looks like were all in this together."

***

That evening after checking the efficiency of the dead bolt several times and the comfort of the pallets, I decided that I had better sell the car and get some more money. I was running uncomfortably close, even with the return of the $11.70 from the beach boy. Though we now knew his name was Sammy, Beach boy would forever be his handle. Rocco and JoJo were troubled by the thought of having no wheels if I sold the car. "What are we gonna do if we have to go somewhere that we can't walk to? What if we even decide to go back to Pueblo?" JoJo whined.

"The car probably wouldn't make it back to Pueblo anyway," I answered, "And besides, there's always somebody headed that way that we can hitch a ride with."

"Not all three of us," Rocco responded, "And if we actually

hitchhike it's all but impossible to get anyone to pick up more than one hitchhiker, let alone three."

"Look, if worse comes to worse we can catch the bus. It don't cost all that much to catch a bus," I said—though I had not caught a Greyhound bus since I was a kid. "Besides it's just a matter of time before I get pulled over. Everything's wrong with the car, its tags are expired and I don't even have a title, or registration. If we get pulled over and one of us has got something on us… it's all over." For that argument neither of them had an answer.

"What time is it JoJo?" I asked. I had given up on my watch, which had altogether given up working, though I still wore it. If you slapped it up against something it would run for about fifteen to twenty seconds and then... fizzle.

JoJo looked on his right wrist where he wore the watch he had 'acquired' earlier in the day, and took a glance at the other one he was wearing on the left. "Six-thirty," he said, "Give or take."

I looked at my impressive but worthless watch and said, "Maybe I could get something out of this, if I could find the right wad of sap." So, we decided to clean up the car, shine up the watches, go to the Hill and try our luck.

We rinsed the car off with a garden hose in the impossible attempt to make it look a little better, realizing in the process that we had ruined the cardboard and had to replace it. We then drove to the Hill and kept driving around until we found a good parking spot on Broadway in hopes of finding a ready buyer. We got out and made our way to College Street, which was the pretty much the focal point for Boulder's hippydom. It was still light out and would be so for another hour and a half anyway.

Strange people were, as usual, milling about everywhere, sitting in groups, sitting as couples, or sitting by themselves. They were talking to each other, singing to each other, yelling at each other, talking to themselves, talking to no one… talking to God. Rocco, JoJo and I crossed Broadway and sat down on a grassy area in order to scope out the human landscape and the possibilities.

***

Clarence Mooney filled up the station wagon with gas while the family stretched, snacked and refreshed themselves. Mark washed all of the windows of the car, especially the heavily dead-bug-infested windshield. When they all began to pile back into the car, Steve got the seat by the window on the passenger side behind his mother.

"We should be getting to William's Creek no later than eight-thirty, and that will give us just enough time to set camp in the daylight," said Mom.

The gas station attendant took the money from Mr. Mooney and looked at all of the children that seemed to be everywhere. "Say, where are you folks from?" he said.

"Texas," said Mr. Mooney, "Fort Worth, Texas."

"I take it you're here on vacation?"

"Yes sir. We come out here to Colorado every year for about ten days and do a lot of fishing and camping."

"Are you all interested in seeing a sight for sore eyes?" the withered cashier asked.

"Well, all depends, what do you mean?"

"Go on into downtown, on the highway here, and I'll guarantee you, you'll see a sight that you won't be seeing in Fort Worth. Some of the weirdest people ever gathered in one place on this planet… that is if you exclude the state of Arkansas." The grizzled man laughed at his joke, and the Mooney family began to make their way to see the sights of Boulder.

***

Rocco was on the lookout for someone that he'd bought LSD from in the past. He would much prefer to do business with a proven source than a new one. Even in Boulder one wanted to be as careful as possible, especially if he were dealing in the quantities Rocco was, and especially if you were trying to move the heroin that Joe sent from Viet Nam. Usually though, that stuff was easy enough to move in Pueblo. Pueblo after all was a hard town with a very seamy underside, especially when it came to the Mafia. There again you had to be very careful about who you were dealing with. Whatever happened, neither Rocco nor I wanted to end up like Neil and Eddie.

Several years before, Neil and Eddie had been busted for selling drugs. Before the date of the grand jury hearing, they were approached by a mafia figure whose nickname was, 'The Beard.' He told them he could get the charges dropped under the condition that they would from then on sell for the mafia. The mafia would provide the drugs and they could make good money and be protected at the same time. They both agreed and lived to regret it, as greater and greater demands were constantly placed upon them. The control over them grew to the place they felt tormented and owned by their tormentors.

When Eddie could take it no longer, he testified in a court case against the man who had originally contacted him. It was to be the first of two trials wherein a prominent Pueblo Judge and 'The Beard' were charged basically with suppressing evidence and jury tampering. The Judge was found innocent—his only defense being character references from three local bank presidents. The charges against 'The Beard' were summarily dropped and hence—no second trial. Within a month, Eddie disappeared and that was the last anyone had ever seen of him. As for Neal, he eventually lost his usefulness to the mafia—and to anybody else for that matter—when he cracked up and had to be put into a mental institution. So, we knew that, between the 'law' and the 'mafia' you couldn't be too careful when you were dealing with substances of this quantity and type, even in Boulder.

After sitting for a while, a little business began to come our way—well, at least my way. As we contemplated, we noticed a rather seedy looking fellow walking about nervously asking people if they wanted to score on some pot. In a flash of inspiration I asked JoJo what time it was, set my dysfunctional watch and gave it a hearty slap. When the guy's offer came our way, I said, "You interested in a classy watch?" He got down on one knee while I removed the watch from my wrist, slapped it again on my palm and said, "This my friend, is one posh watch, what do you say we just trade straight across?" I sincerely hoped he would bite fast as I knew there was only about fifteen seconds left before the watch stopped. He seemed in as big a hurry as I was, gave it the once over, put it in one his pants pockets while at the same time pulling a 'lid' of pot out of the other, handed it to me, mumbled something about it being "really good stuff" and ambled away. I glanced at the clear plastic sandwich bag of 'Pot,' stuffing it in my pocket as my eyes combed the area for any overly interested observers. Then JoJo, Rocco and I smiled at each other in what we felt like was a job well done. I resumed my inspection of the people spread out around us and as I did my eyes came to rest on someone that was staring at me intently and who looked vaguely familiar. Then I involuntarily started as I recognized… my coat!

There it was, the coat and the girl who had been wearing it while asleep in the bathtub at Alan's. It looked like a veritable tent hanging on her, especially as she was sitting with her legs folded, leaning up against a tree. I quickly got to my feet and strode the thirty yards to where she sat and said, "If you don't mind…I'd like my coat back." She continued to stare up at me with a rather shocked expression, stumbled around for words, and finally said, "I don't see your name on it."

"Look at the front, where it's been all sewn back together. It was cut up because a man took a strait razor to me. I took it from him, slit his throat with it and came to realize how helpful a strait razor can be…now give me my coat back." I know my last three statements were terrible exaggerations, but they also turned out to be very effective, as she couldn't get out of the coat fast enough. She looked to be about sixteen and without the tent over her, suddenly looked very small. It was sad, really. Here was a girl with nothing, or next to it, and I was taking even more from her. I would have liked to known about her, her life, where she came from, and what in the world was she doing in a place like this. As I was about to try and soften the blow over the loss of the coat, I heard someone in my ear screaming "LARRY! You dog, where've ya been?" I turned to see… Tito. He was beaming up at me like a long lost puppy. He then looked down at the girl, then at the coat I was holding, then back up to me and said, "What are you doing with Renee's coat?" In Tito's presence she, that is, Renee' was now scowling at me once again as if to say, "Take it back Tito, go on…get my coat back."

I looked at Tito, then to Renee', then back to Tito, and thought, "You two really deserve each other," and simply walked off. I got back to JoJo and Rocco and said, "Let's go. Unless you want Tito and company to become an appendage once again, I suggest we move."

They were up in a flash, and we began to make our way back across the street.

***

Steve, Joel, Timothy, Rebecca, Mark, Elaine, Carol, Barbara Mooney and their parents stared out of the car windows at the bizarre sights before their eyes. People, strange people, were everywhere. They were lost, undone, aimless and seemingly hopeless people. It was a wandering mass of humanity with no goals, no aim, no direction and... no God. The Clarence Mooney family was in amazed silence as they drove through it. After a while Steve said to his parents, "Mom, Dad do you suppose that any of these kids... any of these people have ever heard the truth? Do you suppose any of them have ever had a chance to be saved?"

"I just don't know son... I just really don't know. But it's really, very, very sad."

As they turned and made their way out of Boulder, Colorado, Steve Mooney had tears in his eyes and a deep sadness in his heart.

***

We were making our way back to the Plymouth when a girl about the size of Renee' (the coat snatcher) came by panhandling. She had dirty brown hair that came to her shoulders, green eyes, and a rather small square chin. She was wearing a leather coat with long leather fringes, a tee shirt, dirty, baggy blue jeans and the ubiquitous sandals that belonged to that era. "Spare change... spare change... got any spare change?" she chanted monotonously. As she was passing by me, she looked up at me and repeated her mantra. Why I said it, I do not for the life of me know, but I looked her in the eyes and said sarcastically... "Get a job."

She took a few more steps—as did I—was halfway through her litany when it dawned on her what I'd said. She wheeled around and began to scream, "You get a job you *blankety-blank-blank- blankety- blank-blank*." I thankfully do not remember all that she said, but I do know that woven into the fabric of her colorful speech were statements questioning the circumstances of my birth as well as some pretty pointed adjectives followed by less-than-kind references to my character. At that point I began to respond in kind. There we were, hurling curses at each other, she on her tiptoes and me bending down till our faces were only about a foot apart—which is one reason why I remembered her features so well. Finally, lest in my fierce anger I took a swing at her rage-contorted face, I turned and began to walk off. It was never my custom to hit a lady—I use the term loosely—but this creature had pretty well pushed me to the limit. As I took my first step away from her, I distinctly heard her clear her throat and… and… spit. I turned to look at the back of my left leg where it had landed. Without question, there it was in all its gory glory. I looked into her spite-filled and somewhat triumphant-looking smug face and screamed, "YOU SPIT ON ME!" She screamed back, "YOU DESERVED IT YOU JERK!'

This time I knew I had to keep walking, lest I kill her. JoJo and Rocco were leaning on the Plymouth laughing so hard they were crying. At my glare, they stifled their laughter but only momentarily and just slightly in intensity. I drove back to the apartment doing a slow burn as I listened to their snorts and giggles.

Once back to the apartment they said they were sorry and did I suppose we could try out the weed that I'd traded for my watch. I sullenly pulled it out of my pocket, showed it off to Jerry and the Beach boy—the professor was incommunicado—and we all proceeded to roll up a joint. While I did so I bragged about my little coup of obtaining it with the bad watch. Jerry and the Beach boy smiled approvingly at my sagacity. After our first drag we knew that something was direly wrong. Jerry, coughing, took the sandwich bag and began to dig around in it with his finger. After a while, he set it down, looked at me a long time and uttered two short words… "Tree leaves."

Except for finding my coat… it had not been a good day.

***

Steve Mooney opened his eyes. It was still dark outside, but he could tell by the eastern sky that daybreak would come soon. He quietly arose and began preparing for an early morning fishing excursion. As he did so, he thought once again about the hippies he had seen yesterday. The fact was, he hadn't been able get them off of his mind. He slipped on his light jacket, hefted his tackle box and fishing pole and made his way down to William's Creek. He just couldn't seem to get those sad, lost people out of his mind. When he got to the creek he knew what he was feeling... he knew he needed to pray. He pushed it aside with a promise to do it later. This early in the morning was his most enjoyable and successful time to fish. He cross the rocks that made up the bank of the brook. Why couldn't he get those people off his mind? What would become of them? What chance did they have to ever find God and a decent life?

Again, he knew this feeling... this unction. He'd known it from the time he was a little boy. He needed to pray... he really needed to pray. He stepped over some more rocks, and then... he slipped and fell. The pole and tackle box flew out of his hands as he tried to break his fall. He stopped himself from falling into the water but could immediately tell his ankle was slightly sprained. He would probably have some minor bruises as well. He picked himself up and his fishing pole. The reel on his pole was cracked from landing on a rock and would definitely be out of commission until he could patch it up.

"Okay then," he thought, "I'll pray...if that's what you want." And as he had learned from childhood, Stephen Mooney, an eighteen-year old Apostolic young man from Forth Worth, Texas knelt down to the ground and began to pray for the hippies of Boulder, Colorado. He knew almost instantly that this was not going to be an ordinary prayer meeting. It was as if the fountains of the deep were broken up in his spirit. The hot tears that quickly came were just as quickly replaced by a torrent of heart rending sobs as he prayed...groaned...plead and besought his God, his Savior to please...please... save those poor people—those poor lost undone souls that unless God intervened in their lives would never see, never know, never understand, and never experience the love and peace of God that passes all understanding.

Steve entered into a season of prayer that is known in the Bible as, travail. He felt passion, un-bounding passion, as deep and powerful as he'd ever felt it in his life. There were moments when he felt that he would die. He fell to his side and curled up on the ground in racking sobs. For long moments he felt as if every single cell of his being was crying out in agony for the lost souls of Boulder, for the lost hippies and druggies and dropouts from society who, if God didn't save would be lost in their emptiness forever. He knew that without question God was hearing him and helping him reach into the world of the Spirit where heavenly things take place and make earthly things happen.

How long his season of 'travail' lasted he was not sure, but eventually he could feel the burden begin to abate. He lay on the bank of the stream and after a while sat up. He had prayed so earnestly and so hard that already his stomach muscles were sore. His clothes were damp with sweat and his head was pounding. He wiped his face of both sweat and tears.

Steve Mooney knew as sure as he was alive that something had just transpired in the world of the Spirit. But would he ever know what it was all about? Would he ever understand all that had just happened or live to see any of the results? No, probably not. In the life to come, God would no doubt show him, but in this world he would probably never know what his prayer had wrought or brought about. "Oh well," he prayed at last, "God it's all in your hands… and I know that I trust you."

With that he rose slowly to his feet, picked up his pole and tackle box and began to limp back to camp and to his family.

***

The day after I traded my bad watch for the tree leaves, got my coat back and my leg spit on, I was unreasonably depressed. Unless it was the professor that was getting next to me, I had no idea why—though this was by no means the first time I'd ever been like this. There were times, even during the most raucous of parties, when I would sit in absolute silence for hours. The despondency that sometimes hung over me could be as thick as a sopping wet goose-down blanket. Well, today was one of those wet blanket days and the sorrow was with me as soon as I awoke.

I decided that whatever else I did today, I was definitely getting rid of the Plymouth. I arose, stepped over JoJo, and went downstairs towards the outdoor patio that hung out off the back of the apartment by the street. I had to walk by the couch where professor Manson slept, but he was not there and I really wasn't surprised. Last night had been just a little *too much*... even for him.

What had happened was that after the fiasco of my 'tree pot' Jerry broke down and brought out some really potent stuff. We were deep into it when somebody decided that a game of Monopoly would really fit the bill. We were deep into the game, I mean *really* tripping on it (I owned the whole street from St. Charles to Virginia and was working on a trade for Illinois and had a copious pile of money) when the professor came in. It was one of the few times that his presence did not overpower the atmosphere, and we were rather thankful for it. In fact, when we realized that we had broken through the power of his silent but overwhelming personality, we actually became more strident and shrill in our potted exhilaration with the monopoly game.

The professor stood watching us very quietly for about ten minutes. When he perceived that he had lost his intimidating control over us, he placed his hands under the edge of the table and heaved it up into the air, overturning everything from the game to the drinks to the ashtrays. In one fell swoop, everything came to a screeching halt, except the music, which lasted fewer than five seconds longer (Rocco had the presence of mind to turn it off in order to savor the pathos of the moment).

In the deafening silence that followed, we all sat there too stunned to speak. We were already in bad shape—it really was good pot—but this was just a bit too much and *way* too weird.

Then the professor, in what sounded like sincere contrition, said, "I...I don't know why I did that...I ...I am very sorry." Then, worst of all, he got down on his hands and knees and began to pick everything up, very slowly and deliberately. Whereas a few seconds ago we felt a gathering fury, we now—as we watched him on the floor picking up the cards and the money and the motels like a chastened child—couldn't help but feel sorry for this strange, sad, hopeless man. Needless to say, the party was over.

The underlying tragedy was that at one time he really had been a professor at Harvard, a professor of economics no less. However, one day he had simply walked out of his classroom and out of the life of his wife and children and never went back, not even for his car, which he left on the campus parking lot. He just walked out to the road and started hitchhiking his way to California. He did this in 1968—apparently a bad year for a lot of us—and had been at it ever since. I don't know where he got his money to live—no one was about to ask him—but had nevertheless come to be nothing but a sad, graying, long-haired, long bearded hippie who would overturn tables to get your attention if he couldn't get it through the intimidation of his sullen, silent, intellectual presence. I wonder what his wife, or fellow professors would say if they could see him on the floor picking up Parker Brothers funny money.

There was nothing left to say, nor did anyone want to say anything. After a few feeble attempts at humor that died on the lips, we all went to our rooms, leaving the professor to try and pick up the pieces.

So, I was now depressed and he was gone. I wasn't surprised, though I didn't really know the reason for any of it. It's not that tearing up the game was a 'big deal,' but it was just big enough to put him over the social edge, even in our outrageous social condition. I doubted that he'd be back, and again, I didn't even know why. For whatever reason, I was left with a depression that I just couldn't shake.

I went out on the porch, turned to the right, and watched the sun come up from over the top of the trees down the street. I sat in the lawn chair and felt so glum that I wished I had something to knock me out. It was not a good frame of mind to be in.

After a while I rummaged through the refrigerator for something to eat, and found an egg. I fried it in a skillet with some margarine, salted and peppered it down and ate it in three bites. I went back to the freezer, broke some ice cubes out of the plastic tray and made me a glass of ice water. I drank it and went back to my pallet wondering what was wrong. While staring at the ceiling, I fell back to sleep.

About three in the afternoon, I went to the Hill to rid myself of the Plymouth once and for all. I was determined to get rid of it, regardless of what I got out of it. I was developing a feeling that the car was, or was about to be, bad luck. But then again, a sense of impending bad luck was all I could feel anywhere.

I stopped at a red light and saw a familiar face walking down the street to my left. He apparently recognized me and began to smile and wave. While I had not yet placed him—in a world like mine a friendly face is always good to see—I in turn began to wave back. There we were like two long lost friends, waving and smiling until I recognized him and immediately began to turn away. He was the guy I had traded the bad watch to. He must have recognized me at the same moment, for in an instant he dropped his hand and his smile and turned away also. No doubt his thought was, "Oh no! That's the guy I traded the tree leaves to." There we were, two pirate ships passing in the night that... had ripped each other off.

In making my trade for the Plymouth, I was not in my most creative mood, and therefore ended up with a wad of opium bigger than a golf ball, but smaller than a tennis ball. While I knew I had probably made a horrible deal—because I would never sell it, but would no doubt smoke it—nevertheless I was glad to be done with the Plymouth. It was just an accident or an arrest waiting to happen. I walked back to the apartment where we all sat down to try it out. The professor was still not back and we were all but positive that he wasn't coming back because his kimono was also gone. While we all couldn't help but feel sorry for him—except for the beach boy who thought only of the Monopoly game and that he was sure he was going to win it—no one missed him.

Jerry gave my trade of the Plymouth for the opium a much better grade than he did my bad watch for the tree leaves. But Jerry was such a connoisseur of drugs that he wasn't all that impressed with the opium either because it didn't remove his head from off his shoulders and put it in San Francisco somewhere. As for Rocco, JoJo and I, when we could finally stand up, we'd decided that we needed to go to Alan's and share some of the bounty with him, since he had been so good to us and patient as well. We got the beach boy to his feet and had him take us over to the dorms. From what little I can remember of it, it was an interesting drive.

Alan wasn't exactly glad to see us. It seemed that our old friend Tito had taken our meeting on the Hill yesterday as a sign from heaven that he and Sheree' or Renee' or whatever her name was, could come back to Al's place and crash. Al had to physically throw them out and was in no mood for company that had a tendency to stay too long and eat too much. He mellowed and actually smiled, however, when I showed him the opium.

I don't know how it works that people just 'know' when something is going on. Within thirty minutes there must have been ten or more people in the room, and the opium was quickly being depleted. Yet, for all the smoke and laughter and music, my melancholia was not abating. Rather it steadily grew worse. It seemed that—no doubt due to my depression—all I could see was sorrow. I saw misery in everyone's face in spite of their laughter, and even worse, I saw it in everyone's future. Every dismal thought and conclusion concerning life and its wretchedness seemed as clear and inevitable to me as the fact that we were all in that room and stoned to our toenails. The angst of my heart was literally turning into an ache that I could feel permeating my every fiber. I knew that if something did not happen I would have to leave. I was about to break down into tears. And then, something did happen, that I'll never forget as long as I live.

*I was sitting in a chair with my elbow on the small study table, with a wall mirror to my right, my head resting in my right hand. A song was playing in the background by McCartney and his band, Wings. Again, I was on the verge of weeping when suddenly, I began to feel better… and happier, and… happier still. The sorrow of my heart was slipping away and being replaced by a strange…neat… really wonderful feeling. It was being replaced by an… unmitigated joy…*

*in fact it was ecstasy. Then I turned my head towards the mirror and, instead of seeing my face, I saw a large, beautiful green meadow with gold flowers scattered about. At the back of the meadow were huge clusters of trees with a gorgeous array of branches and foliage. Coming up over the tops of the trees was the sun in all its glory. The music was still playing in my ears, but it was incidental. The monumental overwhelming emotion was a rapturous delight the likes of which I had never known.*

I turned my head from the meadow and immediately the wonderful feeling was gone. I was looking back into the room and gloom of the only world I knew, the world of drugs and alcohol and rebellion and despair...and sin. I didn't know or understand what had just happened but I automatically attributed it to the drug. I would have given anything to have that feeling of joy continue, but, alas, it was not to be. In fact the unaccountable despondency hung even heavier about me like a heavy woolen cloak.

Three days later, I moved back to Pueblo.

# 4
# Pueblo

"Home is the place, that when you have to go there, they have to take you in." The poet was right… my parents had to take me in. Not that they minded, but going back home was harder for me to accept than it was for them. As always, my mother treated me superbly and in a few days I was able to regain lost sleep as well as weight. A few days after that, my restlessness drifted back to the surface and I was once again looking for another place to live. I found it when I met my old buddy Larry Weder at a local bar we frequented called Pinocchio's.

Larry had been living on the third floor of an old house that had been converted into apartments on Lincoln Street not far from Central High School (a hold for many a nemesis) but needed someone to help to share the expenses in order to keep it. I moved in at once telling Larry that when the rent came due I would have my portion of it. As always, my mother was good to help me out with some money till I could come up with something on my own.

I had the best of both worlds, as I was out from under my parents attempts at control, but was able to go back home to eat and have my clothes washed when needed. Admittedly, it was a sorry arrangement on my part, but then, most of my arrangements were sorry.

A week later Rocco and JoJo came back from Boulder as well. Rocco lived out the poet's doctrine as well, but as JoJo had no one, he moved in with a fellow orphan he had known since childhood. We were all at loose ends and had no plans about what we were supposed to do with our lives except drink and drug it away. That—we continued to do with abandon. The depression that I'd experienced so severely in Boulder was coming much more frequently than in days gone by. In fact it was almost always present. I thought that in coming back to Pueblo I could leave it on the Hill, but was sadly mistaken. Nevertheless, I did my best to drown the sorrow with booze or put it beyond the ozone with drugs.

I also resumed with fervency a habit of my last year of high school. When low on money we would purchase—rotgut wine. One dollar would purchase a bottle of Thunderbird, Santa Faye Tokay or MD (Mad Dog) 20-20 wine, and with it, one could do oneself some evermore harm.

A cheap thrill that went along with that, was to go down to Union Street—where the 'real' winos hung out at night—and sit on the street curbs with them and get dead-dog drunk. All the while we'd laugh to ourselves about how pitiful they were. Most of these poor souls could speak nothing but Spanish, some could speak English haltingly, while some could speak English only when sober enough to speak at all—which was not often.

When we first began to go down to Union Street the derelicts were very leery of us, not understanding why boys our age would want to be around them. After they got over their fear that we might do them harm, they began to wonder if we were there just to make fun of them. In this they were of course correct, though we tried not to do it to their face, and if need be would pay off their hurt feelings with another bottle of cheap wine. To us, it was just a thrill, a 'kick,' kind of like the field trips we used to take in grade school. These men and their sad, aimless lives fascinated us. While we certainly didn't intend to end up like them, we were interested in what made them 'tick.'

One night after far too many swigs of rotgut, we began to 'drag main.' Dragging Main consisted of simply driving slowly up Main street in downtown Pueblo all the way to Mineral Palace Park, turning left one block and driving slowly down Court Street for eleven blocks, turning left on Fourth Street, going back to Main and repeating the process. You repeated this with several hundred other young people and cars from all over Pueblo county. You continued until you grew tired, it grew too late, the crowd thinned out… or something happened. More often than not 'something happened'—and it was almost never something good. A 'good' event might be that you meet an old friend or even make a new one, perhaps a girl and would end up at a party or bar somewhere. A 'bad' event usually meant that you met up with an old enemy or made a new enemy and ended up in a fight or jail.

There was always a lot of drag racing between the 'souped-up' vehicles, such as the one that my brother Phil had or my friend Bill had. Phil owned a 1957 Chevy Impala with a 67 Corvette engine that had been bored and stroked and possessed a ¾ race camshaft. To this day I really don't know what all that stuff means, but I knew the lingo and knew that it ran like a screaming banshee. The trouble was that he couldn't keep a 'rear end' in it as he was forever destroying the 'differential' when you 'punched it.' Bill had a 1956 Chevy that had more or less the same 'go-go-toys' and ran like a scalded dog. Larry Weder had an old—I don't know what year—Oldsmobile that ran like a run-over dog. Whenever we rode with Larry we were not looking for a race. While it was not nearly as bad as the Plymouth that I'd unloaded in Boulder, nevertheless it would not be finding its way into any road magazine either.

At any rate—after *way too many* head-shaking, body-shivering gulps of Mad Dog—there we were, looking for the 'bad' rather than the 'good,' and found it in spades.

Having found a fairly big bottle of liquid soap in Larry's trunk, we parked by the courthouse that took up the entire block between Main and Court. I went to the southwest corner of the block, stepped out onto Court Street a few feet and stood waiting for my first victim. I did not go out into the street far enough to get run over, but was in it far enough to make a conscientious driver nervous. Most cars had their windows rolled down so that they could see one another and yell out expressions of recognition or epithets of defamation.

Though my categorizing processes were running a little on the ragged edge, I basically knew what kind of prey I was looking for. First, they had to be a male, preferably unknown—though I was certainly not above blessing known enemies—and it helped if they had a look about them that declared, "Yes Larry… here we are and we're asking for it."

When the first driver came by that pretty much fit the criteria, I raised the bottle of soap that was hanging down from my side and—squirted him in the face. I figured the guy was 'asking for it' because he had the temerity to yell at me and tell me to get out of the way. After I'd squirted him in the face, his car swerved around the road quite a bit, but bye-and-bye he regained control once again. A few minutes later another likely prospect appeared and I shot him also. I continued to target those who more or less 'fit the bill.' They basically had to appear to me as if 'they deserved it.' It quickly became surprising how many deserving looking people were out dragging Main that night. In fact—though I was usually loath to ever pick on a girl—I even shot a couple of rather loud-mouthed females who really did need their mouths washed out with soap.

Eventually, the soap bottle was emptied and I threw it on the courthouse lawn. Quite a crowd of kids had gathered to watch the show and after a moment or two, one of them, the tomato throwing Ronnie Garza, brought me the bottle back full of more liquid. It had the same yellow color as did the soap, but we quickly came to realize that it did not have the same subsistence—though it did carry an ammonia fragrance.

I continued my spraying of the deserving until finally a car pulled over whose occupants were not particularly pleased at having been so treated. It was full of some rather large men—all college seniors of the Southern Colorado State College football team—and they seemed very much ready to 'do business.' The only thing that seemed to halt their momentum was the fact that when they pulled over, their car was immediately surrounded by the large crowd that had now gathered. While not everyone in the crowd was a friend of mine, the football players could not have known that and therefore paused for a fateful moment before getting out.

I strode over to the window of the passenger side and asked the inhabitant what I could do for him (I would have shot him in the face with the 'soap' but it was once more empty and Ronnie didn't seem to be able to refill it). The passenger looked up at me and I recognized him. He was a veritable monster who had been a senior at Central when I was in the ninth grade. He took the Colorado State Championship in the heavyweight wrestling division as well as being an all-state offensive tackle two years running. This did not bode well. He was looking at me as if he were not pleased with my actions and might even want to discuss the matter with me, but wasn't sure if this was the right time. His eyes roamed the crowd that had gathered to my back and slowly said, "Ya know Booker… me and you… we'll talk about this later."

There was a distinct threat in his voice and I should have just shaken his hand and said "Sure pal, give me a call and we'll go out for breakfast sometime." But, alas I didn't, and stupidly said "Well… why don't we just take care of it now." I then reached through the window grabbed him by his hair with both fists and began to beat his head upon the dash of the car. The driver began pulling away as the crowd parted hither and thither. After about twenty feet of running along side with my left hand still holding his hair and pounding his head, I—more or less—let go. It was truly amazing the amount of his locks that were still in my fist.

In a few moments someone spotted police cars coming down Court Street and we quickly dispersed into our cars and made haste for parts unknown.

Thus another Friday evening on Main Street had passed… but not before we went back down to Union Street and continued our night watch with the wino's until we had all but passed out. Eventually we weaved our way home to Broadway Avenue, somehow made it upstairs and crashed.

***

After one such night, Larry, his brother Eddie and I made our way home at about 3:00 am and as usual, passed out. About 5:30 we heard someone coming through the kitchen, singing, laughing and loudly yelling, "It's party time! C'mon get up, it's time to party!"

My eyes were in the process of opening but as yet were unable to focus. When I finally made them work, I saw three pairs of legs ending in three sets of rough looking shoes on the throw rug. One pair of shoes were very scuffed with one shoe lacking shoestrings. Another was a pair of work boots that were in the same scraped, dried out condition, with both boots untied, one string brown, the other white—at least it would have been white if it had been halfway clean. The last was a pair of tennis shoes that had been dyed purple which I immediately recognized as being Rocco's. I began the painful process of moving my eyes up the legs of two very dirty pairs of pants and Rocco's bell-bottoms. Eventually my eyes reached arms, shoulders and faces. And there was Rocco holding a large grocery sack and smiling from ear to ear as if he had brought off some great coup. "Let's party!" he insisted again, and from the sack brought forth a bottle of Thunderbird.

I looked into the faces of two Union Street derelicts that Rocco had picked up. One looked to be in his seventies, was grizzled, dirty and had two of the most hopeless eyes that I had ever looked into. He stood there trembling, licking his lips and looking back and forth from me to Rocco to the bag of wine. The man next to him was much younger, perhaps in his forties, but already the look of doom was upon him. He also was trembling, dirty, unshaven and between the two of them our room was filled with strong, foul body odor. Though I had been drunk with both of them before, I had somehow never seen them quite so clearly, nor in this light.

"C'mon man... let's party!" Rocco repeated. He set the bottles of wine on the top of the chest of drawers and turned on the radio to the KDZA rock station. I could not take my eyes off the faces of the men nor could I move, and for whatever reason the men could not seem to take their eyes off me.

Larry and Eddie had already sat up and were smiling at the uniqueness of the situation. It was one thing for us to go to Union Street but it was quite another to bring Union Street to us. Rocco removed the cap off the bottle of Thunderbird and passed it to Larry. The younger of the winos made his way quickly towards Rocco as if to insure that he receive his portion, but the old man and I could not stop staring into each others eyes. It was as if we were both on a search for something. Then I found it and was instantly terrified.

I knew as surely as I was barely breathing that I was looking into the future. I would someday be—*the old wino*. If something did not happen, if something did not change, I knew that—if I lived long enough—I would indeed become that old, pitiful, lost creature. I would end up a trembling, lip-licking alcoholic that would be the brunt of some young punk's idea of a bad joke. Kids would make fun of me as I shambled my way through life from one bottle to the next, until I finally could take it no more and end up like my real father—dead at forty-six of a heart attack after drinking a quart of whiskey a day for the last ten years of his life. It was at that point in the revelation that I moved. When I did, I moved fast and fierce.

I grabbed the old man as if I were tearing him loose from my fate, thrust him towards the door and away from me. The fear on his face was awful to behold but the fear of my heart was greater. When I'd seized the elderly man, the younger man let the bottle that Rocco had given him drop to the floor. It hit but did not break and he immediately leapt to retrieve it and its precious contents. He was on his feet in a flash and began reaching into his pocket for what I knew would be a knife or strait-razor. Before he could get to the weapon I grabbed him and ran him through the kitchen and out the same door through which the old man had just been propelled. I wheeled back towards Rocco and in an effort to get control of myself was barely able to keep from shrieking. With a trembling fear and rage that I could not fathom I seethed, "Get out! Get out Rocco… and don't you ever bring those bums back here again!"

Rocco was backing out of the room with a dazed, hurt expression on his face. In all our years together, we had never had anything like this happen between us. He started to speak but as he did I grabbed the sack of wine bottles, thrust them into his arms and shoved him all the way through the kitchen and out the door, which I slammed and locked behind him. I then leaned on the door, my forehead on the back of my hands, breathing hard.

I could not hear a sound behind me. Larry and Eddie were as stunned as Rocco. When I finally turned around I saw Larry screwing the lid back onto the bottle of wine Rocco had given him. He apparently thought that he needed a drink after the scene he'd just witnessed. When he saw me looking at him he stashed the bottle under his pillow thinking I had perhaps become a temperance crusader and would smash it to pieces. "God help me," I thought, "I'm getting as bad as the Professor."

Still shaking, I made my way back into the room and sat down on the edge of the bed. After long silence Larry said, "What the #%!$& was that all about?"

I sat a while longer, finally, after several deep breaths and said, "Can't you see it Larry… can't you see it?"

"See *what*?"

"Larry, it's you and me… those two wretches… that's going to be you and me… and Eddie. Someday that's us. We're going to be the bums that young punks like us laugh at. We're going to be on Union Street, and not just for a night of kicks and laughs…we'll be trapped, just like those guys. It's going to happen Larry, I'm telling you it *is* happening. When those men were our age they never dreamed their lives would come to an end like this… but look at 'em Larry… they *did end up there*… and they're not going to get out of it until they're dead… and we won't either."

No one spoke. We just sat there staring at the floor, the only sound heard was my still heavy breathing. We couldn't look at each other because in our hearts we knew that it was all too true. Larry began to rub his face with both hands as if he was trying to wake up. He sat up, reached under the pillow, stopped and slowly drew his hand away and finally asked, "What are we going to do? I mean… what can we do?"

The despair in the room was palpable. It was as if we were looking into an abyss towards which we were hurling and could do nothing about. After a moment or two Eddie said, "Let's change."

Larry and I looked at him as if he had uttered an oracle.

"What do you mean… change?" I asked.

"I mean…change… like, change the way we're living. Change the direction we're going, change… I mean change everything…"

Larry was an extremely intelligent guy, but his brother Eddie was never known for being the brightest light on the Christmas tree. In fact—though he was a very nice guy and everybody liked him—he was just a wee bit slow, and Rocco's nickname for him was—'Special Ed.' But that early morning Larry and I looked at Eddie as if we had climbed a great Himalayan mount, reached the top where a Guru of infinite wisdom sat, and where people waited with breathless wonder for his next utterance. That very fact that we took what 'Special Ed' had said as being so wonderful, and profound gives testimony to how deeply ingrained we were with forebodings of failure.

Finally Larry asked, "How do we change?"

"I dunno… quit drinking. Quit the drugs. Get a job or go to college or… or something," Eddie answered. That's when it hit me.

"That's it!" I said excitedly, "That's it! Larry, let's both go to college! Let's go and do our very best to make something out of our lives! Let's do our best to get rich, I mean *really* rich! And the one that gets rich first has to find the other one, wherever he is in the world, and support his drink and drug habit the rest of his life. That way neither of us will end up on skid row!"

Larry looked at me like he just been let out of prison, smiled a genuinely excited smile and said, "Of course… that's exactly what we'll do."

We continued animatedly in that manner for about another forty-five minutes, before the long night we had spent began to catch up with us. As we began to fizzle, Larry reached under the pillow and withdrew the bottle of Thunderbird. "Whaddya say we have a drink to our future. Immediately Eddie concurred, and after a few moments I said, "Sure… why not." We retrieved three miss-matched coffee cups from the pantry and began to make our toasts "To the future!" When we'd finished the bottle, we were pretty much back in our original condition and so tired that we all passed out and slept the day away. We awoke that night, went to McDonald's and bought some 25 cent hamburgers… and started drinking all over again.

***

I did not, however forget the winos that I had thrown out of our apartment nor did Larry or I forget what we had talked about. After a few days of kicking it back and forth, I told Larry that I was going to have to join the Army in order to ever be eligible to get a college education. Larry stated that he was going to go talk to his grandfather who was a preacher and loved Larry very much. His Grandpa always told him that if he ever seriously wanted to make something of himself to come and see him.

I began my 'betterment drive' by talking to some of my other friends about going into the Army. After a week of intense sales pitch, five of us went to the recruiter's office. The Vietnam War was still in high gear and it wasn't everyday that five young men came in wanting to join up. Needless to say, the recruiter was glad to see us. We signed some papers and after a few days went to Colorado Springs for our testing and physicals. Frank—who never did go to summer school and whose diploma was therefore still blank—went with me as well as Bill, John and Edmond, who Rocco had surnamed 'Hair' because of his very long, thick black hair.

We made our way from one room to the next, taking scholastic tests and getting checked out physically. Eventually we came to a room where we were instructed sit down and fill out forms detailing any and all infractions that one has had with the law—even traffic tickets. My tickets and car wrecks alone were enough to keep me busy a long time, let alone every other thing I'd been involved with.

After a while I realized that I was the only one left in the room—everyone else had finished, left and was continuing the process —and I was still writing. The Sergeant who was overseeing this part of the procedure eventually came over, stared down at the papers I had already filled out and began to read. He sighed deeply and stated, "Son you can continue to write if you want to, but I can tell you right now that they're never going to accept you into the service. Your record is just too bad, and that drug conviction will put you over the edge."

I sat there for a long time staring down at the papers. I sighed, looked up and asked, "Don't I even have a chance?"

"Well, you can try… but I really don't think it's going to fly," he said, then turned and walked off.

Nevertheless, I kept on working, finished the legal brief on my life—which was anything but brief—and went through with the rest of the testing and checking.

Several days later the boys and I gathered back into the recruiters office. He had our files on the table before him upon which his hands were folded and resting. He told us to have a seat, cleared his throat and said, "Well, you young men are quite a crew, but I believe you are going to make fine soldiers and serve your country well." He then shifted a little in his chair, looked towards me and said, "There is a problem however with you, Larry. I'm afraid that due to your police record you won't be accepted."

So, my buddies were in and I was out. Seeing as I was the one who had talked them into joining, they were not exactly happy campers.

I stood to my feet and said to the recruiter, "Sir, can I ask you one question?"

"Sure."

"How did I do on my tests?"

He looked down to the folders, pulled mine from the bottom but didn't open it. "Larry," he said, "You excelled in them all. Every area. There is no field you could not have applied for. In fact, I have no doubt you would have received a tremendous amount of schooling while in the service especially had you desired to go into engineering."

I shrugged my shoulders in an act of painless indifference for my buddies, mumbled something about how cookies crumble, and left my friends. Before it was over Bill and Edmund served in Germany but Frank and John went to Vietnam.

Larry did end up going to College. His grandfather was a Wesleyan Minister and he pulled some strings and got Larry into the Wesleyan Bible College in Bartlesville, Oklahoma. None of us could believe it, as we knew that Larry had not a religious bone in his body. In fact, it seemed to us that his bones were extraordinarily polluted. It was like putting a raging bull in a very fine china shop. But, at least it was college and who knew, maybe Larry would somehow strike it rich and I could coast the rest of my life in a financially-supported drug stupor.

Regardless of my hopes for Larry's future, mine were pretty dim. I was on probation and had been since I was fifteen. I'd blown my football scholarships, couldn't even get into the army in time of war, and had absolutely no money to go to college. I wasn't about to hit my parents up for it when I'd barely made it through high school with a D minus average and doled out a ton of heartache.

As to the apartment, while I wasn't exactly a huge 'money maker,' Eddie had absolutely no concept of the word 'work.' So with Larry gone, we had to give up the apartment and I had to move back home. "Home is the place, that when you have to go there, they have to take you in." The guy must have been a prophet.

***

One day while riding with Pinky down by the city park, sipping on some Spinada wine (things were going a little better in the wine department), I saw a car for sale in front of a rather nice home. The moment I saw it my heart skipped a beat. It was a dark green Spitfire Triumph sports car. I told Bernie to pull over. I walked around the car about four times, kept looking inside of it and sighed longingly. I did everything but drool. I eventually approached the house and rang the doorbell. An elderly gentleman answered who, looking at my long hair and rather tacky clothes, paused to give me the once-over, and finally said, "Yes?"

"I want to ask you about the Triumph you have for sale," I answered.

"Yes?"

"Well... what year is it and how much do you want for it?"

"It's a 1965 and I want five hundred dollars for it."

I could not believe my ears but was trying to remain calm. Not that I could even dream of where I could get five hundred dollars—but at that price it was an absolute steal!

"How many miles does it have on it? I asked acting very cool and calm.

"44,000… give or take some," he answered.

"Could I take a look at it?"

"Yes…" he said slowly, "But, have you the money or are you wasting both our time?"

I wasn't about to tell him that I was "just wasting his time," though I certainly didn't have a dime on me, let alone five hundred bucks. Nor that I hadn't the faintest inkling of where I could get five hundred dollars, nor that I'd just spent my last two dollars on a bottle of wine.

What I told him was, "Well, let's just say that if I like it, I think I can get the money… though I do think that five hundred dollars is a little steep," I managed to say with a straight face.

He smiled at me and turned inside the house. In a moment or two he came back with the keys and we approached the car together. It was so beautiful to me that thought I'd die if I didn't get it. I ran my hand along the fender doing my best not to let my slobber show. I didn't know when I'd ever wanted anything so bad in my life. The old man started it up and the engine purred like a kitten.

"Can I take it for a test drive?" I ventured.

He looked at me and gave a little laugh. "Of course you can't take it for a drive. Not without me riding with you… and by the looks of you… I don't think I want to."

I just stared at him with my mouth open. He was a somewhat feisty, nice, articulate little fellow, and I couldn't help but like him. Nor could I blame him for not wanting to let the car out of his sight or for not wanting to get into it with me for a test run.

"I'll tell you how it's going to be," he continued as calm as a swamp, "You come back here with five hundred dollars—cash, and not a penny less—and I'll hold the money while you test drive it. Trust me, you'll like it."

I stood there wondering what on earth I could possibly do

to buy this car. Eventually I knew the only thing I could do, but wasn't sure that I could muster up the audacity to do it. I swallowed and said, "I'm going to do my very best to be back as soon as possible. I know this sounds really stupid but is there any way you could hold this car for me? Just till tomorrow night? If you don't hear from me by then, well don't worry about it… but I really am going to try and buy it."

"Yes, well, I guess I could do that. But just out of curiosity… what are you going to do to get the money?"

My answer—though it no doubt seemed like no big deal to him—was an unbelievably big deal to me. "Well Sir, I'm going home to talk to my dad."

***

Bernard let me off at my house and I approached the door taking deep breaths in order to gain some control of my racing heart. What I was about to do required some real chutzpah on my part. Chutzpah is a Jewish phrase that means someone has unbelievable audacity or gall—such as if someone were to kill their parents, and then beg mercy from the court on the grounds that they were, after all, orphans. For me to go into my home and ask Buzz for five hundred dollars for a sports car after all I had put them through was—supreme chutzpah.

I walked in the front door and noticed for the first time in years that the trash needed taken out. I did it. Buzz had not taken his eyes off of the television set, but my mother was staring at me as if I was painted green and had a bone through my nose. I sat down on her footstool after moving it closer to my dad, cleared my throat and said, "Buzz, can I talk to you for a minute?" He moved only his eyes in my direction and said, "What have you done now?"

"Nothing! Really. Honest. I…I… just want to ask you something… kind of… like if, maybe you could do something for me."

He was now looking at me face on, but with an expression that revealed absolutely nothing except that he was looking at me.

"What?" he said.

"Well it's like this," I began, squeezing the words out through lungs and throat that were constricting terribly, "I have found this really awesome, really beautiful car… it's a Triumph… a Spitfire. A Triumph convertible, but also has a fiberglass top and it's a 1965 and it only has 44,000 miles on it and it's really beautiful, and the guy really seems to like me and that's why he's willing to sell it so cheap… I mean… that's probably why, and honest Buzz you've got to see it… I mean it really *is* something, and I promise you, I promise you, with everything in me… I promise you that I'll get a job and I'll pay you back every single penny…and Buzz you've just got to see it, I promise you it's so, so… awesome…"

My rush of words eventually played out as Buzz just stared at me with an expression that I'd finally stopped to read. Total incredulity. Like, "Boy do you have any idea what you are saying and who you're saying it to? Do you remember the misery I had because of your first car—the car that I bought for you…and you've never paid me a red cent for? What with three wrecks in three months and losing your drivers license… and the fact that in spite of my twenty-five year perfect driving record my insurance cancelled me, and that out of fear of you. And how your brother had to move out of this house lest they cancel him and when he did move they raised his rates atrociously because they were afraid that you'd somehow steal his car and drive it… and how many time I've had to bail you out of jail and put up with your failing grades and truancies and drugs and… good grief boy you're more brazen than a brass monkey!"

While thankfully he never said any of this, he didn't have to… his eyes and expression and *my conscience* said it all.

Buzz continued to stare at me while my mom finally buried her head into the Enquirer newspaper and kind of hunkered down in her recliner.

I swallowed a few times and kept looking at Buzz until I grew embarrassed for being such a fool. I lowered my eyes, let my shoulders sag and said, "I'm sorry, I really mean it. I know that I had absolutely no right to ask you for anything like this. I'm sorry… really."

I turned away on the footstool, as I didn't want him to see the tears that were beginning to well in my eyes and arose to my feet. I don't think I was about to cry over the car that I never had a chance of getting anyway, as much as it had just fully hit me how stupid and rotten I had been to these two wonderful people that had simply tried to do the best for me that they possibly could. Buzz didn't owe me a thing. He'd come into my life and spared me and my mother and brother from God only knows how much heartache, while all I'd ever done was shove nothing but shame and pain back into his face. I was almost to the stairs that led down to my room when he finally spoke.

"Larry… you don't even have your drivers license. The state took it away—remember?"

I turned back, and this time I couldn't keep from choking up… because I knew Buzz…and I knew what was happening in his heart and mind.

"I… I could get them back now… the two year suspension is up. I… I can get them now," I managed to croak.

"Yes, but Larry, it's not just the car… you have to get insurance, and Allstate cancelled us both. Your insurance for six months will cost almost as much as the car… your record is rotten."

All I could do is hang my head and say, "I know… I guess I hadn't thought about that." And I really hadn't. "It's okay… there'll be another time…" I turned again to leave when he cleared his throat and said, "Where is it…the car I mean?" By this time my mother was crying, though she was doing it behind the paper.

Leaning against the wall, with my eyes closed and my throat constricted I said, "It's down by the city park. I don't know the man's name, he's an old man, but I know where he lives… he… he said he'd save it for me till tomorrow night."

"Well… maybe in the morning we can go see it. That is if you're going to be around."

"Yes sir," I said, "I'll be here." And then, really choking up I managed to say, "Buzz… if we don't get it… the, the car… it really is going to be okay. It means everything to me that you'd even think about it." And it really did.

With that I made my way downstairs, laid across my bed and cried like a baby.

***

I drove up to the construction sight and parked the Spitfire where as many of the workers could see it as possible. It was the third job-site I'd been to that day. A framer at the last place told me that I might try this one as he'd heard they really needed help. He winked and whispered to me that, "We need help here too, but the foreman's a world class jerk." Really, his language was a bit more colorful than that but does not bear repeating.

I think the framer felt sorry for me because when I met up with the boss after inquiring his whereabouts from several of the workers, he just looked me over—that is my hair and clothes—and said, "Don't need ya." What he really meant was, "I don't want to see your face around here again, and the back of your head is looking better than the front all the time. So clear out now, hippy boy."

So I came to the Belmont—northeast—area of Pueblo and pulled up at a huge apartment complex that was being erected and began asking around for the boss. The various workers would just grunt and point in various directions. I kept trying to follow out their rather nonchalant hand gestures until finally one guy, who seemed to be about my age, looked up from his chalk line and said, "Just listen for the screaming. When you hear somebody screaming and cussing a blue streak you will have found the boss." His description really didn't sound very promising, so I decided to ask if he thought they needed any more workers. "Oh yeah, he needs help alright, He needs all the help he can get." At that he returned to his chalk line and didn't seem to want to discuss the matter any further.

I went to the very center of the complex that was made up of four large rectangular buildings that were themselves placed in a rectangular formation. I cocked my ear to see if I could pick up anything other than the sound of saws, hammers and the vehicles that were roaming around. Presently I began to hear one of the finest demonstrations of pure shrill profanity that I had heard since the day that my uncle Frank had an old-car-tire-dam (that had taken months and thousands of used tires, completely filled with sand, to build) wash away after the first big rain. He'd built it in effort to keep the St. Charles river from washing away any more of the precious tableland of his farm. When the first spring rain (and flood) came, it carried away almost every tire as well as an acre of freshly sewn corn. It was then that I found out how a retired sailor could really cuss. But now, as I stood in the center of the complex of apartments what I heard might have been even a shade more meaningful. I took a deep breath and made my way towards the sound of the fire-breather.

Thankfully, as I drew closer, his language—if not his anger—began to abate. I began to weave my way through the framed out rooms towards him and whoever it was that had just been seared. Then I saw what I knew must be 'the cusser' storming in my direction. I was immediately both relieved and concerned. I was concerned because of his fierce countenance. I was relieved because if I had ever seen a 'long-haired freak,' I was looking at one now.

Of course I'd seen furious hippies before, but I'd never had to ask one for a job. But then… I'd personally never seen one that *had* a job, let alone be foreman over an endeavor like this. I decided to play it very straight.

"Sir…Sir, could I talk to you for a second?" He stopped and stared at me as if I'd appeared from the ether. I guess he hadn't seen me prior to my speaking and now he seemed irritated that I came from…wherever it was that I came from.

"What do you want?" he more or less snarled.

"Well, do you… do you need any help… have you got any openings you know, for work?" I more or less mumbled.

He stared at me, started to walk off, stopped and said, "What can you do? Anything?" I felt like replying, "Well you don't look like you can do a whole lot yourself," but thought better of it.

"I'm a carpenters helper. That's about it. I'm not great but if you'll give me a chance I'll work hard."

"What I want to know is, will you show up everyday?" he asked, searching my eyes as well as my mouth for the answer.

"I'll be here. I've got a car I have to pay for."

"What kind of car, *and*, who do you owe the money to?" he asked with his head cocked to one side. I thought the questions were odd and really none of his business but said, "It's a '65 Spitfire Triumph and I owe the money to my dad."

He lifted his head from its tilted position and didn't say anything for a moment or two. There was something going on in him, I could see it in his eyes, but I couldn't read what it was. Finally he said, "People pay their bills better when they don't owe it to family. A bank will come get your car if you don't pay for it. Anyway, be here in the morning at 7:00 am. Go to that building over there"—he pointed to the one on the north—"and ask for Tom. Do whatever he tells you to do, and you better be ready to do everything from driving nails to picking up trash to digging a ditch. You'd better work hard and fast. I'll pay you minimum wage. Be ready to work ten hours a day if needed and Saturdays as well. You don't get overtime, and you'll be paid in cash. There'll be no paperwork but I won't cheat you. You'll meet a guy named Fred sometime next week. He's the guy that doles out the money. If he doesn't bring it to you by 5:00 on Fridays go to him and looked depressed, which shouldn't be too hard to do. What's your name?"

"Larry... Larry Booker."

He looked at me cocked his head to the other side and said, "You related to Phil?"

"Yeah," I said, somewhat surprised, "He's my brother."

He stared at me and said, "You just got out of high school didn't you?"

"Yes...and I got a real diploma," I said trying to work some humor into the conversation.

"Hmmm. Well I got news for you Larry Booker," and at this point he took a step forward, "Don't mess with me, and don't mess with anybody here. If they don't have you for lunch, I will." At that point I felt something rising up in me that wanted to say, "I don't think you're big enough and I'm certain you're not tough enough, or your cronies either," but I swallowed my pride and just nodded my head slowly never taking my eyes off his.

"Another thing, don't come to work drunk or ripped, and keep your hangovers to a minimum. If you come to work that way you'll end up losing some fingers, or worse. If you don't believe me ask Fernando over there"—he was now pointing to another building—"why he had to learn to hammer with his left hand. And you're *not* covered by insurance." He turned and started to walk away, stopped and slowly turned around. He now had a different look on his face and again, I could see something, almost like pain in his eyes.

"Larry," he said quietly, "Don't be a jerk. Make sure you pay your dad back for the car. If you don't you'll might regret it for a long time." He turned and was gone.

"What a strange duck," I thought, shrugged my shoulders and started to go back to my car when I spun around and yelled, "Hey!" He turned and looked at me.

"What's your name?" I shouted.

"Jack," he said and kept on walking.

I got into the Triumph—no small feat for a guy my size, started it up, spun out on the gravel and headed towards Rocco's house and then Pinocchio's Bar to celebrate my new job.

The next day I left home at 6:30 a.m. wishing that I'd went home instead of going to Pinocchio's. My head was throbbing and my mouth tasted like the bottom of swamp. Howbeit the sports car was running well and for that I was grateful… because I definitely was *not* running on all cylinders.

I parked the car and sat for a while in an effort to get my bearings and finally groaned my way out of the seat. I slowly walked to the north building and started asking around for Tom. Another 'hippy looking' worker that seemed to be in worse shape than me (at least I hoped his eyes more bloodshot than mine) pointed towards a man that looked to be in his mid to late fifties, and said, "That's Tom… have at him."

Tom was short, maybe five foot two or three inches tall, but what he lacked in height he more than made up for in girth. He appeared to be very strong physically, and you could tell by the way he carried himself that he was 'open for business' of just about any type. His hair was mostly gray, cut short, and over all he bore a most military type bearing. He seemed to be in earnest conversation with a tall gangly figure (kind of like myself) that appeared to be upset. In a moment or two the tall guy had apparently heard enough, for he spun on his heel, strode back across the room and began to ferociously tear some studs out of the wall.

Tom turned towards me and began his approach while at the same time barking out orders to the hippy kid with the bloodshot eyes. He finished him off rather quickly and then said to me, "You the new guy?"

"Yes… Jack hired me yesterday."

"Are you any good at anything?"

"Well, I can drive nails… and pull 'em," I said trying to smile.

"Can you frame out by yourself?"

"Not really… not yet. Somebody will have to point out things and tell me what to do. But if they'll do their part I'll do mine."

"We'll see," he said, and began looking around the building and across the way to where I'd met Jack the day before. Presently he said, "You got a nail bag?"

"No, I don't, but I have a hammer and a measuring tape in the car" (compliments of Buzz—though he was unaware of it as yet).

"Okay," Tom said, "there's a box in the back of that white truck over there," he pointed to a pick-up that had definitely seen better days, "Get a nail apron and nail off the roof of this building. The top four sheets of plywood on the north side have already been done. Do the rest just exactly like they were. I'll be up there in about an hour or so to see how you're doing. Use these nails," he had walked over to a box of nails and kicked it lightly, "and make sure you don't fall off."

He must have seen the look on my face as I was looking across the way at the buildings. They were all three stories high.

"You afraid of heights?" he asked.

"No… not really. I just don't feel so hot today."

"Hangovers will do that to you. I don't recommend that you keep up your pace of night life, that is if you expect to make a living in the daytime." With that he turned and left, calling for the longhaired boy (it was then I found out his name was 'Manny') to follow him.

I then called after him, "Hey! Hey Tom!"

"What?"

"How do I get on the roof?"

"There's a ladder on the top floor. Take it to one of the skylight openings. But hurry it up... I want that roof nailed off by lunch time." So he and Manny went off and I began to make my way to the white truck.

***

I survived the first week, but just barely. It wasn't so much the work, though God knows I wasn't used to it, nor was it my continued drinking, drugging and partying—it was the combination of both. One thing I knew for sure, my first payday was spent before I ever laid hands on it. Buzz, was not amused. If I kept this business up, either my body—or Buzz—was going to give way to trauma. As for the apartment complex where I was working, it was confusion personified and was threatening to become a disaster. And it took less than a week to understand why.

Jack had taken over the job of construction foreman only three weeks before I arrived. Sadly, his father, who was the original contractor, had died of a heart attack only a month ago. In order to (hopefully) save the family business, Jack took his father's place as foreman. He was totally unfamiliar with the operation of this project, and had in fact been singing lead in a rock band in Denver when his father passed away. So he moved back to Pueblo, put on a hardhat once again and was trying to make a go of it. I felt sorry for Jack and wished him well—but it didn't make him any easier to live with. In fact, he was growing worse every day. His screaming was becoming more strident as the pressures and failures grew worse. Good carpenters who couldn't take it, simply walked off the job. And most of them were of necessity being replaced with carpenters... well, with people like me.

Tom was Jack's right hand man and had apparently been with the family business for many years. If it weren't for him the job would no doubt have already gone up in smoke. It was obvious that the better carpenters were staying only because of Tom's entreaties. As Tom could not afford to take out his frustrations on them—he took them out on me and my fellow 'sad-sacks.'

As for Jack, the *only* person he was civil to was Tom, whom he correctly recognized as his 'life-line.' The rest of us caught 'Hades' on a daily and nightly basis. I say 'nightly' because Jack's screaming even worked its way into some of my dreams.

I was not able to nail off the roof of the building by noon on my first day. In fact it took me till noon the next day. At that point I think Jack wanted to tell me to take a hike, but Tom recommended that they give me a few more days to 'catch on.' Since then things had gone a little better, especially after I quit taking anything that brought on hallucinations. The last thing I needed was to be on a rooftop and think that I was on the ground floor, or that I could fly to the next building. And—believe it or not—I actually became more proficient at hammering and even some of the other work stuff.

The tall, gaunt individual, that was none too happy with Tom the first day that I came, took me under his wing and began to give me tips on how to do things correctly. His name was Hanford, but everybody called him 'Hanny,' which he liked better and understandably so.

After Hanny gave me his first couple of suggestions, saw that I didn't mind the advice, thanked him and actually implemented what he said, he really opened up and helped me whenever he could. Before long we were pretty good friends.

Hanny was in his mid to late thirties, and came across as a quiet, forlorn character. I once tried to get him to talk about himself but was immediately made to understand that his private world was not open for discussion. Manny (the hippy boy), said that he'd heard that his wife had ran out on him for some type of a business tycoon and had left him with a little boy to raise. He'd also heard that it wasn't so much her leaving Hanny that hurt, as it was *who* she'd left him for (Manny, as it turned out, tended to hear much of the ongoing scuttlebutt).

"It left him feeling like he was a loser because he had to make a living with his hands instead his brains. Not like the new guy who made a living with his smooth tongue and fancy suits and big cars. She apparently made it a point to drive that home to him several times," Manny said, and then looked down at his own hands.

"She's an idiot," I said, "It sounds to me like she was just an accident waiting to happen."

"Yeah... probably so. But I heard she was a real knock-out."

"Just drives my point home," I answered.

Hanny never did open up to me about his pain filled, private world. Nor did I blame him.

At any rate, in 'Hanny' and 'Manny' I had found a couple of friends at work—though they were very different from each other. Manny made me feel a little better concerning my carpenter skills because as I got a *little* better, his ineptness became more apparent. After a while I came to feel that, if anyone was going to get the 'axe' it would probably be Manny before me—unless I really did something stupid—which was after all entirely possible. Not that I wished that on Manny, but after a few more of Jack's tirades I was grabbing at straws in trying to regain a semblance of self-esteem.

I finally came to the place that I was asking Hanny how to do everything. In doing so, I accomplished two things. One, I found out how to do whatever it was I was supposed to do, and secondly, it seemed to help Hanny to feel better about himself. I also, on occasion, would make it a point to brag on him to Tom. When this got back to Hanny, I was 'in like flint.' In turn he would, on occasion, cover for me when I'd 'muffed' something by either fixing it before Tom or Jack saw it, or do his best to make an excuse for me if they did see it. I sincerely came to like and respect him, and my heart went out to him because of his heavy load in life.

One day I met Hanny's son. He was about six years old, and was sitting in his dad's truck waiting for him to get off work. I'd parked my Spitfire next to it and was about to leave when I heard a voice behind me say, "Hey!" I turned and saw a small, blonde headed urchin stick his tongue out at me. I smiled and returned the favor. He looked somewhat pleased and when I grinned at him he responded in kind.

"Why are you in Hanny's truck? Are you trying to steal it?" At that, he seemed genuinely pleased and gave me an ear-to-ear grin.

"Maybe I am… so what."

"Can you drive it?"

"Of course I can drive it… but I don't have the keys," the urchin said. Then looking at my Triumph he said, "But I'd really like to steal that car. Is that your car?"

"Well… it's mine if I ever get it paid for." Then asked, "What's you're name?"

"Toby."

"Are you Hanny's boy?"

"Yeah, he's my dad."

"I like your dad, Toby. He's a very nice man.

"I like him too. Did you know that he's going to buy me a bicycle?" the boy said with bright eyes.

"Really," I answered, "Can you ride a bike?" I asked him that remembering how long it had taken me to learn how to ride a bike.

"Well, I think that he's going to get me is a bike that has extra wheels."

"You mean a tricycle?"

"No! Not a tricycle! A bike!" he said indignantly, "but it's not going to be a real big one."

"Well good for you," I answered. "Say, what are you doing here? How did you get here?"

"My aunt brought me here 'cause she had to go do something. She watches me till my dad gets off work. What's your name?"

"My names Larry… Larry Booker."

At that Toby's eyes grew wide and said, "Oh… I heard about you—you like to get drunk and get in lots of fights."

I stared at the boy, not really believing my ears.

"Who told you that?"

"I heard my aunt talking—not the one who watches me, the younger one, Aunt Carlene—I heard her telling my dad about you. She said you were not very nice and that all you did was go around getting in trouble and getting drunk and getting arrested and beating people up and stuff."

I could not believe what this child was saying, but knew that these statements pretty much depicted what my life had been reduced to. After a moment or two I said, "How does your aunt even know me?"

"She said that she was best friends with a girl that used to like you and that you used to go out with her and stuff."

"What girl? What was her name?" I asked.

"I think her name was Rhoda, or Rhonda, or something... I've met her and she comes to our house sometimes with my aunt Carlene."

As I listened I gulped and thought, "Well... she does know what she's talking about after all."

I knew Carlene, but not well. I remembered her as being Rhonda Morsline's friend. I had met her at a dance that was held out in Blend. It had not been a great night as I almost ended up in a mammoth fight with a bunch of guys from County High School.

Then I said, "Toby, when's the last time you saw this Rhonda?"

"Oh that was about a month ago. I ain't seen her since. She was a nice lady and gave me some candy, and she was pretty too."

Yes... Toby had indeed met the nice Rhonda that I used to date and had done so dirty. "What a creep I am," I thought, "I'm lucky Carlene didn't say a whole lot worse than she did."

Hanny walked up and threw his nail bag in the toolbox in the back of his truck. "So, I see you two have met," he said.

"Yeah," Toby said, then added excitedly, "This is Larry Booker that aunt Carlene said is such a jerk!" Both Hanny and I had to laugh, and I said, "Hanny, I didn't realize that Carlene was your sister. I'd met her a couple of years ago. I'd like to see her again and... well... maybe fix up some things that I've messed up."

"I'm not sure I want you too—or if you really should... she's best friends with Rhonda Morsline."

"Yeah... that's what Toby just informed me. That's the mess I'd like to fix." Then I said, "Hanny, do you know Rhonda... do you see her much?"

"Naw, I've only seen her once or twice. She doesn't seem to think a whole lot of you though."

"No, no… I guess she wouldn't." At that my mind began to think back to one of the sweetest girls I'd ever dated… and ended up probably hurting the worst. I just 'dropped her'… with a thud. Never a call, never a word, never so much as a gesture to explain why I no longer wanted to date her. I just quit calling and refused to return her calls. When I saw her at a party a month later, I acted like she was part of the furniture. The really stupid thing about it all is that, to this day I have no idea why I did it. And I really do believe that she genuinely loved me. Carlene's right… I am a jerk. I know now that I deserve everything that Norma's putting me through. Then I pulled myself out of my reverie and said, "Toby… it's good to meet you little man. You're a lucky boy to have a daddy like Hanny." I then stuck out my hand, and he reached out his little paw and shook it.

Toby beamed and Hanny didn't do so bad either. Then I said, "Toby, I want you to tell your aunt Carlene that you met Larry Booker, and that he knows he's a jerk and someday wants *not* to be."

"What if I see Rhonda is there anything you want me to tell her?"

Hanny and I looked at each other and until finally I said, "Sharp kid isn't he?"

"Yeah… too sharp," said Hanny.

"Toby, if you see Rhonda… why don't you *not* bring my name up… O.K.?"

"If you say so," he said smiling. At that point he more than ever looked like an urchin.

***

Things were *not* going well at home. Too many parties, late nights, Mom working overtime to get me up in the mornings and by far the worst of all… I had yet to give Buzz a dime towards the car or the insurance. Three weeks had gone by now… and nothing. I could tell that Buzz was trying hard not to explode but it was becoming quite a struggle. No doubt the only reason he held back was for the sake of my mother.

One morning after I had an exceptionally hard time getting up, I could hear him as he went out the back door on his way to his truck and to work. While I could not make out all that he was saying I did pick up on the words, "worthless" and "bum" and "just get out," and as few other things of that nature. It didn't take a rocket scientist to figure out to whom Buzz was referring. I warily made my way out of the restroom, making sure that he was indeed gone. When I came into the kitchen I saw my mother sitting at the table with tears in her eyes. All I could do was kneel down, put my arm around her and say, "Mom… I'm really sorry. I really am… I'll try to do better.

"Larry, can't you just start paying him back a little each week?" she pleaded.

"Mom, I mean to… I really do. When I get paid I always put back some money in one of the folds of my wallet to pay Buzz with, but I get with the guys and, and… well it just kind of disappears. I'm going to try to do better, okay? Please Mom, please don't cry."

I drove to work feeling like the cad that I in fact was. It didn't help that I had another hangover and thought that at any minute I was going to have to pull over to the side of the road and retch.

I parked my car next to Hanny's truck and could already hear Jack screaming. I sat there for a minute wondering if I should just restart the car and go somewhere… anywhere but here. I was not up to listening to an all day harangue.

I actually felt sorry for Jack now that I knew what this whole project was all about. Manny had been more than happy to fill me in on more of the details. Jack's father had been the general contractor *as well as* primary financier of the apartment complex. The venture had actually gone relatively smooth, until one morning the workers arrived on the job site to find that all the trusses they had set up on the northern-most building had fallen during the night. In the process of a cursing tirade, Jack's father keeled over with a heart attack and had died in route to the hospital.

As theirs was a 'family business' if there ever was one, it fell Jack's lot to come back and take over the project. He had pretty much been raised in construction and without question knew how to build. But a vast amount of knowledge about this development was locked up in his father's head and had died with him. To save the family from financial catastrophe, Jack had to give up the lead singer business in Denver, and move back to try and pick up the pieces of his families emotions as well as their company's finances. And he had to attempt this while carrying his own load of personal grief as well.

This grief was magnified in that Jack and his father had not been getting along very well over the last couple of years, mainly due to Jack's complete lack of interest in the business. He was (according to Manny) a very good musician and singer and was doing his best to pattern himself after the recently deceased Jim Morrison of the 'The Doors.' That was no small feat, though it didn't take as much talent as it took 'chutzpah.' So here he was, being forced leave what he loved, and return to a trade at which he'd worked most of his life and abhorred.

All of this together, created in me a real empathy for Jack. Though I had never pictured Jim Morrison with a hardhat and nail bag. I could however see him running around and screaming at people. In fact, it was this picture that helped me hold up under my boss's tirades. I would play a little mental game that Jack was 'Jim'—there actually was some resemblance—and comfort myself that I'd just been cussed out by the great 'Jim Morrison' come back from the dead just to pay me a personal visit and vent his troubled spleen.

I had to be careful however while practicing this mental exercise, because while applying it one time, I started cracking up laughing. The sight of 'Jim Morrison' screaming at me in a hardhat, holding a T-square with a pencil behind his ear was just too much. As I began to laugh, Jack stopped dead in his tracks and demanded, "What's so funny Booker?" I didn't have the heart to tell him, so I wiped the smile off my face, stifled my amusement and simply turned and went back to work. It must have thrown Jack off balance as he turned away but continued to mutter to himself.

All of this information did clarify Jack's remarks to me the first day I'd met him about my not being 'a jerk' and making sure that I paid my dad the money for the car.

I came out of my reverie when Hanny tapped me on the shoulder. He had gone to his truck to get a crowbar and saw me sitting lost in thought. "You coming to work today?"

I looked up at him and did my best to smile though it cost me something by way of head pain. He continued to look at me and finally said, "You know Larry, I actually think you have turned yourself permanently green from all your boozing." I probably would have laughed but I feared my head would explode, and, that he was probably right about my color.

"What's Jack screaming about now?" I asked as I worked my way slowly out of the Spitfire.

"The dry-wallers are scheduled to start on the south building this afternoon and Marty and his guy left the whole bottom-half of it unwired."

"Sounds like we're on par."

"Plus, we have problems that Jack doesn't know about yet. Half the studs in this building are so crooked that those same drywallers are screaming their heads off. They're saying they have to try two and three times before they can even hit the studs in the middle of the sheets."

"And… what's that mean to me."

"This means you're going to have to straighten the studs. Measure, cut and nail in pieces of 2x4 scrap till the stud lines are straight enough for the drywallers. Anywhere you see a bowed one you gotta straighten it out."

"That's gonna take a lot of time Hanny, this whole place is crooked."

"Yeah but you get paid a lot less than the drywallers. As it stands now, they're threatening to go on to another job and not come back till this one's ready. If they do that Jack will freak out of his boots."

These words no sooner left Hanny's lips than we heard what

sounded like an all time record of shrieking profanity coming from Jack. It had an almost animal-like quality about it and even worse, it was heading in our direction. Hanny and I both turned and were more than relieved to find that it was Manny that was about to receive the latest verbal machete.

I was not sure what Manny had done (or not done) but I could tell that this was a 'humdinger' of a fiasco in the making. I could see Manny physically bracing himself against the wall as Jack tore into him in words that cut like a buzz saw. As I watched the exhibition it came to me that Jack would have made a much better drill sergeant than a contractor. But upon reflection, as he absolutely soared to new heights of profane fury, I contemplated that some new kind of 'grungy Rock style' might possibly be in the making. I could picture Jack standing on the edge of a coliseum stage hurling brutally vile curses to an audience that quite simply couldn't get enough of it. I could picture young girls screaming and swooning at his feet thinking that if only they could live with such a man how thrilling life would be. Ahh… if only a talent scout of savant proportions were here to witness this demonstration of sheer, unbridled passion surely Jack would be literally hurled into some type of immortal fame. This was simply a talent that was too great to waste on mere lackeys of the construction world. As Jack continued in his unabated diatribe both Hanny and I became spellbound at the sheer raw beauty of eloquence that we had only dreamed existed. He was now so livid that his face was turning purple and the veins were bulging from his temple to his neck. It came to the place that I knew two things for sure. First, I really believed that even my uncle Frank would have been impressed, and secondly, I could now clearly see how Jack's father died with curses still left within him. His heart was simply unable to compete with his mouth.

The cause for this awesome demonstration it turned out, was that Manny had evidently left last night and forgot to put the air compressor he'd been using into the tool shed. Now, it was missing. Also, he'd left the tool shed unlocked and there were several other expensive pieces of equipment gone. Had Manny not slowly slid his way down the wall and out of the building,

Jack might have slipped past the verbal into the physical and beaten him to death. Jack stopped his infuriated invective only when Manny threw his tools into the back of his car, jumped behind the wheel and sped away. Jack leaned up against the wall in order to catch his breath propping himself up with his right arm. You could see the great expansion and contraction of his rib cage and by the look on his face he was obviously still seething. For a moment or two I thought sure that Jack's dad and Jim Morrison were about to have company.

After a while, speaking to no one, he walked to the mobile structure that served as an office. He was no doubt going to see if the insurance company would do anything about the missing equipment. The way things were going, I had serious doubts that the premiums had even been paid.

Manny returned within the hour, and nothing else was said about the equipment, his stupidity, or his leaving the job site. Apparently the 'driving away' trick had saved him before and more than once. I couldn't understand why Jack didn't just fire him and be done with it. When I asked Hanny about it he replied, "How can he? Manny's his nephew." I was, to put it mildly, 'blown away.' That was one bit of information that the 'tell all' Manny had never related to me.

It was only later that afternoon, when I caught Manny talking and laughing to himself that it dawned on me that it was probably Manny himself that came back late last night and stole the equipment. Though I couldn't prove it, the more I thought about it, I was pretty sure it must be true. When I ran my thoughts by Hanny he said, "Oh, !$#%&! yes! That punks been stealing the place blind ever since he came on the job."

This realization left me literally sick to my stomach. It was more than the theft—it was the kicking a man when he was down… and Jack was after all, 'way down.' Furthermore, Jack was Manny's own family. I also realized why Jack was *so* infuriated. In his heart he probably knew that Manny had stolen the stuff, and but for family dynamics—that I knew naught about—he could do nothing about it. After I realized the truth of Manny's duplicity I was ice cold towards him and could tell by his reaction to me that—he knew that I knew... and was 'lying low' because of it. From that day on we spoke hardly to one another.

It was not that I'd never stolen. God only knew how much my buddy's and I had heisted through the years from homes and stores and cars, but I'll never forget the day that I was sitting in the den in Tony's basement and I saw hanging on his parents' wall a bronze placard displaying the 'Ten Commandments.' There they were as 'big as Dallas,' and as I began to read them I immediately began to cringe inside. I made my way down the left-hand side of the two sided bronze plaque and sub-consciously began to tick off in my mind the ones that I was guilty of breaking.

"Thou shalt have no other gods before me."

"No… I'm not *real* guilty there… I *know* that God is God."

"Thou shalt not make unto thee any graven image"

"No… I've never done that."

"Thou shalt not take the name of the LORD thy God in vain"

"Ooh… God help me… I cuss like a sailor."

"Remember the sabbath day, to keep it holy"

"I usually try and be a little better on Sunday… sometimes I even go church."

"Honour thy father and thy mother"

"Oh God… I'm so sorry… I treat my parents so shabbily… but I really do love them."

"Thou shalt not kill"

"God, you know that I've never killed anybody… I may have really put the hurt on some… but I've never killed a one of em."

"Thou shalt not commit adultery"

"God you know… I mean, I think you know… I've never actually done that."

"Thou shalt not steal"

For whatever reason, when I read this commandment my heart smote me to the core. It was like a knife in my heart being twisted back and forth. Presently I prayed, "Oh God… I really am sorry for all the stuff I've stolen… God, I won't do it any more." After reading that commandment I never made it to the last two. I just couldn't take anymore. But I did make a resolve in my heart to never steal again. And—in one of the few promises that I'd made to God and been able to keep—I never did, except... almost... one time.

So when I realized what Manny had done, it bothered me deeply. Not that I thought that I was a better person than Manny—I knew better than that—it was just that I could see, at least a little, the enormity of how bad his actions were, and that God really must hate it. Of course I never said anything about my suspicion of Manny to anyone—that was something you just didn't do, but I did watch my meager tools more closely after that, and made an obvious point to Manny that I was doing so—even if they were all but worthless.

Maybe one of the reasons that the commandment 'not to steal' stood out to me so strong was because of something that happened to me a few years before with one of my friends.

Pete and I were very close friends. I was in the middle of my seventh grade year when one day Buzz asked me if I'd seen the set of 'bits' that went with his soldering gun. They were a very nice set that—if a guy knew what he was doing—could perform some pretty nifty feats of soldering. They were missing and Buzz actually went so far as to insinuate that one of my 'cronies' must have taken them. I was highly insulted, as I knew that none of my buddy's would do that to me—or Buzz either one. Nevertheless I did ask Pete about them, as he was my only friend that had been over to our house since Buzz had last seen them. Of course Pete denied any knowledge of it, as I knew he would. Pete was just not that kind of guy and except for a little more grumbling from Buzz that pretty well ended the affair.

Four months later, I was at Pete's house where he and I were building slot car racers. Slot-car racing was the rage at the time and my brother Phil had put together a car that was really fast. Naturally, I wanted to build a faster one. In the process of putting the body together I needed some tape to hold some glued parts together while it dried. Pete told me that there was probably some in one of the lower, left-hand drawers of his desk. As I opened the second one down I stopped in mid-motion. There lying in the bottom of the drawer was the complete set of my dad's soldering bits. I stared at them scarcely believing my eyes. By and by Pete knew that something was up as I had slowly stood and now seemed frozen. When he realized what I must be seeing, his shoulders slumped and we were both speechless. I slowly closed the drawer never touching the bits, turned and faced Pete who was looking sick. I said, "I hope you like them." Then I walked out his house and never spoke to Pete again in my life. I never told Buzz or anyone else—ever—until now.

I could not bring myself to tell Buzz nor could I now bring myself to tell Jack—what they had both suspected anyway. All I knew was that I now abhorred stealing. It was too bad that I also didn't hate drugs and alcohol.

***

Buzz and I finally had our 'melt-down.' I stormed out the door swearing that I'd never, and I mean *never* return. At that moment I meant every single non-pious adjective and verb that came out of my mouth (Jack seemed to be rubbing off on me). Buzz also seemed to be in equal earnest in his denunciation of the mere thought of my returning to his house, that was henceforth and forever closed to my "sorry #%@!!&%$#! face." So thorough was his censure, that upon later reflection, I was surprised that he'd even allowed me to take the Spitfire out of the driveway. He may have thought that in trying to prevent that, we might have come to blows—or, then again, he might not care if the car left… as long as it left with me in it. At any rate, we had just had our worst 'stem-winder' argument. Buzz and Phil had been in a few of these, but for some reason this was Buzz and I's first really big 'lollapalooza.' I'm not sure what started it, but surely the fact that Buzz had just got home from a hard day at work, couldn't have helped, nor Jack's eight hour harangue which had set me on edge.

However it started, the blow-up ended with the subject of the money that I owed him—and was not paying—my coming in late, my smelling like a brewery, and my choice of friends—who were admittedly 'a pretty sorry lot.' Our exchange escalated until finally something 'gave way' and we went at it big-time. Normally, mom would not interfere in our disagreements but this time she was so fearful that it might get out of hand that she began steeping in between us. At that point I made my exit, with her helping me out the door.

I drove off in a huff, certain that Buzz would now take his verbal fury out on mom. Poor woman, she deserved better than this. The sad thing about it was that, outside of discussions concerning me, I never knew my parents to get into a heated argument about anything. I was invariably the cause of the problems and was the one that had the problem. And as much as I hated to admit it—I didn't blame Buzz one bit. He'd every right to be infuriated with me, for more reasons than I could count—let alone my failure to pay him back for the car. More and more, I was coming to hate myself and what I'd become.

But here I was, driving off in another rage and I didn't even know where to go. Were it later in the day I would definitely go to Pinocchio's or over to Rocco's. Rocco's Mom loved me to pieces, though I don't know why. Probably because she didn't have to put up with me. But, it was too early to go there as Rocco's dad might think that I was merely mooching another meal—and God knows I'd already mooched enough meals there. I really wasn't up to seeing him glower over the top of his tea glass at me.

I guess I could go down to the city park and sit on the bluff overlooking the Arkansas River, where I sometimes went to just, sit and think. At those times I would turn to the easy listening music station on my car radio—music that my friends would gag over—and simply relax. Just now though, that didn't appeal to me. What I needed was someone to talk to. Someone that I could *really* talk to. Not just one of my buddies who would agree with my every conclusion about how messed up the world was in general, Pueblo in particular and my dad in absolute fact. The funny thing was that, however angry I might be with my parents, I *never* allowed *anybody* to speak ill of them. Which was seldom a problem anyway. My friends liked my parents and loved to come over to my house and eat Beulah's cooking. Especially Rocco who had mooched a few meals of his own—which was a fact lost on his dad.

So… where to go?

Then it hit me—Betty—my cousin Betty's. Yes, that was it! I'd go to her apartment. Granted, she might not be home, but more than likely at this time of day I'd catch her.

Betty was about seven years older than I, which made her about 26, (which at the time seemed really old) and was definitely a 'free spirit.' When my brother and I were little, we'd spent a lot of time with Betty and her mother—my Mom's sister, Ida—and Betty's brother, Ronnie. Ronnie was an extremely wild boy. He'd spent time in reform schools and was almost always in some kind of trouble or another. It had been that way from his earliest youth and now that he was in his late twenties, he kept finding his way in and out of various jails across the country. He was very talented artistically and could draw most anything—for that matter so could Betty. Though Ronnie liked my brother and I, he loved to torment us whenever he got the chance.

Once when we were very young, Ronnie had a B.B. gun. Phil and I thought that owning a B.B. gun was the single greatest feat that a boy could bring about. We begged Ronnie, literally on our knees, to let us shoot it, but he would not hear of it. Rather, he would point the gun at most anything and everything, tell us exactly where he was going to hit it and then prove his skill by shooting it. It would be a few years later and not until I owned my own BB gun that I realized what a feat that was; BB guns not being known for their accuracy. But with Ronnie nothing was exempt or safe from his unerring marksmanship. The real thrill to us was that he had enough guts to 'do stuff like that.' At least Phil and I thought it was guts. Mom's explanation was, "There is something wrong with that boy."

One day, I began to agree with my mother's judgment. We were out on the prairie and begging Ronnie to let us shoot the gun—Phil especially so. Ronnie finally said, "Okay Phil… I'll tell you what, you start running as fast as you can in that direction, right now, and I promise I'll let you shoot the gun." Phil didn't think twice, he just took off as fast as he could in the direction that Ronnie had pointed with the gun barrel. I would have run even faster had he made me the same offer but was immediately thankful that he hadn't. Waiting until Phil was about 50 feet away, Ronnie raised the rifle with one hand, barely aimed and shot my brother squarely in the rear end. Even after all these years, I can plainly picture my brother grabbing his bottom, running and jumping and screaming at the same time. Ronnie nearly died laughing. I was not about to laugh as I now fully realized that I was not safe from Ronnie either. Also, had I laughed, Phil would have killed me as his temper was awesome to behold when stirred, and his memory also was very, very long. [The sad thing was, when we finally got BB guns ourselves, Phil ended up with a BB in the middle of his right eyeball.]

As for Betty, she was always an unusual girl and as I said a 'free spirit.' She was always good to me, and kept life interesting as she was forever getting into 'some new thing' or fad or fashion or craze or trend, be it religious or artistic or some type of study or philosophy. When we were little I remember walking with her—for what seemed like forever—to a big Catholic church. I had no idea why we were going there or what was going on once we got there. Nevertheless, she would take us and I enjoyed the diversion. When I asked her to explain to me what the man in the black robe was talking about, she shushed me with a serious look and the slowly pronounced... enigmatic word... "*God*." At that I tried to pay even more attention... but it still made no sense... and, by and by I would fall asleep, tired from the walk and bored stiff with what seemed to me to be, 'sacred dullness.'

So, with nowhere else to go that fateful day... I decided to go to Betty's. I just hoped that she'd be home as she had a way of going wherever her whims would lead—be it Kansas or South America or Disneyland.

Parking the Triumph, I began to make my way up to her third-floor apartment. Most times I tended take stairways three steps at a time—unless I was drunk—but today my heart was just too heavy. I knew the heaviness was more than from my clash with Buzz— it was the whole sad picture of my life. From drugs, to alcohol, to court systems, to depression, to failing grades, to gang fights, to sorry friends and bad girlfriends, to winos, to ineptness at work, to feeling genuinely guilty for not paying Buzz, to wrecking cars, to my many arrests, to nightmares, to disappointing my family, and my teachers, and most of all disappointing myself—I was to put it quite simply; 'a world class loser'—and I knew it. What's more, though few would believe it, I knew it far better than anyone else.

That the doorbell on Betty's door was broke was obvious. Equally obvious was the fact that whoever broke it had done so by beating on it till it fell apart. I hoped that the condition of the doorbell had something to do with a previous tenant and not Betty. I certainly intended to ask her. I knew she was home from the far-eastern, mystical 'music' that was blaring inside. I began to knock loudly hoping that she could hear me above it. I knocked once more a little louder but still received no response. I began to wonder if the dangling doorbell had anything to do with someone's displeasure over the music and it's volume. I knocked yet again with a greatly increased intensity and finally heard the music go dead.

A small voice from the other side of the door tentatively asked, "Who is it?"

"Betty, it's me, Larry... your cousin Larry," I answered.

The door opened slightly until stopped by the security chain. Gradually a single eye appeared and the right half of a mouth whose lips instantly turned upwards into a smile. "Larry!" Betty called heartily while shutting the door and fumbling with the chain. Soon I heard the tiny clank of it dropping, and the door swung open wide. I was then met by a rushing, hugging cousin.

Betty was a 5 ft. 5 in. wisp of a girl, with dark brown hair that could be anywhere in length from her waist or to the bottom of her ears, depending on her latest whim. One thing for sure, however long her hair was, it was always kept in a 'low maintenance' mode. She was dressed in blue jeans (almost a given) with a deep blue pull-over sweater, and was shoeless. Her hair, by the way, was down to her shoulders.

"Come in! Come in here!" she squealed with genuine delight. "Where in the world have you been keeping yourself? Here sit down, sit down right here and tell me what's been happening with you!" She exclaimed excitedly, while maneuvering me towards a very well-used sofa. "What can I get you to drink? Would you like some hot tea? I can make you some hot green tea in just a jiffy."

I had known when I chose to come to her place, no one would be more pleased to see me than Betty. As for the tea, I couldn't even remember the last time I had hot tea let alone whatever it was that Betty was talking about. "Sure, I'll have some tea. But hey, I don't need it this second. Sit down a minute and take a breather. Tell me what's been happening with you."

At that, Betty sat down on a four-foot square piece of thick carpet that sat in the middle of the room on top of the carpet (I guess it had been placed there for that purpose). She pulled her knees up under her chin, wrapped her arms around her shins, rested her chin on her knees and said, "No Larry, you tell me why you're here! You are very troubled. Something is wrong and I want to know about it. You're not drunk or stoned... but I can tell that you've been that way a lot lately. *And* you've been very, very upset within the past hour. So, Larry... what's wrong with you?"

"Wow," I thought, "there you have it. What else is there to say?" I stared at her for a moment and replied, "Betty, you and the whole world know that I'm a druggie drunk... and it's obvious that I'm not loaded this minute. Furthermore, I've spent half my life in trouble. What I don't know is how you figured out that I've had a bad hour?"

"It's written in your spirit, Larry. You're heart is heavy. There was no joy in you when I hugged you. You weren't excited to see me, like I was to see you... yet you came *here*, I didn't come looking for you. Something is on your mind that is weighing you down. Now what is it?" Betty said and asked matter-of-factly.

I mulled over her remarks, thinking more about Betty's line

of reasoning than what she had correctly deduced. I really was impressed. I was further impressed that she now allowed me to mull all of this over without interruption. It was a nice touch, which put me completely at ease, especially when, without saying a word, she got up and went to the kitchenette and began to make tea. During the entire water boiling process she said not a word, and I frankly enjoyed—and needed—the silence. Her thought-provoking words, questions and silence gave me time to ruminate and sort through the 'stuff' that did indeed weigh on me. It was quite a lesson that I never forgot. Betty should have gone into counseling.

Why *was* I so dreadfully miserable? What in the world was wrong with me that in spite of very good parents, tremendous opportunities, the concern of many wonderful people who had sought to help and befriend me, certain natural abilities, and a somewhat likeable nature, I was forever coming up short. However good things started out, however much promise I might show, things always went wrong and usually fell to pieces. What was wrong with me that I couldn't get along with my dad in spite of his obvious love for me? Why couldn't I get good grades in spite of it being easy for me to do so, even if I only halfway tried? Why couldn't I hold a job, or spend a paycheck wisely or stay sober?

Yes, Betty… there is a lot weighing on me… and I've done it all to myself and don't even know why or how to stop. And my depression… Oh God, my depression… would it ever go away. Yes Betty, something intrinsically basic in me is missing and for the life of me I don't know what it is and therefore I can't find it.

***"Larry… you are never going to be happy without God."***

"What? What did you say?" I said, jolted out of my reverie.

Betty was kneeling in front of me holding out a cup of tea and viewing my face with a disconcerting earnestness. Again I said, "What did you just say?"

"I said… Larry… you are never going to be happy without God."

And I knew. In that brief moment of time I knew that her

words were the truest, most powerful that had ever been spoken to me in my life. I sat in speechless shock.

Betty had the grace to say nothing more. She let me simmer in a prevailing, momentous silence while her words sank deeply into my being. I could literally feel the power of her statement and it was as if every part of my body was involved in digesting it. It was like the moment one feels when they've been hovering over a highly complex picture puzzle—thoroughly stuck—and looking for a piece that you swear was somehow left out of the box—when suddenly, there it was. You knew before you picked it up and slid it into place that this was the one missing piece you'd been looking for. And the finding of that piece seemed to be a turning point in the assembling of the rest of the puzzle.

I will carry with me, as long as I live, that one single moment of epiphany and destiny, that I found sitting in my cousin Betty's apartment.

Part of me wanted to bellow, "Eureka! That's it! I have found it," but all I could do was sit speechless with my mouth hanging open. Finally I managed to say in a low voice, "Betty… you are right. You are absolutely, totally… right." Having said that, I again fell into an emotionally-filled silence that mere words could not express. It seemed that something had entered into the atmosphere of the room and was driving her words into my heart.

I now knew, as clearly as I had ever known anything in my life, that from that moment on it would be impossible for me to be happy or even function without God. Though I had no idea whatsoever what 'having God' entailed.

To this day I am thankful for Betty's silence. Wherever she had learned to use it so well, it was put to good use that day. In fact, I barely remember anything else that was said that afternoon. I do recall her bringing out a Bible and reading to me about the 'gifts of the Spirit' and asking me if I thought I possessed any of them. I really didn't know what she was talking about, but pointed to a couple of the words from the list. Soon afterwards, I made an excuse for leaving. I saw Betty one time after that—and not again for several years. But her deed was done and I knew what I had to do. The only problem was, I didn't know how to go about it.

After leaving Betty's, I immediately went home. I walked in the front door, sat down on a footstool in front of Buzz—blocking his view of the television—took a deep breath and said, "Buzz… I'm sorry. I want you to forgive me. I was wrong. I am as wrong as I can be. I owe you for the car and I promise you that I'm going to pay you… I mean it, I really do want to. But, but… I can't stay here… I've got to leave Pueblo. I've got to get out of this town. Everywhere I look I get into trouble with my friends and just 'blow it.' It's like I'm stuck in a rut and can't get out. If you don't mind, I want to move… to Denver. I want to get a job there, get settled, make a change in my life and, and… if you'll please be patient with me, I'll pay you back every single penny. I promise Buzz… I really do promise."

Buzz stared at me. After a moment or two, he sighed deeply as he'd heard promises before a-plenty. After another moment he said, "Okay Larry… I'm for whatever can help you. We can't go on fighting like this… your mother can't take it and frankly, I'm sick of it. When are you leaving?"

I thought his answer a little abrupt in light of the emotions that I had been feeling, but then again, Buzz hadn't felt what I'd felt in Betty's home. As to when I was leaving, I hadn't thought quite that far ahead, but I began to think furiously. Buzz and Mom both kept silent—it was apparently a good day for me to do some much-needed thinking. After a bit I said, "I'll give a one-week notice at work—at the most two. Probably my boss will just tell me to hit the road. If he does, I'm going to leave immediately. Otherwise I'll wait till then." That pretty much was the end of the discussion as I arose and went downstairs.

I went to my room and lay down on my bed. I folded my hands behind my head and stared up at the ceiling. My thoughts were, "How in the world can I find God, and, what's going to happen when I do?" After a while my mother brought me a sandwich, some potato chips and a Pepsi. My mother, God bless her.

***

The next day I gave Jack a week's notice telling him that if he needed me I'd stay two weeks. He snorted in amusement at my last statement, looked around for the drywallers who had yet to arrive. "I tell you what," he said at last, "You straighten up the studs in the walls for the sheetrock, and I don't care if you leave today." He must have realized by the look on my face and that I was starting towards my car that if he really wanted the walls fixed he'd have to do better than that. So he quickly continued, "But hey… if it takes you a few days to do it that's fine. I really need it done… okay Larry?" I turned back, without a smile, and said "Sure Jack… I'll try and knock it out quick."

So I went back to my measuring, cutting and nailing, Jack returned to his screaming, and after a while the drywallers showed up and resumed their griping. Hanny came by to tell me that he was sorry to see me go, and I could tell that he genuinely meant it. Manny continued to 'lay low,' but I noticed that he had a new set of tires and rims on his car.

That night I called Tyrone in Denver having heard that he'd moved in with his older brother and sister. I asked him if there might be room for me there until I could line up work and get an apartment of my own. He welcomed me by saying, "Sure that'll be fine… in fact I'd like to move with you into an apartment when I get a job. You see my brother's kind of slow, and my sister… well she can be 'high strung' around the edges." With that settled, I at least had a place to stay in Denver and could leave my parent's home (yet once again).

Three days later I was still working on straightening up the studs in the apartment complex, when I drove a 16-penny nail through a copper water pipe in the bathroom area of one of the apartments. I had been nailing in boards, trying to straighten out the studs and hadn't paid attention to the pipe system on the other side of the stud. The water pipes of that particular complex had been air tested two days before, and I was exceedingly thankful that the water meter had yet to be installed. I looked to my left and three rooms back the drywallers were working furiously in my direction. Furthermore, they were still grumbling at what they thought was shoddy work on my part. At that same moment I heard Jack scream an epithet towards someone upstairs. I then looked in the other direction, at the few walls left to straighten up and then back to the drywallers. I looked at the nail in the pipe for a long time… and finished driving it in till the nail head was flush with the stud—and kept on working. Tomorrow was going my last day and I just wasn't up to another session with Jack.

By that night the bathroom had been sheet rocked and by the time I got my cash and drove off the next afternoon it had been mudded and taped. I was glad that I would be in Denver when they turned on the water for the first time. In my dreams however I could still hear Jack screaming at me.

***

That night I paid Buzz $20.00 towards the cost of the Triumph, and went to celebrate leaving town—and blew the rest of my money. I went to bed that night and before I passed out, wondered if there was any hope for me and God to get it together. When I awoke the following afternoon I got my mother aside and 'borrowed' $15.00 from her. Buzz was somewhat mollified over the $20.00 I had paid him and I felt about '$5.00 better.' That evening after a delicious 'Beulah Supper' but still fighting a hangover headache, I left for Denver with my little Triumph packed to the gills.

My last thoughts as I saw the sign letting me know that I had left Pueblo County and had entered El Paso County was; "God… when I get to Denver… please be there for me."

# 5

# Denver

I called Tyrone from a phone booth in Littleton and got the directions to his house one last time. I was unfamiliar with the city of Denver save for the major highways that ran through it, but Tyrone was a born traveler who understood how to give and take directions and could get you where you needed to go.

When I arrived at the large, old, two story home that served as apartments for three families, Ty was sitting on the porch and eagerly waved me on up. It's always good to see a friendly face and therefore, it was always good to see Tyrone. Tyrone was a cheerful survivor, who had the ability to adapt to most any situation. He'd been raised a good part of his life in the same orphanage as JoJo but I don't know exactly *why* he was in the orphanage as (I was about to find out) his mother was alive and well. Though curious, it was none of my business and I thought it better not to ask.

When I met her, she came across as a very congenial woman who seemed as glad to see me as Tyrone. His older brother and sister were congenial as well and I deeply appreciated that they allowed me to come into their rather small apartment home.

Rolly, Ty's brother, was indeed, very simple. I personally think he was mentally handicapped but the family denied that it was quite that bad—so who was I to say. He appeared to me to be in his mid 30's and looked like a rather rough character. As he rarely ever said anything he left the impression of being a little dangerous, but Ty assured me that he was completely safe.

Tyrone's sister's name was Rose. She was 23 or 24, and was pretty though you could tell that life was taking a toll on her. She had a little boy, Tico, who was two and a half years old that was cute and vivacious. Her husband was somewhere back in Texas, apparently in some kind of trouble and again, I certainly didn't feel it my place to ask what kind. It was understood that Rose and her husband would someday get back together but no one really knew when.

Tyrone had moved to Denver not too long after our trip to South Dakota. I didn't bring up the subject of Theresa Bordeaux, and as he offered no information, I figured that her decision to call it quits was final. That had to be tough on Ty as she really was a beautiful and great girl. But Tyrone was tough, and as I said, he was a survivor.

Though he had been in town for five or six weeks Ty had not yet obtained a job. One reason he hadn't was that he had no car—well none to speak of. His sister had a 1964 Chevy Impala that had definitely seen better days. Tyrone said the battery was bad but that they'd had no money to buy a new one. He thought it would run well enough though it also needed tags and the tires were almost bald. Also, Tyrone's drivers license had lapsed and he'd never pushed to get it renewed.

I quickly gathered that one of the reasons Ty and his family were so open to my moving in was the fact that I did have a car. Tyrone almost immediately asked me if we could go looking for work together and of course I agreed. For one thing, I was more than happy to have someone that knew Denver ride with me, and when it came to sharing costs—including gas—I knew that Ty would be more than fair—once he had a job. Another hint as to how much my car was appreciated was perceived when Rose asked me if it would be possible for me to take her to the grocery store to get some milk for Tico—before my car was unpacked. I said "Sure," and was immediately glad that the Spitfire was so small as it seemed that everyone wanted to go for the ride. The total trip took about fifteen minutes and I did my best to pay attention to the neighborhood in order learn it as quickly as possible. I asked Rose how they were doing on food and though she didn't come right out and say it I got the impression that things were pretty tight. I gave her five dollars and told her to use it for what they needed. It wasn't much but I could tell that it was much appreciated. Later that night we had tacos for dinner and I must say they were very good. Almost as good as Beulah's… but then by that time I was also very hungry.

Before dinner was over I found out that Rolly received a small Social Security check due to his… problem, and that his mother took in ironing from some of the people of the neighborhood, while Rose had a job in some type of factory to which she caught a bus every weekday morning. Ty and I decided to head out first thing in the morning and start looking for work. He said he'd been keeping close tabs on the help wanted sections in the paper and thought we might have some luck—now that we had transportation.

As we finished the last of the tacos, Tyrone went to the fridge and brought out a bottle of Spinada Wine. "I've been saving this for a special occasion. Whaddya say we have a toast or two to our future success." Rolly had left the table after only two tacos and Ty's mom was already in bed. Rose had begun to wash up the dishes and seemed totally uninterested in our celebration of future success. As for me, I was extremely and instantly uncomfortable.

"Tyrone," I said quietly, "there is something I need to tell you.

"Yeah…?" he said.

"I've quit drinking. At least I think I have. Well, at least I want to." Tyrone looked at me as if he wasn't sure what he'd just heard.

"You what?" he said.

"I've quit drinking. At least I want to…and I know I need to. And Tyrone, I'm going to tell you something else… I'm going to try to live for God." His mouth fell open, and his hand that had been on the neck of the bottle now slid down it till it rested on the top of the table. I noticed that the room had grown quiet and when I looked over at Rose she was standing motionless with her hands in the dishwater. Slowly her neck turned and she stared at me. You'd have thought I'd just told them that I had typhoid.

"Well… Larry," Tyrone finally said, "when did this happen?"

Wondering where to start, I cleared my throat and said, "It's a long story Tyrone, but do you remember the morning that we went up into the hills above Pierre and watched the sun come up? Do you remember how the only thing sticking up out of the cloud bank was the cross on the top of that steeple? Tyrone, that really got to me. But that was just one incident out of many. Off and on I've thought about my need to change for a long, long time, several years in fact. Then about a week or so ago it came crashing in on me like a ton of bricks and I knew I would never be happy if I didn't live for God. So… here I am. It's a big part of the reason I knew I had to get out of Pueblo. Ty, I've got to change. I've got to… or I feel I'm going to be sucked down the tubes and end up a wino, or crazy, or dead. I just can't keep it up anymore, I can't take it much longer."

When I finished, Tyrone and his sister were if anything, more quiet, but in a moment I noticed that Rose slowly returned to washing the dishes.

When Ty finally spoke he did so by first clearing his throat. "Larry, I admire you, and I mean it." He had now re-gripped the Spinada bottle and brought it to rest in his lap, as if it needed protection from me. He continued, "I think you're right, about the booze… and I wish I had the guts to do the same. Of course you know we're Catholic and that we believe… we feel that we are going to heaven, as long as… well, as long as… well you know… as long as we keep doing what Catholics do."

I didn't know what to say to this, or if a reply was needed. But I managed with, "Well, I know this Ty, me and booze and drugs, we just don't get along well anymore. I know I'll manage a lot better without them and I'm going to try. Something else I decided on the way up here is this, I'm going to go to church… everyday. Not necessarily to church services, but to a church… somewhere. I'm going to go there to pray and I'm going to do it every morning before work—or before I look for work—and I'm going to do it every evening when I get off from work."

I noticed that Rose had once again stopped to listen and that Tyrone had now gripped the wine bottle with both hands. He leaned forward in his chair, looked me in the eyes and said, "Wow, Larry… you've really got it bad don't you?"

"I guess so," I answered, "But I know me, and I know what I've got to do."

We sat silent for a while, both lost in our own thoughts. Then we started talking about this and that, and rambled on until we finally decided that we'd better get some sleep.

Rose and her mother slept in one bed at the far side of the single bedroom, Tyrone and I shared a bed at the other, while Tico slept on a divan. It was not a very large room and I hated the arrangement but, alas, had no choice. The only alternative was to sleep in the hallway or on the bathroom or kitchen floor. Tyrone's brother slept on a pallet with a blanket and pillow at the end of the hall in a large bay window that gave a distant view of the downtown skyscrapers of Denver.

Before I went to sleep I heard Tyrone whisper my name and say, "Are you awake?"

"Yeah… I'm awake. I'm just thinking," I whispered back.

"Well… I'm glad you're doing what you're doing… and, Larry, I…I hope you're able to pull it off. I really do."

"Yeah, Tyrone… I do too. I really do. I'm sorry though if I disappointed you. I mean… after all… we've been drinking buddies a long time." He didn't say anything, and I knew that he was thinking also.

With that said, I went to sleep… my first night in Denver.

***

The next morning Tyrone scanned the 'help wanted' ads in the Newspaper, circling with a pencil anything that seemed to have some promise. Rose had boiled a few eggs before leaving to catch the bus for work. Ty's mom was already busy with some ironing but had to stop every few seconds to corral Tico who was in high gear from the moment he opened his eyes—which I thought surely must have been 4:00 a.m. Rolly was gone before I awoke and when I asked about his whereabouts Ty just shrugged and said, "I don't know where he goes. Nobody does, nor does he tell anybody. He may be home in an hour or maybe he won't be back for a day or so. It's just the way he does."

When Ty and I got into the Spitfire, the first thing I said was, "Ty, which way to the nearest church?" He took it totally in stride and said, "Take a right at the corner and you'll have to go left after a few blocks. I'll tell you when."

We made our way to a large Catholic church not too far from his house. I parked the car on the street and told Tyrone that I'd probably only be fifteen minutes or so. He said that would be no problem, as he needed to go to confession anyway. With that, I locked up the car and we entered the church together.

It was indeed a large church, larger than the one that I visited in Pueblo before seeing my probation officer, and much larger than the one me and the guys used to visit some Sunday mornings when we were in high school. The church was very dark and I must say had somewhat of a foreboding air about it. Tyrone made his way into a confessional that a woman had just come out of and I made my way down towards the front. I sat in one of the seats by the aisle and waited. I don't know what I was waiting for but waited anyway.

After a while I noticed a woman kneeling at the front with a candle burning on the rail just above her bowed head. I kept watching her as after a while she crossed herself, slowly rose to her feet and shuffled out. I saw that she was very elderly and supposed her to be pious. Once I saw that she had made her exit from the church, I rose from my seat and went to kneel at the exact same spot where she had knelt and where the candle still burned. I don't know why I imitated her actions, but maybe subconsciously hoped her piety had sort of 'paved the way' for me. I knelt there for a few moments not sure exactly what I should be doing, but finally began to pray…

"Dear God… dear, dear God… would you please help me. I really am such a mess… God, please forgive me… help me… I want to be saved… I really do… I want to go to heaven. Oh, Jesus, please… I don't want to go to Hell. And, God, I don't know what you want me to do with my life… but whatever it is, God, please, please let me do it. Don't let me mess my life up anymore than it already is. God… please, God, please, please, please, Jesus, help me…"

And with many other such words, I began to try to… well, live for God. After a while I turned to see Tyrone sitting and watching me intently. I finished up quickly, rose and remembering the old lady, crossed myself. Tyrone's interest was piqued and I could tell that he would be asking me questions as soon as we were on the road. He didn't wait that long. As we made our way out the door and were on the steps he said,

"Larry, are you going to become a Catholic?"

I hadn't even considered that prospect, but I thought about it for a moment or two and said, "Probably not."

"Well I just wondered. I knew you weren't Catholic… but… but… why are you doing all that stuff that… that… well, you know… Catholics do?"

"I don't know Tyrone. I really don't. To be honest with you, I don't know what else *to* do. I've never really done much of any of this stuff before. Though I usually do stop to pray before I go see my probation officer at the Catholic Church up the street."

"Really?" Ty responded. "Well did you pray today that God would give us a job?"

"Yeah… yeah I did. I did it just before I turned and saw you. Do you think God heard me?"

"Larry, if God ever heard anybody, he probably heard you. The mere novelty of seeing Larry Booker in a church praying had to get his attention. I'll tell you… it has sure got mine."

So Tyrone Ortega and Larry Booker made their way out into the world of Denver, Colorado—to find a job.

***

It was a disappointing day but at least I learned a lot about how to get around Denver. I was amazed at how easy it was once you learned the layout of the town. Somebody, I decided, had really done their homework in city planning. Also, Tyrone would have made a great tour guide. I was amazed that he knew so much about the town after having lived here so little time. His answer, when questioned, was that he'd spent a lot of time in Denver through the years and that after just a few days of being back the knowledge tended to return to him pretty quickly. He also pointed out that Denver had been laid out in a system that was very easy to learn.

We returned home and I again had to take Rose to the store—Tyrone's mom to one of her friends house—and I even took Rolly for a joy-ride in order to be fair. I wouldn't have minded the requests so much, but after having been in the car most of the day, I wanted to get out of it. I know the Tyrone would have been thrilled to take them—but I wasn't about to lend out my pride-and-joy car just yet—not even to him. One thing that came out of all of this running around was it greatly increased my desire to get the family's Chevy running. That night, after a supper of fried potatoes and eggs, I asked Tyrone, "Have you been able to start the Impala since you've been here?"

"No, but I'm pretty sure that it runs. Rosie says it does and she's pretty smart about that stuff."

"When was the last time it was started, Rose?" I asked her.

"About three months ago. I asked a neighbor to give me a jump-start with his jumper cables. Tico was really sick and I had to take him to emergency… I had no choice. So we got it started and I drove it."

"Did you make it okay?'

"Yes, but at the hospital that night I couldn't get it started… not even with a jump."

"How'd you get it home?"

"I took the bus down there two days later with a gallon of gas. A nice man poured it in the tank and put some in the carburetor then gave me jump. I was able to get it home but that's been it. I can't afford to get it going and fix all the stuff it needs."

My heart went out to this girl who had life so hard and a future so bleak. After all, what did she have to look forward to in her life but just more of the same that she was facing right now? That is unless her husband came back, and from what little I'd picked up, that was unlikely and even if he did, matters probably wouldn't improve much.

"So," I thought, "I've got to do something to help." Though I was under no illusion about my ability as a mechanic, I thought that surely if I could keep my old rattletrap of a 57 Plymouth running, I could do *something* with the Chevy. So I said, "Tyrone, let's go check it out." We found an empty bleach bottle and drove to the nearest station and filled it with a gallon of gas. On the way home I said, "Tyrone… we need a battery."

"Yeah I know. But where?"

As it was dark I headed for a rather nice neighborhood and started driving up and down the various streets. I hated myself for what I was about to do… but kept driving anyway. After a while I saw what I was looking for and pulled the car over and said, "Tyrone… stay here and keep your eyes peeled for anybody that might cause trouble. You see that garage? I'm going to get a battery out of that Lincoln. If an outside light comes on, tap the horn, just once… if somebody comes out honk it twice. If the cops come, drive away like everything's normal, but again, just tap on the horn as you go. Go home and I'll see you there eventually, that is unless I call you from the police station." Then I smiled, got out of the car and walked down the sidewalk about fifteen feet and then up the driveway like I owned the place.

Everything went smooth, even to the point of using the garage owner's tools to remove the battery. I walked calmly down the driveway and to the car, put the battery on the floorboard, got into the Triumph and off we drove.

Twenty minutes later I had placed the battery into the Chevy, poured a little gas into the carburetor and Tyrone began to crank the engine. After two or three sputtering efforts the engine finally came through and started up. It gasped and coughed and wheezed but eventually began to even out. The car, without question needed a tune up and probably would suck gas like a pig—but at least it was running. I jumped in the passenger seat and said, "Let's go!" Tyrone took off and we went first to a gas station where I bought six gallons of gas for about a $1.50 as well as two quarts of oil for another 70 cents. It took both quarts to bring the oil level up to par. We then began driving around in order find out everything that the car needed, which was quite a bit. When we'd spot something we'd write it down so we could figure out how much was going to take to make this a viable vehicle.

The only problem was, the longer we drove, the more miserable

I became. What kept going through my mind was the words, "Thou shalt not steal… Thou shalt not steal…Thou shalt not steal," and here I was stealing again. My level of condemnation was growing in quantum leaps as I thought of the prayers that I'd made both at the beginning of the day and when we'd stopped again at the church that afternoon after searching for jobs. In the afternoon session I had put a dime by the candle rack, taken one candle out and placed it on the wooden rail where I knelt. I then told God, "God, I don't know what this candle is supposed to do… but God please let it do it." That was less than four hours ago and here I was riding around in a car that was running off a heisted battery. Finally I said, "Tyrone… let's go home."

"Sure, if you want. But do you think we know everything we need to know?"

"Yes, I know everything that I need to know about this car. Let's go home."

"Okay… whatever," Ty said, and began to weave his way home on the back streets of Denver while staying away from any major thoroughfares.

When we parked in front of the apartments I got out and popped the hood of the Chevy. I then removed the stolen battery and put it back into the trunk of the Spitfire. Tyrone was staring at me like I had lost my mind. "What are you doing?" he said at last.

"We're taking the battery back."

"Why?!"

"Because it's not right. It's… it's not right to steal," I said quietly.

Tyrone's response was only to gulp. Then he shrugged his shoulders, sighed and started to get into the Triumph.

"No, I want you to drive again so I can jump out and put the battery back."

As I was heaving the battery up over the grill of the Lincoln to replace it, my right hand slipped off and it fell to the floor with a heavy thud and snap as the case broke into pieces. I couldn't believe what just happened and was almost sick over it.

As it fell I leaped back lest it land on my foot. Though my foot was spared I did get splattered with battery acid on my pant leg. I stood very still, hoping that the sound had not alerted anyone in the house and held my breath waiting to hear the sound of my car horn. When nothing happened I reached into my pocket and withdrew a piece of paper upon which we had been making the 'needs list' for the Chevy. I tore off the bottom half and began to write on it with the pencil, *"Dear sir (or Madam), I am very sorry about your battery. Believe it or not, I really was returning it. Sorry I dropped it. I am trying to live for God and be a better man. I didn't do very well tonight. Again, I'm sorry."*

With that, I quietly made my way back to the Triumph and went home. Though I felt bad about the broken battery... nevertheless I felt *much better* than I had thirty minutes before. I didn't know if I was making progress or not, but I knew that in the morning I had some more stuff to talk to God about.

***

Two days later I found a job. Tyrone had seen an ad that, 'guaranteed $450 per month,' doing sales work for 'Howsing Enterprises.' We called immediately and found out that it was a job selling Kirby vacuum cleaners. Tyrone was not interested, which was surprising, as he seemed to me to be a natural-born salesman. But if he wasn't interested, I was.

I called Howsing Enterprises back, told them a little about myself (very little actually) and was told to come in for an interview. Had it not been for Tyrone's thorough directions I would never have found the place, though I actually arrived 20 minutes early, and that after watching a candle burn almost halfway down at the cathedral.

I sat in a waiting area that held five chairs, all five of which were filled by expectant applicants. Promptly at 9:00 a.m. a thin young man with short, styled hair (that was also thinning), white shirt and tie, navy blue slacks and black wing tips came around to each of us to write down our names and ages. He introduced himself as 'Robert Clarry' and was a walking champagne bottle of 'bubbleliness' just waiting to be uncorked. As I was the last one he approached he looked at me and said, "And you must be Larry!"

"Yes," I answered, "Larry Booker."

"And you are eighteen I see?"

"Yes" I answered again. I would have said, "Yes sir," but as he looked to be no older than eighteen himself, I just couldn't bring myself to do it.

"You look older than eighteen."

"Yes, I've been told that since I was fifteen. Sometimes it comes in handy." I could have told him about the liquor stores where it came in handy but that was not germane to my purposes just then. One of the applicants, a young man, stated that he was twenty-three but didn't look a day over fifteen. I stared at him a moment or two and thought, "I'd rather look older than younger," but at the same moment wondered if I'd always feel that way. "When I'm forty I don't want to look like I'm fifty," I thought to myself, but then realized what silly a line of reasoning that was. I knew there was no way I'd ever live to be thirty let alone forty. It just wasn't in the cards for me.

Rob then addressed the group: "We'll be calling you in one by one for your interviews. Whatever happens, you'll be informed of our decisions within three days at the latest, more than likely it'll be within two. We appreciate you coming in and we'll start calling in each of you within fifteen or twenty minutes. Right now we'd like you to come and sit in on one of our daily staff orientation meetings. This is how we start each of our days here at the office."

After this speech, Rob led us into a room where nine men and three women were seated in rows and engaged in small talk. There was seating available for twice that many and the area between the chairs and the wall they were facing was a distance of about twelve feet. The wall was painted azure blue and had three beautiful, matching framed items hanging upon it. On the right was a dry erase board upon which were written the words, "*Number 1 in the Great Midwest!*" On the left was a sales chart that depicted the ups and downs of company sales and revealed that things seemed to be going 'up' on a pretty continual basis. Between these was a large photo of a man with brownish red hair, combed back and cut to perfection. The symbolism was obvious—the man in the center was the reason for the success on the right hand and on the left.

The man must have been in his mid to late forties, had an expansive smile that revealed a mouthful of white teeth, and had the quintessential tan. The photographer had even somehow captured a twinkle in his eye. Maybe it had been placed there after the photo was taken, but still, it was impressive. About two and one half feet out from the wall and framing it, were a set of gorgeous maroon drapes with royal blue edging that were pulled back with matching tie-backs and topped by a cornice. Out in front of the drapes on the left hand side was an American flag that hung from a golden pole and was held upright by a heavy, engraved brass base. A matching base and pole, which flew the Colorado state flag, was on the right. The entire setting give one the impression of a stage, which, as it turned out, was exactly what it was.

Presently, an attractive woman with blonde hair and a maroon dress entered the room and faced us with as bright a smile as I'd seen since our high school cheerleaders rallied us on the football field. She threw her arms wide in greeting as if she were a hostess giving warm welcome to a ball being held at her mansion. The men and women who had been seated, now stood, (Rob also among them) and they placed their right hands over their hearts and followed the woman's recitation of the pledge of allegiance. We newcomers of course did the same.

I was taken aback, but at the same time somewhat impressed with what I'd experienced thus far. I thought this a strange way to conduct business for a company that sold vacuum cleaners. But the show was only just starting. When we'd finished the pledge of allegiance, Rob actually—led us in prayer.

Now I *was* amazed, but not nearly as much as my fellow applicants. One of the girls—there were only two—eyes were now wide open as well as her mouth and appeared to be in shock. One of the men, who appeared to be in his thirties, was giggling, but was trying hard to contain himself. All of us were shocked at the orientation so far. As for Rob, his prayer was a pretty pitiful affair, even by my sorry standards, but the blonde-headed woman seemed pleased enough as the smile she had entered in with never left her face for a moment, even when her eyes were closed in reverence.

The prayer itself—as best as I can remember it—had something to do with "Help us to be a blessing to our world" and "May we ever show a positive light" and "May we ever represent the values held by the owner and manager of this fine establishment, Mr. Dallas Howsing and his wonderful wife Sheila."

He concluded the prayer by requesting that God would help us all to be "successful distributors of the amazing Kirby cleaner to the wonderful inhabitants of the greater Denver area and beyond." There was a hardy "Amen!" from a few of the followers, but I noticed that on the whole it was pretty weak. The 'regulars' sat down and we followed suit. Presently one of the men began handing out some thin, books. I received mine, passed on the stack to the applicants at my left and opened the book to see what information it contained. It was a songbook. A *songbook*?! I could not believe what I was seeing or what was happening. I looked around the room one more time to make sure I was not in a church service.

Rob stood once more, faced us all and said, "Let us turn to page 34." The members of the 'Kirby flock' dutifully obeyed, and we visiting 'sinners'—who probably used Hoover's—did the same. My fellow job applicant who had giggled during the prayer was now snorting audibly and his shoulders were shaking. In spite of that I could see that he was still making an effort to control himself. Mrs. Howsing shot him a sharp look but her smile remained intact. Then, oddly enough, as I watched her stare at him, her smile grew even wider.

One of the faithful on the front row had risen and now reached behind the curtain and pulled out a contraption that I'd never seen before. It was a five and a half foot pole that at once reminded me of a pogo stick. When I saw him operate it I was sure that's what it had once been. Towards the top of the pole there was attached a pair of eight inch cymbals as well as small bongo drum with what looked like a rubber tipped mechanical drumstick attached. There were also three different-sized, hand-squeeze, air horns, as well as a kazoo hanging on a two-foot long string.

The man placed the kazoo in his mouth and after a moment Rob called out, while simultaneously gesturing with his free hand, "And a one and a two and a three," and with that, began leading us in song. The man holding the 'pogo stick' simultaneously began banging (what they affectionately called) the 'Boom Box' up and down on the floor to the rhythm of the song as he also accompanied us on the kazoo. With every hit on the floor the cymbals clanged together and the drumstick beat the bongo. At the semi-appropriate moments he would squeeze one of the air horns. He was, without question, the original 'one man band.'

The song we had turned to on page 34 was played to the tune of "A Bicycle Built for Two." However instead of the lyrics;

"Daisy, Daisy give me your answer true
I'm half crazy all for the love of you,
It won't be a stylish marriage
As I can't afford a carriage,
But you'll look sweet upon the seat
Of a bicycle built for two,"
These lyrics read:
"Kirby, Kirby I'm in love with you
I'm half crazy over the things you do,
Your power to clean is thrilling,
While germs you are a killing…" etc. etc. etc.

At this juncture the giggling, snorting, shaking applicant could take it no longer. I literally thought he was going to fall out of his chair, and he was almost in tears. We knew that is was over for him when the 'usher'—the man that had handed out the song books—came over and (though I could not hear it) no doubt asked the man to leave as he was disrupting the service.

At this juncture the blonde lady lost her smile—if only for a few seconds. As we were sitting towards the back of the room we could see what was happening, but with the noise of the singing accompanied by the Boom Box, few of the faithful realized what was afoot. The 'giggler' never returned to the service nor was he there for the interviews. I guess he decided that he needed to do something else to make a living. Were I not so desperate, I would have been sorely tempted to leave as well, but really needed *some kind* of a job and needed one badly. And, to be honest, my curiosity about Howsing Enterprises was at an all time high. I thought the scene hilarious as well, but I did want to know if these people were serious about themselves or if this was just some 'tongue-in-cheek' operation where they liked to interject the absurd into the daily routine to keep boredom at bay.

I therefore sat through the song service, sang with the others and stifled urges to laugh as well. We sang another song that morning, and while I can't remember which one it was, it also was a take-off from some famous old number. That was what the entire songbook contained.

After we finished singing and the 'usher' had picked up the songbooks, Rob once more spoke to us. "We are so happy to have with us this morning, Ralph and Susan and Johanna and Larry," presenting the names of the job applicants to the faithful. It was interesting that he'd already omitted the name of the giggler (whose name by the way was Alan). The established sales people dutifully clapped for us. Mrs. Howsing clapped and looked on us all as if we were her very own children and had just received some type of tremendous award. After we acknowledged their applause with stupid, embarrassed smiles, Rob proceeded to the very heart of the morning's program… the introduction of Mr. Howsing himself.

After an introductory oration that would have made Caesar blush, Mr. Dallas Howsing came through a side door behind the right hand side of the curtain. I say that there was a door—not because I could see it, or had heard it, but because there was no way that Mr. Howsing could have stood behind the curtain that long simply in order to make such a grand entrance.

Dallas Howsing was as immaculate as his photo but there were lines about the eyes and mouth that hadn't shown up in the picture. The carefully arrayed hair and perfect tan were there however, as was the 'twinkle' in the eye, at least… somewhat. The 'twinkle' was so entwined into his effervescent personality that it just seemed to emanate in his eyes. He was adorned with a perfectly pressed, navy-blue pinstripe suit with matching red tie and a handkerchief that was folded and displayed perfectly in his coat pocket. His shoes were black, wing-tip, slip-ons that were shined to mirror-like perfection. As for his teeth, they were as perfect as the photo and he was grinning even wider for us than he had the photographer.

Mr. Howsing immediately began to pour forth some first-class praise for each and every member of his company. His most laudable oratory was saved that morning for none other than Robert Clarry. He spoke of Robert's willingness to go far above and beyond the call of duty in his effort to better Howsing Enterprises, and by way of reward he was not only earning the unbelievable sum of $1100 per month but would be receiving in December—only a little over two months away—a bonus of over $2,000. It seemed, at that moment that everyone in the room was salivating and that Robert appeared as pleased with himself as a cat licking cream from its whiskers.

Mr. Howsing went on to tell us that this was only the beginning and that everyone in the room that momentous morning would be doing the same and much more as we "Continue to persevere and grow with him and his dreams for the company."

He carried on in pretty much this same vein for another ten minutes and then—as he received an ovation—smiled and waved and began making his exit. But Dallas Howsing could not leave a roomful of people before shaking many hands, cupping some of them with both of his and smiling away every shadow.

The sales people were now ready—yea, more than ready—to take on the world and go forth to conquer in the name of Howsing Enterprises, not to mention Kirby. Before these pumped up sales people left the room however, they were very careful to shake our hands and encourage us to "join the team." I noticed that Mrs. Howsing had exited to her office and had shut the door behind her. The sales force then picked up paperwork and appointments from a rather dour, heavy-set, middle-aged secretary named Doris who looked as if she would put up with no back talk, even from the likes of Robert Clarry.

The four of us who remained—the new applicants—were now left sitting where we'd started and wondering just who it was that was going to conduct the interviews. Presently Robert came out of an office apologizing for the delay but that he'd had to answer an important phone call. He informed Ralph (a very nervous, thin, balding man of about thirty-five) that he would be seeing him first and asked the rest of us if we would like some coffee while we waited. Both Susan and Johanna said they would, but I politely declined, as I really didn't care for the taste of coffee—unless it was in 'coffee nips.'

Three hours and four cups of coffee later, I left Howsing Enterprises feeling like I was about to starve to death. I now wished I had taken the time to eat some of Rosie's hard-boiled eggs.

When all was said and done, I got the job—so did Ralph and Susan and Johanna and no doubt—had he not laughed his way out of the place—Mr. Alan Giggles could have had one as well. It was pretty obvious that, save for extreme cases, anyone who wanted to try a hand at selling Kirby vacuums could have the opportunity to do so with 'Howsing Enterprises.' I never did find out what other 'Enterprises' there were besides vacuums, but nevertheless the name had an impressive resonance. In fact I used it myself when I called Mom and told her to tell Buzz that I'd "secured employment with Howsing Enterprises."

When she asked me what is was I'd be doing, I answered, "For now I'm involved with sales."

***

Things overloaded rather quickly at Tyrone's. Four adults and a child in a one-bedroom apartment, regardless of it having two beds and a settee, was just too much. Tension grew especially acute when little Tico decided to split the night air with a scream for water, or mommy or Uncle Ty, or sometimes even his daddy… who was somewhere in Texas doing whatever it was that nobody talked about. Furthermore I was not used to sharing bed space with anyone—let alone Tyrone. Nor was I used to sleeping in a sweat suit but was now forced by circumstances and decorum to do so. All of this together got old pretty fast. It was not that Ty and his family were not good to me or even one time made me feel unwelcome, but I felt like a fifth-wheel and a crowded one at that.

The fact that I had not yet sold a single vacuum didn't help my disposition either. I had sold none so far, though I had demonstrated it in four different homes. When I returned to the office with my third "No go," Robert Clarry laughed and said, "Three strikes... you're out!" I didn't especially appreciate his humor as it had a certain cutting edge he threw in for good measure.

So my desire to get out on my own was growing daily. Tyrone also wanted to leave, and wanted to go with me so we could share expenses. He had not yet, however, landed a job though he seemed sincere in his efforts to find one.

One very good thing that happened and surprised me completely was that after my fourth day at work—two of which were spent in learning all about the 'Kirby Cleaning Machine' i.e. vacuum and how to "let it sell itself"—Mrs. Howsing asked me if I needed any money against my future paycheck. I stammered out that "Well, yes I could use a little." When she asked me "How much?" I said, "I don't know, maybe fifteen or twenty dollars... would that be O.K.?"

She gave me $50 from the petty cash fund and had me sign a paper that verified the loan. I was so taken aback that from that day on I referred to her with more respect as, "Mrs. Howsing"—and not just when speaking to her. She insisted that I call her "Kit" but I referred to her only as "Mrs. Howsing" except on one occasion. Nor did I any longer consider her to be a shallow person or a 'dumb blonde.' I'd come to view her actions, her 'affectations' during the morning orientation 'service,' as being done solely for the sake of the company. She probably thought it was a stupid scene as well. I now saw her as a genuinely kind human being who was willing for the sake of the company to go far and above the call of duty.

The money was a God-send and that night when I showed up

at home (after going to the cathedral to pray) with quite a few groceries you'd have thought that Santa Claus had just come down the chimney. Even Rolly smiled—well, sort of.

After three more fruitless demonstrations, Howsing Enterprises decided that I'd better take Robert out with me on my next call to "show me the ropes" and help me make a sale. This was even more important to them than it was to me as the $450 a month guaranteed salary was based on the statistics that when a Kirby Cleaning Machine was demonstrated properly a certain percentage of the U.S. population would purchase one. In other words, if I would present the machine in a decent manner and use a modicum of sales technique to ten different customers at least four would buy the product—thereby guaranteeing my salary. I had as yet to produce one sale in spite of my seven opportunities to do so. Clearly the machine was not at fault, so "Larry needs some help."

Personally I was glad to get the help, though I didn't exactly 'mesh' with Robert Clarry's personality. Nevertheless, I couldn't help but respect his success. On one of the walls of the refreshment room was a chart displaying the names of the sales people, the number of demonstrations they had given and the number of sales made from these appointments. Robert of course had the highest percentage of all—and that by far. As I said, my percentage was a dismal, '0' out of '7.' Even Susan, who been hired the same day I was and was a rather shy and mousy girl from New York (accent and all), had a sale to her credit—though, as she told me in confidence: "The guy bought it 'cause he felt sorry for me."

I had as yet had no one feel that sorry for me, though God knows they had reason to. In fact, one rather brusque, middle-aged lady, half way through my demo started putting a sales pitch on me to buy her car. The bad thing was, she was so good, if I'd any money at all, I'd have bought it. When she was through—after I'd admitted to her that I couldn't buy the car because I was broke—she walked over to me past the front of the car (we were outside by that time and looking it over) and reached both of her hands up and put them on my shoulders and said, "Son, I didn't even *intend* to sell you my car. I'm trying to show you how to sell something! Put your heart in it boy! Don't come in here holding your hat in your hand acting like a beggar and all but apologizing for your product and feeling like any minute you deserve to be thrown out. If you're going to be a salesman—SELL! You've actually got a very good product. It almost sells itself."

As it turned out she'd been a top Amway distributor for years. When I asked her why she had allowed me to come into her home in the first place, she answered, "Well for one thing I was bored. Secondly, I thought that you possibly had a sales technique that I could use and incorporate into my repertoire." But even she didn't buy a vacuum cleaner out of pity. So, again, I was thankful that Robert was going with me to "show me the ropes."

I stared at the chart on the refreshment room wall that revealed our sales abilities—or lack thereof—and dreamt of the day when I too would be a grand success. Susan 'the New York mouse' interrupted my reverie by saying, "If you think Robert's good, they say that Dallas Howsing was awesome. He had a 90% sales average when he was out in the field. But they say that he was nothing compared to his father."

"What do you mean?" I asked, "How could his father do better than that?"

"His Dad had a 100% sales record the last few years he sold vacuums," Susan answered as proudly as if she were talking about her own father.

"What?!"

"Yes, it's true! Every single time he stepped into a house—he didn't leave until he'd sold a Kirby. And in one day alone he sold 120 vacuums."

I was astounded and asked incredulously, "Who told you all this?"

"Doris, the secretary. She's worked here for 27 years." Susan replied, and then almost whispering said, "And guess what? She can't stand Robert. She told me privately that he's an insufferable pig and that someday his arrogance will get him thrown out on his..."

At that point the insufferable Robert interrupted Susan's

dialogue by slapping me way too hard on the shoulder and saying way too loudly, "Well, Larry, let's go out and make some sales, huh? Whaddya say?! Think you can do it?!" Without answering him I stood up, smiled at Susan who smiled back with pity in her eyes, grabbed my coat and walked out to the car.

After sharing a few jokes, doing some backslapping with some of the other salesman, and getting our appointments list from Doris, Robert Clarry finally sauntered out to my car and said, "This is a small car… but nice. How many vacuums can you fit in it?"

"I've only got one in it now, but I guess I could put one more in… but not the attachments that go with it." Robert pondered this a moment and said, "Put your stuff in my car and I'll get two complete more units. Today… we *are going to sell.*"

And… the insufferable pig was right.

We came back to the office that night having sold all three units and the attachments for two of them. We'd given five demonstrations that day, and for a while I thought we might sell a fourth vacuum during the last demo, but alas, it was not to be. I had a hard time with Robert's 'pushiness' but it was in the last home that I saw what a jerk Robert Clarry could really be.

Not that he started out the day that way—except with me—nor did he ever begin a demonstration that way. When we entered into a home he was the epitome of graciousness and appreciation for the time this obviously busy housewife had allotted us to come in and clean and shampoo one room of their home for free, or do a free mattress cleansing, or after allowing us to give them the free demonstration give them their free set of steak knives. Gradually as the 'demo' progressed there would be a subtle but profound shift in the dynamics of the relationship. Before long, Robert was the 'Host' and the housewife was the 'visitor' who ought to be thankful that Robert didn't run her out for being so stupid as to even think of not buying a product as great as this Kirby.

Not that this was his 'modus operandi' in every single situation, for Robert was a master at 'getting a feel' of just who he was dealing with and how far he could go. If the personality of the householder was strong, Rob would bide his time and move much slower and seemingly be more acquiescent in his demeanor—that is until he had overpoweringly demonstrated the amazing things that the Kirby Cleaning Machine could do (things that never ceased to amaze even me) and then he would begin to hone in for the kill.

One very effective trick was to vacuum the mattress of the homeowner with a special attachment that had a cloth inserted to catch and reveal the 'stuff' that, "...is imbedded in the bed... human skin that is constantly shedding, night after night, that works its way into the innermost being of this mattress, to lay dormant, save for the fact of the gathering and growing bacteria that is inexorably infecting this place of supposed sleep and rest. A place where you come to retire and refresh yourself from your daily toil, only to be met by microbes that are bent on robbing you of your health (and I might say, peace of mind) and happiness." At that point Robert would wave the cloth—that really did have an amazing amount of 'stuff' on it—in front of the face of the now frightened housewife and say, "Tell me! Would you rub your child's face in that?!" And if they ever reached out a finger to touch the substance Robert would quickly pull it away and in solemn tones say, "DON'T TOUCH IT... it will make you itch like crazy!" And with many other such like things, Robert Clarry would... make sale, after sale, after sale.

Believe it or not, we actually did end up selling one more vacuum that day. At the close of the last demonstration, Robert waxed exceedingly bold. The poor beleaguered woman had been verbally badgered and beaten, and had had so many financial figures and "last chances" thrown at her as to make both our heads spin. Finally Robert said, "Look lady, I'm tired of messing with you! That was my *final* offer!" At that point he stared intently at his expensive wristwatch and said, "It is now 4:15 p.m. You have until 9:00 in the morning to call me and accept this offer or I'm through. Do you hear me? The deal will be off at 9:00 a.m. Do you understand me? That's 9:00 a.m. and it's over! And believe me... I am not playing any more games."

After packing the vacuum away in silence… save for the woman's plaintive apologies for not being able to say "YES!" without her husbands permission, we walked out the door and got into the car. As soon as Robert got behind the wheel he started laughing uproariously and talking about how the world is "absolutely full of stupid people." As for me I was sick. I almost wished that Robert had seen me pat the poor woman on the shoulder and whisper, "Don't worry… it'll be okay." I really didn't know *what* would "be okay," but I didn't know what else to say to the poor distressed creature.

As we made our way back to the office, I asked Robert why he had treated the woman so ruthlessly. He laughed again and said, "Well Larry… you sell em your way and I'll sell em my way. All I know is that, so far I've sold a bunch… and you ain't sold nothing." To that I had no reply. But I did know that if in years to come, Robert D. Clarry ever came knocking on my door to demonstrate a vacuum… I'd deck him.

After I'd cooled down a little, I asked Robert about Dallas and his father and their sales success. Robert became animated and said it was all true. As for the 120 vacuums that Dallas's dad had sold in a day, it was to a motel chain and while they had bought them at a very good price, the bonuses alone had greatly fattened the Senior Howsing's portfolio. Robert Clarry went on to assert, yea, *vow*, that before it was over—he would beat them all.

The next morning a minute or so before 9:00 a.m. and just before we started service, the phone rang and Robert Clarry happened to answer it. "Howsing Enterprises," he said cheerfully.

"Do I have time, do I have time?!" A very anxious voice said at the other end of the line.

"Who is this?" Robert asked with a blank look in his face.

"It's Jennifer. Jennifer Aldrechi. Do I still have time to get the vacuum?" the poor woman all but howled into the phone.

The light went on in Robert's face; he looked at his expensive wristwatch and in a serious voice said, "Madam, you have exactly fifty-four seconds left to make up your mind."

"I'll take it!" she exclaimed, "I'll take it!" At that Robert smiled, made the arrangements, hung up the phone and laughed like a lunatic.

Of the four sales we (Robert) made that day I got credit for two—they were after all *my* appointments, but Robert received the money for the other two as well as the rather hefty bonus. While I really needed the money and was glad to get it, I felt cheap and dirty. I decided then and there that it didn't matter if I starved, I would not treat people like Robert Clarry.

When the secretary, Doris, handed me the check on Friday she said, "Well Larry, did you enjoy your time spent with Mr. Clarry?" I stared at her for a long moment to see if she was trying to somehow trick me (she was, at times, a hard woman to read) and finally said, "Frankly, no. And if I have my way I'll never go out on a call with him again."

Doris sighed and said, "No and I don't blame you. Larry, don't think they're all like that. Dallas… Mr. Howsing was never, ever that way. That's why Kit loves him so much. And as for his father, Stimson Howsing was a dream. A real gentleman. A first class human being who deserved every honor that ever came his way. Larry, I'm telling you… you don't have to do it Robert's way."

I patted her chubby little hand and said, "Thank you, Doris, thank you for telling me this. You know, you're actually a nice lady yourself… when you let yourself be. Almost, a doll." At that she blushed and said, "Get out of here," and as I put the check in my coat pocket she added, "By the way I subtracted the $50 that Kit loaned you."

"Thanks. And listen, please tell her for me again that I really appreciate it." I then went directly to the bank and cashed my first paycheck. And the same night I returned to stupidity.

***

On the way home—after cashing my paycheck and stopping at the cathedral—I stopped to buy some more groceries. Though I passed by the temptation several times, I finally stopped and put two tall six-packs of Coors beer in the shopping cart—to celebrate my first check. While Tyrone was a little shocked with my purchase he was much more pleased. He had reason to celebrate as well, as he had finally landed a job washing and waxing cars for a car dealership. After supper and after the two six-packs were gone, we returned to the store for two more. Whereas I had not been drinking, the first two six packs would have been plenty as I did not want to get drunk. But after awhile Rosie eagerly joined us, and even Rolly grabbed two cans and left. Hence the need for more.

That night that I realized I had to move from Tyrone's home and that I needed to move quickly. Rosie was a lonely and frightened young woman. Whether her husband ever came back into her or not, she feared a life of lonely misery. Before the evening was over, I was made to understand that she somehow hoped I could be her answer. *That...* I assured her was never going to be the case. The last thing she or Tico needed was me messing up their lives even more. I went to bed, and though I'd had plenty to drink—could not sleep for fear of what would happen if I stayed here one night too long.

The next morning I was determined. First I went to the cathedral and for the first and only time in my life entered the confessional. I guess the priest could tell by my awkwardness and ignorance of language procedure that I was not used to this. He kind of coaxed me along into confessing to 'falling off the wagon.' This may have amused him—especially as he probably drank as well. I know the priest in our part of Pueblo got drunk quite often, even with some of my buddies, but I hoped that this one wasn't like that. Nevertheless after I'd confessed as best as I could he said to me, "Son, you're not Catholic are you?"

"No sir," I answered quietly.

"Would you like to become one?"

"I... I don't think so... if you don't mind... I mean if that's okay."

"Yes, it's okay. I... we, of course would like for you to become a Catholic... but, you don't have to if you're not ready. Now, according to our faith, I can now forgive you of your sin. Would you like for me to do that?"

I was quiet for a long time and thinking very hard. Finally I said, "No sir. If ... if you don't mind, I think I'll go ahead and go out there and get it... get it cleared up with God directly... I mean if that's okay."

"Yes son… that's okay. And it's been good talking to you."

"Yes sir… it's been good talking to you too." As I started to get up he said, "Son?"

"Yes sir?"

"I'm not supposed to ask this… but as you're not Catholic I think it will be alright. What's your name son?"

"Larry, my name is… Larry… Lee" (I decided not to tell him my last name—he might, after all, tell on me).

"Larry, I've noticed that you have been in here quite a bit in the mornings."

"Yes sir… and I try to come every evening also."

"May I ask why?"

"Well, I've been pretty bad most of my life… and I'm really trying to get it together." He was very quiet at this and when he finally spoke he said, "I wish you well, Larry, I really do. And I hope you find what you're looking for."

"Thank you," I said, and left for the front of the church and a fresh candle. That day I paid a quarter for the candle. Of course I never got to see the priest because he was behind the screen, and except for returning that evening to pray I never went back to that Cathedral again.

***

I didn't know Charles very well, having only met him a couple times at various parties throughout the past few years. He was a year older than I and had graduated from Central High. As he was never quite 'in the flow' of the rivalries between Central and South there had never been reason for Charles and I to be at odds. He was rather on the small side, a sort of quiet guy that tended to keep to himself. Once he warmed up however, he had an engaging personality and a sharp sense of humor. Add to those qualities the fact the he was good looking and you have a young man who never had a shortage of girlfriends. All in all, he was the classic 'Lover not a fighter' type of individual. Charles had been living in Denver ever since he'd graduated. During my short stint in Boulder, Alan had told me that Charles was somewhere on Pearl street. But Pearl, like so many streets in Denver, was several miles long, and this told me almost nothing when it came to finding him.

I decided to call Marcy and ask her if she knew of Charles' whereabouts. I had not talked to her or Tom since JoJo, Rocco and I had stopped, partied, spent the night and left their home a wreck on our way to Boulder earlier that summer. I called her right after our morning 'service' at Howsing Enterprises hoping that somehow she'd not already gone to work. After letting the phone ring about twelve times, I was just about to hang up when I heard a more than groggy voice say, "What?"

"Hello… hello… is this Tom?"

"Yeah. Who's this?" he answered, sounding as if I were interrupting his dieing process.

"It's me, Larry… Larry Booker." He seemed to perk up a little… but not much.

"Larry. Humph… heard you'd moved to Denver."

"Yeah I did. I'm living with Tyrone's family but I really need to get out of there." At that the line grew very quiet and I realized that Tom thought I was throwing out a hint that I come live with them. To put his mind at ease I continued, "That's why I'm calling… I'm trying to get a hold of Charles… Charles Fanner. I heard that he lives on Pearl street, not to far north of Speer Avenue, but I have no idea where and his name's not in the phone book.

I could almost hear Tom's sigh of relief and he perked up a smidgen more. I got a picture in my mind of him opening his eyes a little and maybe even pulling the covers from off his head where he'd hidden upon hearing my voice. "Charlie lives probably… ten blocks from us. I don't know his house number but I know it's at the corner of Pearl and… something or other… on the south east side of the intersection. I think it might be 5$^{th}$, but I'm not sure. Anyway it's a blonde brick house and if he's there he's got a white falcon… I think it's a 62 or 63. I know he's got a phone but I don't know the number. I think Marcy's got it somewhere but she ain't here. By the way he hates being called Charlie… it's *got* to be *Charles*."

"Man, Tom, thanks a lot. I'll call Marcy after work and see if she's got the number. What time does she get home?"

"About 3:30… 4:00. Sometimes later if she's got to get something at the store. Hey how come you ain't called us or nothing since you been to town?"

I really didn't feel like going into my 'temperance' routine… especially since I fell from it last night, so I just said, "Tom, I been meaning to, but I got a job selling vacuum cleaners and I have to work weird hours, days and nights … whenever I can get into a house to do a demonstration."

"Yeah well, we don't need no vacuum," Tom interjected. I was a tad shocked at his abruptness but had to laugh nonetheless.

"Don't worry. You've gotta be rich to own one of these." Then I added, "Hey, if I go over there tonight and see Charles maybe I can drop by then."

Tom actually sounded somewhat enthusiastic and said, "Yeah, try and do that. Marcy'd be glad to see ya. But hey… were trying to knock off the partying and save it for the weekends only. We found out that we couldn't keep it up. Besides…" and at this point he paused, "People come, party like animals, leave our house a shambles… and we're the ones gotta go to work." I knew then that me, JoJo and Rocco should have cleaned up a little. But I pressed on and said, "Yeah, I don't blame you. In fact Tom, and I know you're not going to believe this but… last night I downed a few Coors and it was the first time I drank anything since I moved here… and I haven't taken any drugs, nothing, not even a joint."

At that, there was definite silence on the other end of the line. When Tom spoke he asked, "Why?"

It was my turn to be quiet. What to I tell him now? I thought, "Oh well, why not? He's going to hear it sometime."

"Tom, I'm trying to do better. I mean really better. I've been praying… quite a bit of praying actually… and I'm trying to live for God." The silence now was deafening. All I could hear was his breathing and he seemed to be having a hard time doing that.

I finally said, "Are you there, Tom?"

"Yeah, I'm here. I'm just… thinking that's all. Just trying to take in what you said. Did you know that Charles is an atheist?"

I didn't know this about Charles or any of my friends. Except for one of my cousin Betty's boyfriends from Nicaragua, I'd never met an actual atheist before that I was aware of. Not that, until this point in my life, it had ever mattered.

Tom continued, "He ain't no flag waving atheist or nothing, he just don't believe there's a God. I don't know what he'll think about a Bible-thumper moving in."

"Well," I said slowly, "It's not like I'm out to convert him or anything, or anybody else for that matter. I'm doing well to keep my own head above water. I just need a place to stay and I want to stay out of trouble… if you know what I mean."

"Yeah, I think I do. Look why don't you come on over if you can. You don't need to call first. If nobody's here there'll be a key in the mailbox, come on in—we shouldn't be gone long.

"Tom, that's really nice of you. I'll…"

"Today's my day off. They put me on swing shift as we're trying to put out a lot of tennis rackets before Christmas. Marcy will be glad to see you." Then he added, "But Larry, go slow on the religion stuff… especially around Marcy. It really makes her nervous. Me… I was raised Catholic… my parents are very devout… probably too much so. It made me and my sister almost hate it. My grandma is absolutely weird. So, you know… go slow."

"Tom, you can relax. I have no idea what the Bible is even about. I only know one verse and I can barely find it. All I want to do is get it together before I destroy myself."

"Yeah… yeah… I can understand that. Larry… really man, I'm happy for you, I really am. I hope it works. I wish it could have worked for me… but it didn't, and I don't know if it ever will. But look, call Marcy and try to find Charles. If you have a problem finding his place, let me know and I'll take you over there."

"Thanks, Tom… I really mean it… thanks a lot." At that we hung up and I went out to keep the three appointments I had that day. "God," I prayed as I headed to the first one in Arvada, "I know I'm a mess… but please don't give up on me… and, God… please help me sell a vacuum today." And He did.

***

That night, about 11:00 p.m. I moved the last of my stuff into Charles' house. He'd had two roommates, but both had moved out within the last two weeks and Charles was sweating about how he was going to pay the rent. As for my 'Christianity' and his atheism, if I had entered his house that night wearing a priest's frock, carrying a crucifix in one hand and a Bible in the other—as long as I had some cash in my wallet—he would have crossed himself and said "Amen, Brother… move on in!"

I'd made it a point to tell Charles that I was trying to 'go straight' and that it was for religious reasons as well as to avoid self-destruction. His eyes opened wide as he listened (his eyelids were usually half closed in a somewhat bored expression) but he quickly recovered himself and said, "So, tell me about your job. What is it exactly that you do?"

Tyrone understood completely why I was moving out (well… not totally completely) and asked that I relate to Charles that he also wanted to move in once he'd received his first paycheck. As for Rosie, I could tell she was hurt and at one point I thought I caught her weeping silently. But she said not one word the entire evening other than… "Goodbye," and didn't even shake my hand. The girl was tough. She had suffered a lot in life and developed deep survival instincts. Ty's mother hugged me, said, "Good-bye," and told me what a fine boy I was. Tico laughed and Rolly grunted.

Charles was thrilled to hear that Ty wanted to move in and said, "The sooner the better and the more the merrier!" When I asked Charles if he knew where the nearest cathedral was, his answer was, "How the #%*! should I know?" When I went to Marcy's and asked her where one was, she gaped at me and said, "Larry… you're really serious about this religion bit aren't you?"

"Well… it's not actually a 'bit'… but yes, I am serious. I feel better about myself than I have in years. And I'm doing a whole lot better mentally and physically. Marcy, I don't think you know how bad of shape I was in."

"Yeah… well, Norma told me she thought you were going under… with the drug thing I mean."

Hearing Norma's name, threw me into a quiet tizzy. I don't think Marcy—or Norma, or anyone else—ever knew how much I really liked—and probably loved her. She drove me crazy (even into rages) with her madcap ways—but I loved her just the same. It was not until I absolutely knew that over the long haul of life we simply could not make it together that I painfully gave up. Now, in Marcy's astute presence, I made an effort to sound completely calm and casually asked, "How is Norma? Is she still in Grand Junction?" Then my heart stopped beating while I waited for the answer.

"She's doing okay. Her grades aren't much to speak of, but she's not failing anything. She'd like to quit and go to work somewhere but her Dad won't hear of it."

Norma's father—as I've stated—really did like me. I don't think he liked me going out with his daughter, and in that regards he no doubt wished that I would go away. But he was fond of me as a person and no doubt thought, "If this hoodlum is going to hang around and maybe end up related to me, I have to try and help him… fast."

"I'm glad he's not letting her quit," I said, "What about her mom, how's she?"

"Oh she's okay. You know I haven't seen either of her parents, or Norma either for that matter, since I moved up here. Norma calls a couple of times a month, but that's about it."

"So when did she tell you that I was 'going over the edge?'

"The last time you were here and left my house a wreck," Marcy said with a definite bite in her tone, "I told her all about it. That's when she said you were a bigger wreck than my house could ever be… that is unless it burned down."

"Well, well" I said, "That's nice of her," but didn't say anything more… for it was, alas, too true. Finally I mustered, "Well that's why I want to know where the cathedral's at. I'm trying not to burn down."

"Just go north on Pearl. You'll go… oh I don't know, it's quite a ways, maybe ten or fifteen blocks… but stay on it till you come to Colfax. Take a left and it's almost immediately on your right. I think it's at the corner of Colfax and Pennsylvania, but maybe it's Logan. Anyway you can't miss it… unless you're stoned."

I didn't miss the cathedral and thankfully I had made it another day without being stoned or drunk. I parked my car in the parking lot that lay to the east of the church, climbed the steps and entered. It was much like the cathedral over by Tyrone's house, only bigger. I stood in the entrance and let my eyes adjust to the light, then seated myself on the back row of pews. As I sat, I began to pray.

"Jesus… I hope you're hearing me. I'm going to go down to the front in a few minutes, and I'm going to pray some more. Please meet me there, and please listen to me. If it's possible… please, make *something decent* out of my life." With that I arose and went to the front. Off to my left I saw the rows of candles, some of which were lit while most were not. I approached them, took an unlit candle… lit it with one that was lit… put a dime in a little wooden box… took it back to where I'd been standing, knelt down and began to pray.

***

It was not so much that I 'fell off the wagon' as that I slowly 'slid off.' But nevertheless—I was definitely off. Once Tyrone moved in—and had a little money of his own, he and Charles started partying, and inviting fellow party-goers over… and inexorably I slipped back into my old ways. At first—as I'd done back in the ninth grade—I told God that all I would do was drink. Then the pot got me, then the… well then it was whatever came around that we could—or couldn't—afford. The irony was that I still went to the cathedral every morning—unless I just couldn't get out of bed—and every evening—unless I was still in it. A further irony was that every night before I went to bed, unless I passed out, I knelt by my bed and prayed. The focus of my prayers however had changed as well as my lifestyle. Whereas I used to pray for my friends, my brother (who was now married and had a child on the way), his soon-to-be-born baby, and my parents, I now could only ask God to please forgive me and pull me back out of the drugs and put me somehow on my feet again.

I still went to work—most days, but they could tell that something had changed. Whereas there had been somewhat of a 'spring' in my step, I was now, for the most part, 'dragging around.' And most mornings, the 'boom box' and the songs promoting Kirby salesmanship about killed me… especially my aching head.

One morning after Mrs. Howsing greeted us all with open arms, and Robert Clarry had taken the floor once again, she came back into the room, tapped me on the shoulder and motioned for me to come with her. I followed as she led me into her office. She told me to be seated, while she sat down at her desk and began ruffling through some papers. After a moment, she found what she was looking for, laid it down in front of her, scanned it and then looked up to meet my eyes.

"Larry," she said, "I note that your sales have been picking up." They had, and I was extremely thankful for it—I'd even told God that morning how much I appreciated His help—after I'd asked for forgiveness.

"Yes, I seem to be finally getting the hang of it… but I've got a long ways to go," I replied.

"Then what's wrong?"

"What do you mean?"

"Why are you drinking and doing God-knows-what-else? What are you trying to do to yourself?"

To this day I have never been able to figure out why so many people—good people—have taken an active interest in my welfare. It's not that it bothered me… I just didn't understand it. I can only figure that God in His mercy kept weaving these people in and out of my life. On this particular day I was especially taken aback as I knew that Kit Howsing simply did not interfere with people's lives—especially the sales people of Howsing Enterprises. So, that morning I tried to bluster in her presence.

"I… I don't know what you mean?"

"Oh Larry, knock it off. You know exactly what I mean. You come in here with bloodshot eyes, looking like death warmed over, all but holding your head in your hands while we play that stupid music. What's wrong with you? You're nineteen going on forty and if you keep it up you'll never reach thirty."

"Funny," I thought, "She expressed my sentiments exactly—

even down to the music and age of death."

I took a breath and answered, "Kit… Oh! I'm sorry… really… I always mean to call you 'Mrs. Howsing."

"I told you weeks ago that you can call me Kit."

"Well, I'd rather not. Really. Anyway, I don't know what's wrong with me. I was doing better, I really was, and I just kind of… slipped up. I moved into a place with a couple of friends and well… I got caught up in the party stuff again."

"Larry, I have no authority over your personal life, nor do I want it. I know and you know also that there are people who work here that are probably in worse shape than you. I just happen to like you, I think you have potential and I don't want to see you throw it away, that's all. You could make a lot of money in this business, I know that you can, and believe me, Dallas *does*. But not that many people stick with it, because it's not for them. And I don't see selling vacuums being for you either—not for the long haul. But I do think you can make something good out of yourself and your life can make a difference, somewhere. Don't blow it Larry. Trust me, life is very short and it screams by. Don't waste it on a bunch of foolishness that will kill you in the end."

With that she went back to shuffling through papers and never looked up. I knew the interview was over. I stood to my feet, and started to leave, but turned back and faced her. "Mrs. Howsing?" I said.

"Yes?" she said looking up.

"Do you ever pray?" I asked her. She looked a little surprised, and curious. "Yes, I sometimes pray. I suppose everyone does on occasion. Why."

"Well, I just thought that, if you did… maybe you could pray for me… you know… just sometime." Tears immediately welled in her eyes and she actually had to struggle to keep her composure. I was not sure what nerve I had touched, but I knew that Kit Howsing was a much more complex person than I'd thought. After a moment or two she cleared her throat and with a rasp in her voice said, "Larry… I promise you that I will pray for you." She then smiled a kind of broken smile and turned her eyes quickly down to the papers still in her hands. Her hands trembled for a moment, I heard her take a deep breath and then the papers were as still as stone.

I said, "Thank you, Mrs. Howsing… thank you very much," and left.

***

That day I sold another vacuum cleaner to a very pleasant elderly lady that I think just wanted to help me out. Looking at her elegant house I realized two things. One, she would probably never miss the money, and two, I doubted that the Kirby would ever be used… at least not by her personally.

I went by the cathedral on my way home, knelt and told God how much I appreciated the sale and for having Mrs. Howsing care so much about me. I also thanked Him for all the wonderful people in my life that had shown me love and concern. As I thought about it, I was able to compile quite a list of these special people. Between family members, parents of my friends, many teachers, counselors, more than one medical doctor, several very patient probation officers and even a few merciful policemen, many attempts had been made to help Larry Booker. I then asked God to again please help my brother Phil's baby that was going to be born in April. I asked that God would please be with that baby, and not let it mess up its life like their Uncle Larry had done.

Then I went home, told Charles that I'd made another sale. When Tyrone got home (he was back to using the bus system as I had proved to be to a little too unpredictable) we all decided that this was cause for yet another celebration.

We sat there that night making ourselves drunk by offering 'toasts' to everything from "Long live the Kirby Vacuum" to "Long live John, Paul, George and Ringo… well, at least may they live to be sixty-four."

As the evening progressed, I kept glancing at the Bible that was sitting on the fireplace mantel. I finally arose, picked it up, sat back down and spread it open across on my lap. I then looked up at the guys—who were definitely looking at me, and said "Hey guys, whaddya say we study the Bible?"

The room grew quiet as Ty, Charles and Lyle—a guy we'd known in High School who was coming over more and more, and staying longer and longer—gazed at me through eyes that had already began to blur, and now fogged over.

Presently Lyle said, "What did you say?"

"I said, let's study the Bible. Let's read some of it and talk about what it means."

After an interminable silence he spoke again, "You're serious aren't you?"

"Absolutely. I'm dead serious, and I think it'd be an awesome thing to do."

Lyle was an inimitable character even among the peerless characters I knew. He was a year older than I and, for the most part, through our high school years, we pretty much hated each other. He was considered a 'bad dude' that you just didn't mess with. About 6' 1" weighing 225 lbs. of solid muscle, he was a tremendous athlete that excelled in every sport.

He'd made a powerful impression on many of us early on while in the seventh grade gym class at Pitts Junior High. Me and my fellow, rather scrawny, twelve and thirteen year old, shy shower takers, whispered about how "Lyle Legston" actually "*had hair on his chest*." We were all envious, and it sent shock waves of fear through us as well.

Though Lyle and I had never actually gotten into a fight, we came perilously close to it several times and were always leery of each other. It was not until the end of my junior year that we began to relax in each other's presence and begin to almost like each other. That summer we slummed around at a lot of the same parties and developed a wary friendship. It was not one of the better *seasons* to be around him however as he had determined that (now that he'd graduated and was 'his own man') he was not—I repeat, *not*—going to bathe nor use deodorant the entire summer—and he was true to his word. Thankfully he would swim in the Arkansas River at least once a week, but never once used soap or shampoo. His hair was to his shoulders and was as greasy as possum meat, and at times his body order was rancorous. Lyle thought it was funny and at a reasonable distance, so did I. And believe it or not, during those days he still had several girlfriends. Go figure.

And here he was now, spending more and more time at our place and often 'crashing' on the couch. I had the distinct feeling that he was 'oozing' his way into a steady position as more and more of his clothes were making their way into the hall closet. Lyle was ever into the 'free lunch program' of life.

At any rate, here we were, and I now pushed the point of our need to study the Bible. Only because it was such an unusual notion, Lyle jumped on the bandwagon and Tyrone was game—as he was for just about anything. Finally even Charles acceded saying it would be "good mental exercise."

We decided to start at the beginning—the book of Genesis. Our first argument was over how to pronounce the name of the book. Lyle—ever opinionated—was adamant that it was pronounced Gen-iss'-e-sis, while Tyrone said it was Gen-ee'-sis. As for me, I really wasn't sure but thought it was Gen'-i-sis, but had no way to prove it. Tyrone stated that a priest in the orphanage taught them it *was* that way, and that it had something to do with the Hebrew language. With a reference like that I found it hard to refute him, but Lyle needed no such backing and merely stated that any '*expletive depletive*' could see that his pronunciation had to be the correct one. Charles had no opinion, other than to say, "And this my friends is why the world's on fire."

After agreeing to proceed in spite of our differences, we worked our way through the Creation but it took a good hour. I won't even go into the various theories expressed, but as we talked and drank and smoked, our words and ideas flowed with ever increasing if not muddled freedom. Even Charles became excited and inserted some thought-provoking suggestions as to how we really 'came to be.'

The highlight of the evening was reached when we got to the third chapter. It was then and there that the 'light shined' and we were for once in complete agreement. It was here that Charles elucidated in slurred solemn tones, "In this instance, the Bible is without question… on target." The verse we all agreed upon was the one that revealed Eve's part in the downfall of man.

"And when *the woman* saw that the tree was good for food, and that it was pleasant to the eyes, and a tree to be desired to make one wise, *she took of the fruit thereof*, and *did eat*, and *gave also unto her husband* with her; and he did eat."

Well, there it was, as plain as the nose on your face. It was the woman's fault. That pretty much ended the Bible study for the night as we all meandered off into our own personal horror stories of 'mistreatment' at the hands of women. Before it was over—and even deeper drunkenness had set in—Tyrone was weeping over Theresa Bordeaux and I was getting pretty maudlin myself over Norma. I couldn't even bring myself to talk about Molly Mae and her dog Scotty. Had I done so, and been able to tell the story in all its painful detail of hopes dreamed and dashed, I think we would have been so depressed as to give up on women entirely—at least till our discussion was over, or one came walking through the door.

Thus we spent another night in ruining our next day's effectiveness. Nevertheless, before I crawled into bed, I knelt by it (a very easy thing to do in my condition) and prayed. I asked God to once again forgive me for my drinking, I thanked Him again for helping me to sell another vacuum and asked Him to please help me sell one tomorrow. I finished up by asking Him to please forgive all the women of the world for doing what they did—whatever that was. Then I remembered my mother—and how good she was—and had to thank Him for her. Then I thought of my grandmother—and how good she was—and I thanked God for giving me probably to two best women He'd ever made. It dawned on me that Mrs. Howsing had been awfully good to me… as well as my third grade teacher, Mrs. Holloway… my aunt Arvie… Then I remembered the statue of the Virgin Mary that stared at me every morning and I thanked Him for her also.

Somewhere in the process, I fell asleep, well… passed out, while still on my knees. I awoke freezing about 4:00 a.m., realized where I was, crawled into bed and finished the night.

I awoke at nine, realized I was missing the opening service at Howsing Enterprises, lay there a while thinking about what Kit Howsing must be thinking of me—and rolled over and slept the day away.

***

Thanksgiving Day was approaching and I was quite frankly starving for one of my mother's meals. I informed Doris that I was going to be leaving for Pueblo Tuesday night after my last appointment and probably wouldn't be back till Monday. She didn't look up from her paperwork and merely grunted something about "not even knowing when I was gone."

Lyle bummed a ride with me to Pueblo—it seemed that he was bumming everything else as well—and we headed out at about 5:00 p.m. I did not stop to pray at the cathedral, as I wanted to get on the road. Interstate 25 heading south was busy as usual, but once we got past Littleton, traffic picked up pretty well. The sunset that night was gorgeous, but then it almost always is as the sun settles down over the Rocky Mountains.

As we headed south, Lyle began to ask me questions about my interests in the Bible and my praying. He was for all intents and purposes fully settled into our house now and had apparently noticed me praying sometimes before I went to bed, and was curious as to how far I was going to go with all this stuff. I told him that I didn't seem to be going very far at all since I'd gone back to my drinking and drugging, but that when I was 'straight' from that stuff, religion really did affect me in very good ways.

His answer was, "Larry… anybody that goes straight does better. That doesn't mean you gotta be a Jesus freak."

"Lyle, I don't think I can go straight without Jesus… and I'm not kidding either."

"It don't look like to me that you're doing so hot *with* Him," Lyle snickered.

To that I didn't have anything to say, except, "I don't think I've ever really had Him yet… but I want Him… I really do. And if I ever find Him, Lyle… you will be able to tell it."

With that, he grunted, dropped the subject and asked me if he could borrow five bucks. My reply was, "Lyle, why don't you just ask me to *give* you five bucks. Your definition for 'borrowing' is not the same as the dictionary's.

"Okay, Larry, if that makes you happy. My only desire is to make a better Christian out of you… Will you please *give* me five bucks? And remember, before you answer that the Bible says that it's better to give than to receive." I turned my head towards him and said, "How would you know that?"

"How would I know what?"

"How do you know it says that in the Bible?"

"Oh, it's there."

"Where?"

"Somewhere. Go home and ask your mother. Better yet, ask your father if he likes *your* definition of the word 'borrow.'" With that, Lyle leaned his head back on the seat and went to sleep. I continued to drive and stew and remember why I couldn't stand Lyle Legston for so many years.

As I drove into Pueblo I turned off the highway and went over to Belmont to see how the apartment project was coming along without me. Though it was dark I could see that there were shingles on the roof now and it looked like every building had doors in place. I could also tell that the sidewalks had been poured and they were in the process of landscaping. I was genuinely glad to see it going forward. Some of the men must have been working late for I saw Hanny's truck and almost stopped to see him, but thought better of it when I also saw Jack's truck. I was sure that if they had already turned the water on, Jack would surely kill me on sight. So I drove on by and wished them well.

I hadn't told my parents what time to expect me just in case there was a good party going somewhere. Though it was only Tuesday I knew someone, somewhere in Pueblo was bound to have something 'going down.'

There was indeed a party that night. Not a big one, but one nonetheless that I knew that I'd enjoy. It was at Georgia and her husband, Hayne's home and there were only about fifteen people coming. The way I found out about it—and received an invitation—was that when I took Lyle to his parents' home I went inside and used the phone to call Norma's house and say "Hi" to her parents. Well… really, I was hoping that maybe Norma would be home for Thanksgiving and I could talk to her. And it worked out as I'd hoped. I said hello to her mother, chit chatted a while and asked if she'd heard anything from Norma. "Oh Norma's here! She got in late last night. I think she's in the shower… would you like for her to call you… oh wait, here she is… Norma! Norma, it's Larry, he's on the phone… he's down from Denver. Yes, yes… he would like to talk to you… Larry… Larry, you would like to talk to Norma wouldn't you?"

I thought I was going to die… and felt like screaming, "*of course I want to talk to her … why do you think I called?!*" But of course what I actually said was, "Uh why yes, yes I'd enjoy speaking to her… that is if she's not busy." I was able to sound calm but I was holding the phone so tight that my knuckles were white. I was also very anxious that Lyle's 'homecoming welcome' would come to an end and then he'd bring his mouth over to my phone conversation and start butting into places that he didn't belong.

"No, no I don't think she's busy… Norma! Norma! You're not too busy to talk to Larry are you? You know it's Larry Booker."

"*Oh come on… give me a break,*" I muttered to myself.

"What's that? What did you say, Larry?" At that point, mercifully, I heard Norma's voice as she grabbed the phone away from her mother.

"Larry! Larry, is that you?!"

I felt my heart leap inside me at hearing her voice again, but was determined to 'keep cool' and show that I was 'on top of my feelings.'

"Yes… is that you, Norma?"

"Oh don't be a nincompoop… of course it's me you ninny."

She had not lost any of her vim and vigor… and that certain refreshing something that had always drawn me to her. And I remembered once again why I'd loved her so.

We proceeded to have one of our wild-and-wooly conversations where among other things she explained her mother's talkativeness. "She's been hitting her diet pills again… you know trying to slim down for the holidays. But she's about to drive us all crazy. I'm trying to talk Daddy into giving her something to slow her down, but he says it won't do any good because she'll just take more of her pills in the morning anyway. But I told him that it didn't matter about tomorrow… he had to do something or none of us would be getting any sleep and Wendy—my sister—is going to be coming in sometime tonight and that if…" At that point I cut Norma off and said, "Norma… Norma!"

"What?" she said.

"Norma… have you been taking diet pills?"

"Well… I've had one, or two… Why?"

"You sound a little wound up yourself."

"Oh, but I'm okay, I took these—and they're actually a little different from my Mom's, I got these from a guy in Grand, you know, Grand Junction, at school—and I took these this morning, well actually about eleven, to help me drive down here, because I've really been tired, but when I took these I always do okay—there not like my mother's…"

"Norma!" I interrupted again… "Norma it's okay… it's okay. I was just wondering. Listen what are you doing tonight?"

"Oh! I'm going over to Georgia and Hayne's—they're having a little get together—Larry! You come! I know they'd love to have you—Georgia was just asking me about you the other day, we call each other all the time…"

At that juncture, I saw Lyle carrying in his last little knapsack and I knew I had to get out of there quick before he thought of someplace he needed to go. I interrupted Norma by telling her I'd meet her at Georgia's somewhere around 8:00 or 8:30 and got off the phone.

After the drive from Denver, putting up with Lyle, and having received only a sliver of sleep the night before, I was very tired and the short but frenetic talk with Norma and her mother had finished wearing me out. I decided to go home and see if I could get a thirty-minute nap before I went out on another binge.

I parked my car in front of my parents' home, bounded up the front steps, rushed into the house, hugged my mother, answered her host of questions rather perfunctorily, and then begged to be allowed to go to my room to rest. She asked me if I was hungry and though I was, I was actually too tired to eat. I told her I would eat a little something when I got up—asked her to please wake me in a half hour and went to my old bedroom in the basement.

I lay down on the twin bed I'd known since the fifth grade and all but passed out. But before I went to sleep I thought once again of the fact that I'd missed my prayer time at the cathedral. It bothered me so much that I decided to utter a few words before I crashed. "God," I said, "I'm sorry... I really am. I'm sorry about everything. If there's any way that you can still help me, please do so... please don't give up on me, God. I want..." But by that time... I was asleep.

I awoke and saw on the illuminated clock that it was 9:30. It took me a moment to gather my thoughts as to where I was and why I was even there. As my mind coagulated I realized that... here I was, once again, downstairs, in my bedroom... and I became overpowered with the memory and feeling I'd had here years ago—the night I'd freaked out in the house with Edmond, Richard, Loren and Bernard. I thought of the promises that I'd made that night to God. Promises that I'd never 'whiff' again... and never smoke, or drink, or do pot, or LSD, or speed, or cocaine, or heroin, or shoot up anything in my arms. As I lay there it crushed me that I'd broken every promise thousands of times—except one. As yet I had never allowed anyone to put a drug needle into my arms, and I ***sincerely*** believed that the only reason I was still alive was that I'd not broken that one last promise. And if I ever did, I thought surely that God would kill me. This was not the first time that the possibility had occurred to me and I actually thought about it quite often.

Just a week ago, Pam Rique had come up from Pueblo with some 'smack' and had proceeded through the course of the night to shoot up everyone but Tyrone and me. Tyrone would never shoot up as he'd lost too many friends and family to overdoses and was deathly afraid to fool with 'the needle.' I wouldn't do it because I was deathly afraid that it would be the death of the wretch called Larry Booker.

I lay on my bed thinking of the many, many times I should have been dead—but was somehow spared. I knew, and even my friends knew, that I'd been extremely lucky. "Larry's the cat that always lands on his feet," was Rocco's succinct way of putting it, and I had to agree. I then began to talk to God again and said, "I don't even know what to say… but thank you God…thank you for sparing me so many times."

Then I remembered Norma and Georgia's party. "Oh man!" I said and jumped to my feet cursing myself for sleeping so long. I quickly slipped on my shoes, grabbed my railroad jacket and keys and ran for and up the stairs.

"Mom! Why didn't you wake me!?" I said while hurrying past her.

"Because if you're too tired to eat, you're too tired to go running around!"

I didn't feel like arguing so I just kept moving towards the front door. Buzz had not been there when I'd got home—I think he was at his brother Raymond's… working on his car or something—and he was not in the front room now watching television, so I figured that he'd already gone to bed. I was out the door and headed for my car when I heard, "Larry, wait!" I stopped and turned to see the sweetest woman God ever made standing with a paper plate piled with chips and a breathtaking—as only Beulah can make—sandwich. "Mom… Mom… you are too much." I took the plate in my left hand hugged her with my right arm, kissed her on the cheek,, jumped into the Triumph and drove away.

I arrived at Georgia and Hayne's at about 10:00 p.m.. Things were still just getting underway and as it was a small affair I hadn't missed much. They'd brought out the beer and wine (a much better vintage than my usual) and the pot was flowing freely. We all caught up on what each was doing now and who lived where and with whom.

I didn't sit by Norma as that spot had already been filled by guy named Rick whom Rocco had nicknamed the 'Z Man,' and who apparently saw no need to move. What really fried me however was that Norma did not move to sit by me, and was evidently enjoying things the way they were. Words cannot express how I would have loved to break Z Man's neck, but I acted as if neither he nor Norma were even there. I purposely made it seem as if I were oblivious to her presence and spoke to her only when forced to by her repeated questions. The entire—what was becoming miserable—situation would have been alleviated instantly had either she or Z Man moved. But they did not and I acted more distant than ever, though I felt as if I was dying on the inside.

I attempted to quench my anger by drinking and smoking and drinking some more. It became obvious to all that I was headed for 'obliterate city,' but rather than pass out I actually became more and more loquacious as the night progressed.

Somewhere around 1:30 in the morning I began a monologue whereby I 'held court' for about two hours. I was totally drunk—and stoned—but could still talk... and talk I did. I talked about God. I talked about the fact that people should live for Him and quit the drinking and drugging, and (though I obviously do not remember all that I said that night) I remember talking about 'Fatima' (Portugal) and the 'miracles' that took place there in 1917, between March and October of that year. I mixed what little I knew about that Catholic phenomena (I think I got some of the info out of one of my mother's Enquirer magazine) and what little Scripture I had of late been reading and about some of the things that were happening in our world and spun a pretty frightening tale. When I saw that I was making Z Man nervous, I pulled out all the stops and did my best to scare his shriveled little heart to death. I was oblivious to the effect I was having on everybody else, though I kept my eyes roving over them all. As far as I was concerned, the only two people in the room were Norma and the Z. After a while, Norma was as ashen as Z Man, but... I couldn't care less.

As I wove my tale, no one moved and no one spoke. It was as if I were animated and every fear I'd ever felt, every desire I'd ever had, every prayer I'd prayed, every thought I'd ever thought, every experience I'd ever experienced came rolling out of me that night. Though I did not stop until after 3:30 in the morning—no one nodded off or left.

Finally, I just 'ran out of gas' verbally and 'pulled over to the side of the road.' I stood to my feet weaving back and forth, looked at them all coldly and said, "I am going to bed." I stumbled my way down into Hayne's basement, lay down on the couch and went to sleep.

What the 'party' did after I went downstairs I'll never know. No doubt I was the subject of an interesting discussion, and I know that most of the people left, for when I awoke—to run into the bathroom and vomit—at 5:00 a.m. they were almost all gone. Artie was still there and was asleep in the recliner, and Georgia and Hayne were in their bedroom. Gary was passed out on the floor, as was Bernard. "Funny" I thought, "I didn't even know Gary and Bernard were here." I again looked at my watch and saw that it was ten minutes after 5:00 am.

I decided then and there to go down to the Arkansas River and watch the sun come up, think about God and maybe even do some praying. I went to Artie first, then Gary and finally to Bernard and tried my best to wake at least one of them up. I wanted somebody to go with me so I could talk some more about God. But for all my efforts they were out cold and were apparently not going to be in the land of the living for some time. So I left them to their unconsciousness, grabbed the last two cans of beer out of Hayne's refrigerator and piled into my car.

I really had no business walking, let alone driving, and I remember only sketchy bits of what happened. I do remember thinking about Norma and getting angry all over again. I also remember thinking about how really messed up I was as a human being. I thought of every wasted opportunity, and wasted effort that my life had produced. I thought of all the heartache and grief I'd caused my family and so many other people. As my inebriated, stoned mind went through this trek for the thousandth time of my life, a rage entered into my drunken bosom, and all my inner frustrations began crawling to the surface. To vent these feelings I pushed to accelerator to the floor. I remember entering the west end of the city park and beginning to take the curves of the road as they presented themselves. I was determined to take every curve and not to let up on the accelerator. I distinctly remember hanging hard onto the steering wheel and trying to force the car to turn to the left… and I remember the left side of the car beginning to rise…

Then… I knew I was standing… but didn't know where. Where was I? Where in the world was I? I thought I was alive but could see nothing. I heard something to my right and as I turned my head I was able to see. What I saw was an approaching police car with its lights and sirens blaring. I looked to my left and there down the road was the central circle of the city park. I then looked in front of me and there, five feet away, was what was left of my car. My beautiful Spitfire Triumph… was no more.

It lay upside down upon its fiberglass top. It had been completely flattened to the top of the body, as had all of its windows. Though I would not know it until the next day, both the top as well as the windows were shattered—but were all still in one piece, and there were no 'holes' in them. Meaning, that I could not have been ejected through any one of them. Each of the four tires and rims were bent out to the point that they were as flat as the undercarriage of the car. All in all, the Spitfire took on more the appearance of a pancake than that of an automobile, or as if it had already been through a car crusher. Both doors were jammed shut and, as I found out later— completely so. My beautiful little car had become a flat, sealed coffin.

And there I stood… staring at what should have been my fate.

The sirens died away and the next thing I knew someone was calling my name. I could not respond and it seemed that I were in some kind of a trance. Finally, I felt someone take hold of my right arm and give me a little shake.

"Larry… Larry… are you alright?" I turned my head slowly and looked into the officer's face. It was obvious that he knew me… and his face seemed familiar but I could not place it.

"Larry… do you need to lay down? Are you okay?"

All I could do was look at my car and every now and then at the officer. After a moment or two, the policeman said, "Larry… can you hear me? Can you walk, Larry?" Then I felt a slight tug on my arm as he began to lead me towards the open back door of the police car. I went with him as if in a dream… a dream…yes, a dream. There was something… something had just happened… but my mind, I couldn't bring my mind back… something… something unbelievable had just happened but I couldn't pull it up from what seemed like subterranean depths.

I watched the officers as they set out markers and every now and then would stop and wave some car around the scene, though there weren't many cars going through the park that early in the morning. I looked down at my watch and it read 6:20. Where had I been… what was I doing here?

That was when it hit me, and I remembered. As the officer walked over and softly closed the door on the police car, I began to cry. I cried as I'd never cried in my life. I fell over on the seat and with sobs… great wracking sobs and wails, I literally went to pieces in the back seat of the last police car I ever sat in.

I knew what had happened… and I couldn't believe it… but knew that it was true nonetheless. In fact it was the most 'truthful' thing that had ever happened in my life.

Someone had just talked to me… and I to Him. Someone who knew *everything* about me and *everything* I'd ever done in my entire life. And I knew that I had just been spared. My miserable, wretched life had been spared. I should have been dead and *would have been killed* had He not saved my life. I also knew that He had talked to me about other things… but what they were I do not know to this day. But I know it concerned my life and its purpose… and that it *had* a purpose… and that I'd been spared in order to *fulfill that purpose*. And I knew one other thing. *I knew I'd heard that Voice before*… someplace, somewhere… I'd heard it… but it was as if it was just beyond the reach of my consciousness… and I couldn't quite get a hold of it. I'd feel like I was about to touch it and it would slip away… just a little further… as if it simply was not meant to be…

So there I lay… big, tough, wild and crazy Larry Booker crying like a lost little boy in the back seat of a police car… while the officers stood at the door looking unsure as what to do. Had I fought, or cursed, or been silent he would have known exactly what to do, especially with me. But neither of them were prepared for this.

After a long time (long enough for a tow vehicle to come, load and carry my car away) I sat up, but would still from time to time, break out into sobs and lean against the door. Both officers were now in the front seat and finally started the car and began to drive me away.

There I was, nineteen years of age (I'd had my birthday on the 17th of that month), been on probation since I was fifteen, in and out of jail, and court and trouble and now the police had me in the palm of their hand. Even the most simple blood/alcohol test and I was finished. There were two crushed cans of beer in what was left of the car as well. I was about to be sent up, probably to the state penitentiary. But at that moment, I didn't care—I had something much more important on my mind. God had spared me, and had something very important for me to do before I died.

In the midst of my thoughts I realized that someone was asking me something. I was not sure what was being asked, so I raised my head. I still had not said a word, nor did I feel that was really able to communicate. So I indicated with a motion of my head that I was listening.

It was the policeman on the passenger side: "I said… where do you want us to take you?" I took a deep breath and managed to croak out the words, "What… what do you mean?"

"What I mean is… where do you want to go, Larry… we're not taking you to jail. Tell us where you want us to take you."

I could not fathom what I was hearing. Pueblo police officers were not known for their compassion. What's more, they knew me, and were more than aware that the narcotics division had been trying to put me away for a long time—ever since Larry Weder and I had laughed at them in the courtroom after our attorney, Mr. Biddle had struck a deal with the D.A. But now, for the second time that morning, I was about to receive an unbelievable display of mercy.

I lowered my head, and whispered, "Betty's… could you take me to my cousin Betty's. She lives just off Abriendo… by the library."

The police cruiser kept going straight as we headed in a different direction than the jail. I laid back down on the seat and began to cry once more.

***

After I, through many tears, related my story to my cousin Betty (to my relief, she never doubted a word) she let me go to sleep. About noon she took me home to my parents. My mother grew ashen and began to cry as I related what had happened to the car, while Buzz kept total silence and never spoke a word—not even when I told him how sorry I was... and that I would someday pay him the monies owed.

Norma heard out about the accident and immediately called and begged me to let her father examine me and make sure I was all right physically. She picked me up within a few minutes and we went to meet her father in their home. He did a thorough examination, asked me a ton of questions and poked me everywhere. When all was said and done, I had an abrasion on my left knee and a light cut on one of my left knuckles... other than that, there was nothing to show that I'd been in a most destructive car accident.

After he was satisfied that I was indeed 'okay' he proceeded to give me an in-depth lecture—no doubt for Norma's benefit also—on the dangers of drinking and driving. On his way home he had stopped at the police yard to see my car—what was left of it—and told me several times through the examination and lecture that I was a 'walking miracle.' No doubt what bothered him the most was the thought that his daughter could have been with me just as easily as not.

Though I am ashamed to admit it... the same night of the wreck, Norma and I went to Frankie's house and proceeded to get stone-cold drunk. I was however, to put it mildly, very contemplative and had almost nothing to say to anyone. Z Man came to the get-together at about 9:00 p.m., saw Norma and me together and immediately left for greener and safer, pastures. As for Norma, she sat by my side the entire evening.

I spent Thanksgiving Day with my parents. Though we were not a religious family, my mother made mention of the fact that they were thankful that I was still alive and in one piece. She later reassured me that Buzz was thankful as well, though we had not been able as yet to look each other in the eye. The thought that I had destroyed that beautiful car, and had paid him a mere pittance on it, made us both sick. And, sad to say, in spite of my assurances, we both knew the chances of him getting the rest of his money any time soon were pretty meager.

It was at this point in my life, I came to completely hate myself. I hated what I had become… but couldn't seem to do anything about it. It was as if I were helpless against the onslaught of my own passion and stupidity. I now felt that even my praying was but a feeble, stupid effort and seemed to do me no more good than a band-aid placed upon the finger of a cancer victim.

Except for Norma and Betty, I had as yet told no one what I'd really experienced in the park. I knew I could tell Norma and not be laughed at. That was one of the main reasons why I liked her so much… I felt I could tell her anything. And, thankfully, the feeling was mutual.

A big part of our ability to share things was because of an unbelievably bizarre event that happened to us once, well twice, when we were together. We had been at a party about a year before, had both taken some mescaline and were smoking pot in the basement. The room we were in was small and darkly lit. On one wall was a poster of a Crow Indian Medicine Man called 'Mescalito.' He was considered by druggies to be the 'patron saint' of the hallucinatory drug world. In the poster he was sitting on his haunches with his arms wrapped around his legs, covered with an old Indian blanket and holding what looked like a little opium pipe in his left hand. He sat there with a very intent expression his face and it seemed as if his eyes were boring through you.

I sat next to Norma; we were both in very bad shape, and began to 'trip.' I looked at Norma, she at me, and then at 'Mescalito.' Suddenly, it was as if a motion-picture reel was moving frame by frame with each one revealing a slight change in Mesalito's features as well as his surroundings. When the 'film trip' had finished he had been transformed into my good friend, Bill. Bill was sitting—squatting, on a rock and holding a plastic baggy in the same hand as the pipe had been. He was wearing a leather coat with leather strips dangling from the sleeves. I turned from Bill to Norma and we looked at each other with looks of astonishment on our faces as we *were* up in the mountains *not* in the little room in the basement. Then the 'trip' began to work its way backwards and Bill was changed back into Mescalito and the surroundings back into the small dark room. At that point I looked again into Norma's face and said, "Man, Norma… I just really, really had a weird trip!" She avowed that she had experienced something extremely strange also but we did not talk about it… we just got up and left the room.

A few months later, in the spring, Norma, Loren, Bill and I went up to the mountains to do some drugs. While we were there, Norma and I were sitting on the ground next to each other. We were very stoned when suddenly Norma and I looked at each other, and then we looked up to see Bill sitting—squatting on a rock and holding a plastic bag in his hand. He was wearing a leather coat with leather strips dangling from the sleeves. It was the exact way we'd seen him months before. Then the 'trip' started in reverse. It was as if a motion-picture reel was moving frame by frame with each frame revealing a slight change in his features as well as the surroundings. The next thing I knew I was *back* in the room and staring at 'Mescalito.' I turned my head to see Norma turning hers towards me… we stared at each other and we *were* now in the dark little room. We then both looked back towards the poster. The 'trip' then repeated itself exactly as it had the first time, and in a few moments we were back in the mountains, staring at Bill. At that point I again turned my head towards Norma and we stared at each other in fearful astonishment.

When I started to speak and ask her what exactly she had seen, she jumped to her feet very frightened and said, "Please, Larry, don't… not now… I can't talk about it right now… really… I think I'm about to lose it." I knew better than to press something as eerie and scary and intimate as that, so I backed off. It was not until much later—and when we were both 'straight' that I brought it up and we compared notes. Her experience… was exactly like mine, point for point.

Whatever it all meant… and however much the devil—or whatever was involved… we knew from that moment that we could pretty well talk to each other about anything.

But that night, as I spoke to Norma about the car wreck and my experience with the voice, I sensed an discomfort in her that I'd seen in her before, but never paid much attention to. Though I knew her uneasiness might well have something to do with the bone-numbing spiel I'd delivered at Hayne's the night before, nevertheless I now fully comprehended that Norma was not real comfortable when the subject of God was discussed.

So after telling Betty and then her, I pretty much kept the experience of hearing the Voice to myself. Eventually I told Loren and Tyrone as well, but to others—when asked about the accident—I merely asserted that I now knew that there was something special for me to do with my life.

That Sunday night I caught a ride back to Denver with Alan as he was on his way back to Boulder. I never dreamed I could miss a car as much as I missed the Triumph and had no idea what to do about my job. I could probably hitch a ride to work with Charles (so much for going to the cathedral in the mornings) but how would I ever get around to the appointments and give demonstrations?

As for Charles and Tyrone, they were full of questions about the accident, and I told them as much as I could remember—except for the part about the voice of God. Though I eventually confided it to Tyrone, the further in time I got away from it, the more ludicrous it sounded—even to me. But still, I knew *it was true… and that it really did happened!*

***

It was during the course of Tyrone and Charles inquisition that it hit me what I could do for transportaion. Tyrone's sister's car! If I could just get a battery, and if they'd let me use it, I could still somehow make it.

Charles dropped me off at work the next morning and immediately Robert—who was standing outside—asked me where my Triumph was. I told him it was "history" and that I'd "totaled it in a wreck." It was the one time that I thought I saw a spark of compassion in the man. He said, "Man, Larry… that's a tough one. Was it insured?"

"No… all I had was liability."

"Man… I really am sorry." And the strange thing is, that for whatever reason, I believe he genuinely was.

I entered the office, saw Doris and gave her a quick wave. She in turn gave me a quick glance and went back to her paperwork. I entered the room where we held the daily services, and took a seat in the back, while Robert began his shtick for the day. I couldn't wait to get out of there and make a beeline for Kit Howsing's office. While I dreaded telling her what I'd done, I also knew that if there would be any help coming… it would be from her.

After a grueling inquisition on her part as to my sobriety the night of the wreck, I finally admitted to her that, "Yes ma'am… I was as drunk as a three legged skunk… and then some." And, "Yes ma'am, it really was one of the more stupid things I have done in my life." And, "Yes, ma'am I have in fact gotten my rotten self into a mess this time."

It was at that point that I interrupted Mrs. Howsing and screwed up the courage to ask her for another loan. She stopped talking and looked at me as if I'd just fallen out of the sky. "You want me to do what?"

"I want to know it I can borrow some more money… until my next sale… maybe you know… another fifty?"

"What in the #%$&!% for?" she asked. I was rather taken aback as I'd never heard Mrs. Howsing curse before. But then I'd been told for years by Buzz that I had the ability to make a saint cuss.

"Mrs. Howsing, I think I can lay my hands on a car if I can get a battery for it… but it's probably quite a gas-hog, so I'll need a little extra for gas… until I make my next sale."

After staring at me for what seemed like ages, Kit Howsing reached for her purse and proceeded to open her billfold. She thumbed through a wad of bills, took one out and handed it to me. When I protested that it ought to come from petty cash in order to keep better records she said that she would rather loan it herself than have to listen to Doris tell her what a fool she was. That short speech pretty well let me know where I stood with Doris, but I took the money and promised to repay her—which, believe it or not, I did.

That night, Charles took Tyrone and I over to his mother's house. We stopped at a Western Auto and purchased the least expensive battery possible, but one that hopefully could crank the behemoth Chevy in the middle of a Colorado winter.

The Chevy had not been moved since the night of the great 'battery fiasco.' We put the battery in, and Charles turned the key. It cranked okay, but did not start until we chummed the carburetor with some gas. I hoped to goodness I wouldn't have to do that every morning. The tags were expired and it was filthy, but at least it was a car. Tyrone had to make many profuse promises to his sister and I in turn had to make many profuse promises to Tyrone before we were actually ready to leave.

During the time that Ty and I worked to get the car running Rosie came out holding Tico in her arms. She seemed genuinely glad to see me and kept asking why I never came around to say hello. I shuffled off a few excuses as to how busy I'd been and that I'd been meaning to... etc., etc. I asked if she'd heard anything from her husband and immediately wished I hadn't. A pain-filled expression crossed her face as she said, "No, no... I haven't." After a moment or two and without another word she started back towards the house. I called after her and said that maybe I could stop by sometime before Christmas. She smiled a faint, unbelieving smile and walked through the door. In retrospect, I was glad she didn't believe me because I never saw her again.

After many more, profuse promises, Tyrone was finally able to break away from his mother and we drove away from the house. The first thing we did was go to a gas station and fill up the tank and the second was to go to a car wash. By the time we were finished, the car didn't look half bad, but the experience made me curse myself once more for totaling out my sports car. My poor car… and my poor, poor dad.

While washing the car we were reminded once again that the tags were expired. This placed even more of an onus upon me because of the promise that I'd had to make to Tyrone that I would take him to work *every* morning. With the tags expired, I knew I'd have to take as many back streets as possible and stay off the main thoroughfares. As Tyrone's workday started earlier than mine I would have to get up much earlier in the mornings—a thought that I relished not at all. One good thing that might come out of the deal was that after I dropped him off I could probably make it back to the cathedral in time to pray a while before I headed to work.

Thus I spent my December of 1971. As much as I hate to admit it, I continued to drink and smoke and drug. I also continued to read my Bible (through bleary eyes) and be miserable because I knew what a vile wretch I was. I would kneel and pray beside my waterbed, in the basement of our house, asking God to please continue to have mercy on me and somehow help me to fulfill whatever it was He'd spared me for. I would arise in the morning with headaches, shakes, dry mouth and blood shot eyes. I would drive the back streets of Denver, take Tyrone to work—and if I didn't have an appointment at that time of day—pick him up and take him back home. I would pray at the cathedral most every morning and as many evenings as possible. Because it was December and people were spending their money on other things, no one (except Robert Clarry) was selling many vacuums. Especially me. Due to lack of sales, and my lack of keeping appointments, I was reduced to going to the blood plasma donor center.

There I would lay on a table, surrounded by the wino's and derelicts from that part of Denver and let them take what seemed to me to be a copious amount of blood, extract the plasma from it, mix the remaining blood with an anti coagulant, some saline, and put it all back into me. The process usually took from two to two and a half hours. From it I would receive enough money to buy two six packs of beer and a carton of cigarettes.

What a life… and for this I had been spared?

One day, when I had no appointments whatsoever and was just not up to being a door-to-door vacuum salesman, I went with Charles to score on some drugs. We entered an apartment building not too far from where we lived and walked up to the third floor. After knocking some kind of a special knock, the door opened and we entered a very dreary apartment, its walls covered with posters of rock stars, furnished with various weird lamps, artifacts and a very strong smell of incense. We were met by a thin, bearded man that looked to be in his thirties and his, greasy-haired, barely-clad wife that might have been in her mid-twenties but who was going on fifty physically. While the business was transacted I noticed a little boy looking at us out from behind an old wingback chair. He had short brown hair and beautiful, sad blue eyes. He wore a tee shirt with holes in it and old blue jeans with matching holes, a pair of red socks with holes, and absolutely no smile whatsoever. I caught a glimpse of him peeking at me from behind the chair and at first I acted like I didn't see him. I arose from where I was sitting (the man immediately stared and did not take his eyes from me) and strolled over to the wingback chair and sat down in it. The father, apparently sensing no danger, proceeded in his dealings with Charles.

After a moment or two I began reaching my right arm around the right side of the chair and acted like I was grabbing for the boy that I knew was still there. I did it in a kind of clumsy, silly way so as not to frighten him and after a while heard what I thought might have been a giggle. Then reaching back into my pocket I brought out a half eaten roll of Certs and held them, palm open around the back of the chair. My hand lay still for maybe ten seconds until the Certs were snatched out of my hand. Before I could bring it back around I felt something on my palm and the boy made a beeline out the door an I could hear him running down the stairs. The father and mother—or whatever they were—were oblivious to the boy and didn't even look up when he went out the door. When I brought my hand back around I could see that the little boy with the sad blue eyes had replaced my Certs with his spit. I stared at it for about five seconds.

During that short time, an entire world of perception and despair rushed through my mind and I had no compulsion whatsoever in wiping that poor little boy's spit on the arm of his parents chair. My only regret was that they didn't see me do it.

Charles in the meantime had gotten into some kind of a rap session with the man—I think the woman was mute—and it didn't look like he was going to be finished for a while. I found the atmosphere suddenly nauseating so I got up—immediately the man's eyes were upon me again—and I told Charles I would be waiting in the car. The last thing I heard Charles saying to the man was, "Don't worry about him, he's okay."

I walked down the stairs and out to the porch and began down the steps to the sidewalk when I heard a voice say, "Hey! Hey mister!" I turned to see the little boy sitting on a porch swing, sucking on a Cert with great pleasure.

"Hey what?" I replied.

"Hey yourself, that's what," he said with a self-satisfied grimace.

"Is spitting on people your way of saying 'Thank you'?" His answer was a shrug and then he held what was left of a Cert between his front teeth, up on end where I could get a view of it.

"What's your name?" I asked.

"None of your business. Are you going to do all that dope yourselves?"

I stood, horribly transfixed by the boy. I had no idea what to say, or how to make something so terribly wrong into something with even a smidgen of decency in it. I finally just smiled a stupid smile and said, "Do you know a lot about... about what your daddy sells?"

"He ain't my daddy. My daddy left a long time ago. He left when he heard I was coming. I know about it cause my mom tells me all the time. That man, he ain't my daddy. He thinks he is, but he ain't. And yeah, I know a lot about dope. What do you want to know?"

I was getting more ill by the minute. Before me was a wizened old man caught in a little boy's body, and a shame-filled world. And what was worse—I was part of why it was so shameful. It was people like me who helped create a world that turned out kids like this. Cynical, messed up children with very little hope in life for anything decent. I suddenly didn't want to talk about drugs or his messed up parents and life, so I tried to change the subject.

"Hey, do you know that it's almost Christmas?" I said, and then, for whatever reason, I tried… me of all people… I tried to inject a little bit of something pure into the boy's heart. "Do you know what Christmas is really all about? Have you ever heard of Jesus?"

His beautiful blue eyes suddenly widened and he stared at me in surprise.

"Ask your mom to tell you about how a baby named Jesus was born a long time ago. He came into the world to help people… he came… he came… to save them."

When I said that, it was too much even for me. I didn't know what was wrong, but I felt like crying. Crying for myself and my messed up life and crying for this little boy and his messed up existence and crying for this mad, messed up, stupid world.

The little boy was looking at me very strangely, with his head at a tilt as if inspecting me to see if I was real, or maybe just an apparition. Then he straightened his head, and with a voice as cold as the grave, and seething with anger he said, "Mister, you're crazy."

Till the day I die, I will never forget that child and the effect our meeting had on me. I felt as though I'd been shot. Not by his words, but by his life, his emptiness, his jaded outlook. So young… he was supposed to still be innocent... but he was so… so… old and worn-out.

God only knew what his young eyes had been forced to see and his young ears had been forced to hear in his short unhappy lifetime.

I turned and finished walking down the steps and went to the car. I got in and sat motionless. After a few minutes Charles hopped in laughing and telling me what a great deal he'd got and, "This stuff's going to blow our ever livin' heads off."

"I don't want to hear it." I said looking out the passenger window.

"What?"

"I said I don't want to hear it." I was now looking straight at Charles.

Charles looked hurt. "What'd I do man? I thought we was gonna' have a good time. Did I say something wrong? What is it?" I really didn't want to talk about the boy… it was far too depressing, and I wasn't sure Charlie would get it anyway. So I just shrugged my shoulders, sat quiet for a while and said, "Charles, it's not you… it's me. I… I'm really messed up… I'm not thinking right and I don't know what's wrong. Well… that's not quite right… I do know. But it's just all so weird and… well… forget it. Let's just go home."

Charles looked at me, shook his head, started his car, turned on rock radio and sang along to the music of Ozzy Osborne, and drove home.

***

That night I knew what I had to do and what I was *going to do*… at least I hoped. Charles brought out the stuff he'd scored, and true to the dealer's word it "took our heads off." Well, for the most part. While I was unquestioningly, 'ripped' I was nevertheless miserable. I couldn't get the little boy with the sad blue eyes off my mind. In fact the drugs made it all the worse. He was all I could think about. My mind went wild with macabre scenarios of the boy in his teens, and then his twenties. I couldn't get him past his twenties because I was sure he'd be dead by then. A poor little boy who absolutely never had a chance.

As for me, I'd had plenty of chances, and blown them all. Yes, we were poor when I was little—but I didn't know it, and my mother was every boy's dream. She was good and kind and loving and generous to a fault. I cannot remember my mother ever one time being selfish about anything. Everything possible was done for my brother and I. The philosophy mom lived was, "These boys didn't ask to be born... I'm the one who got them here... and I will raise them the best I know how." And she did.

As for Buzz, again... he saved us. That's all there is to it. He came along like a knight in shining armor and saved our family. While my mother had worked like a dog to provide for us, her resources—except for love—were all but zero. Buzz took us in, provided amply for us and he gave us his name. Yes, he had his ways, and they were different, but who doesn't. This I know for sure: of all the fathers of all my friends, I wouldn't trade Buzz for the lot of them. He really was... my dad. But if a boy with all the breaks I'd had—could turn out so despicable, what chance in the world would a little boy have like the one I met today?

"Larry... LARRY!!... What in #$!%&! is wrong with you!?" It was Lyle. It was about the third time that night he'd asked me that question... but not quite in that strong of terms.

"I'm sorry guys, I really am. I don't mean to be the party-pooper. I was just really affected by that kid today." I'd finally told them what was eating on me after the second time I was asked what was wrong with me. I'd went into it pretty deep but it made them all kind of uneasy, so I finally just shut up. I knew my being bummed out was bumming them out and I hated it. In the past, whenever a guy started acting like I was acting now, if I couldn't pull him out with humor I could get pretty ruthless with him verbally. Then, they would either snap out of it, or leave. And most left. And here I was, acting the biggest donkey of them all.

So I finally decided then and there to let them know what my plans were. "Boys... I'm going to do something in the very near future, and I may as well tell you about it now." At that they all began to listen up and Tyrone even turned the music down.

"You guys have known for a long time my... feelings... and struggles with this 'God thing.' You know that (for whatever good it's done me) I've tried to pray and read some of the Bible. Tyrone, you saw, before we moved over here, that for a few weeks I had actually quit drinking, drugging, smoking... everything. I was better off then than I'd been in years." (It was a pretty well known fact that since the latter part of my ninth grade year, I'd either been drunk or stoned *every day* except for when I played football in my senior year.)

"Well... I'm going back to giving it up... for good. I mean I am really going to give it all up. I am quitting all drinking and drugging completely as of New Year's Eve."

At that point they all began to smile a little—except for Lyle who smiled broadly, so I continued, "It's more than a New Year's Eve resolution. I mean it—I'm through. And if I can't do it here... well, I will be moving."

"Where?" Tyrone asked, a little surprised.

"I don't know... I haven't thought it out that far yet... but I will... believe me I will." And with that I rose to my feet and said, "Look guys, I know I've been rotten company lately... and not just tonight. Ever since I had the wreck, things just haven't been the same. I know it and you know it. I don't mean to be a downer for you... I just have to ride this God thing out... completely. I know that I will never be happy without Him. And to do that I've got to go all the way." Then I walked out of the room through the kitchen and downstairs to my room.

***

The next couple of weeks seemed to drag by. I still drank, and drugged but my enthusiasm for it was all but gone. I sold two more vacuums—not enough to keep afloat but not quite bad enough to drown either. I still went to the cathedral most mornings but hardly at all in the evenings due to trying to pick up Ty from work when I could. I would however pray every night before I went to bed. The main thing I prayed about was December 31st. I kept asking God to please have mercy on me and help me to really kick all the useless garbage out of my life. I also asked Him to somehow show me where I should move, as I knew I could not stay here. The downward pull of my friends was just too strong and I had to get away from it. So, again, I asked Him over and over to somehow lead me and show me where to go.

As time went on, three plans of action began to formulate in my mind, but I kept them to myself as I figured I'd already stretched the limits of my friends' minds. In my resolve to change at News Year's I was still adamant. Lyle was especially, cynical and skeptical. But I couldn't blame him. After all, he'd heard me talk about God for almost three months with a cigarette in one hand and a joint or drink in the other. But whenever one of them, or someone who'd heard about my resolve, would ask me—I'd tell them emphatically, "Yes… come midnight, New Year's Eve, Larry Booker is absolutely, unequivocally, finished with drink and drugs forever." I knew it was a mouthful, and my track record wasn't exactly on my side… but I knew that it was essential for my life to ever mean anything at all.

At work I had dropped a hint to Doris that come New Year's, I might not be coming back. She never even looked up and her only remark was, "We'll give your appointments to someone else." I couldn't bring myself to say a word to Mrs. Howsing, but I knew that Doris would pass along the info. As for Robert Clarry, I would not miss him—nor would he miss me.

The day finally arrived.

The boys had put together a *big* New Year's Eve party at our house—no doubt for my benefit and for the benefit of the curious and dubious. This didn't bother me, as I understood completely. Had it been Lyle proclaiming all this time that he was going to change—I probably would have laughed in his face—though in my heart I would have been rooting for him, hoping that he could actually pull it off.

It seemed that everybody was there. That is, at least of our friends who had migrated to Denver or Boulder from Pueblo. There was also a number of 'Denver-ites' who'd been invited or heard about it and were looking for a good and raucous time.

In the early hours of the party there seemed to be a lot of interest in my 'resolution' to go straight, and I was peppered with questions. Thankfully, as the night wore on and people got more inebriated or stoned or both, their focus on me blurred and they gave themselves over to getting blasted and plastered.

As for me, I more or less parked myself in a chair in the corner and rarely moved. To be sure, I smoked and drank and did some pot, but I could not 'pour' myself into it. I sat and smiled and drank and smoked and carried on small talk with this one and that—and I *thought*. I thought about what it was going to be like to not drink and drug anymore.

The thought of giving up cigarettes was wonderful. They were very hard on my lungs as I always tended to be susceptible to bronchial problems, and cigarettes without question made it worse. It was not like I'd been smoking all that long anyway. I actually hadn't got into it seriously until my senior year when we were busted and my Aunt Arvie saw me on television. That was just before Joe Arguello went back to 'Nam and he and I and Mick and Edmund and Larry Weder almost sold the farm.

My thoughts took me from one subject to the next. Once I'd contemplated the drug bust I began to wonder about Larry... Larry Weder. "Man, I wonder what he's up to?" I mumbled. Someone had said that not long after he went to Oklahoma—to the Bible college, that he'd gotten a real bad case of religion. That he was into it up to his eyeballs! I just couldn't picture Larry that way... but Oh God... I hoped it was true! I hoped with all of my heart that it was true!

I was jerked from my reverie by the screams of my drunken and drugged out friends. "Ten... nine... eight..."

"Well, here it comes," I thought, "My life is about to change"

"Four... three... two... ONE! HAPPY NEW YEAR! HAPPY, HAPPY NEW YEAR!"

And so my friends that I loved and would always love, brought in the year of 1972 with a bang. Friends that had been closer to me than family. Friends that I knew that under the right circumstance I would—and almost had several times—die for. But I knew that now—right now, this minute—I had to get away from them. As they were totally caught up in the spirit of the moment and were paying attention to nothing but mayhem, it was not going to be hard to do.

Some guy I didn't know, was sitting on the floor next to me with his back to the wall. He had passed out cold and was drooling on himself. I took the one joint I had in my shirt pocket and slipped it in between his lips. I screwed the lid back onto the quart of Coors I'd been holding between my legs and sat it down between his. Neither this or the cheering of the party-goers was able to arouse him from his stupor.

I looked at my cigarette, said "Good-bye" and rubbed it out in the ashtray, then quietly got up and began to slip my way through the crowd. I received a few rambunctious hugs from both guys and gals and some girl I'd never seen before gave me a kiss as we both kept on moving away—her to her party and me to my room.

I slowly worked my way through the kitchen—which for some reason was exceptionally full and was just about to turn the corner to go down the stairway when somebody bumped into me hard. I turned to see who it was and—it was Tyrone. He was laughing uproariously and turned to see who it was he had just crashed into. When he saw it was me and saw that I was headed to my room he stopped laughing. We looked into each other's eyes and he managed to whisper hoarsely, "Larry… my friend. Good luck… I really want you to make it." With that he slapped me on the shoulder, started laughing once more and turned away.

I walked down the stairs hoping to goodness that no one had gone into my room. Thankfully, it was empty and I shut the door and locked it. I lay down on the bed and stared at the ceiling. I could hear the crowd upstairs as the party began roaring into full swing.

Then I began to pray.

"God… this is me… Larry. Larry. You know, the one you have spared so many, many times. God, please… please, God… forgive me. Forgive me for the thousand upon thousands of sins I've committed. Forgive me of my drinking… and my drugging… and for breaking so many of the promises that I made you that night… the night when I freaked out so bad and thought I was doomed forever…. Oh GOD! Forgive me… forgive me." And thus I prayed… and prayed… and prayed.

After a while, as I prayed, something began to happen. At first it was so slight as to be almost imperceptible… but then I felt it a little stronger… and then a little stronger still. It was something that was very strange for me to be feeling right now, because after all, I was in the middle of repenting and asking God to forgive me. But what was happening was that… I was beginning to feel happy, and I mean happy! Really Happy! It was growing in me and I could now feel it coming on stronger… and stronger… and then so strong that I was now smiling… I mean really smiling. I mean 'stupid grin' smiling. Then I started to laugh. I mean a *clean* laugh… a… a *good* laugh, a hearty laugh! And it kept coming, and coming… and getting more and more … powerful… yes, very powerful. I said, "Oh God you can't keep this up… if you do I'm going to start screaming it's… it's, *so good!*" Then it happened… I did start talking out loud… saying… "Glory!" And it felt good to say it… in fact it felt wonderful. So I said it again a little louder… "Glory!" and then a little louder… and yet louder still! Finally I was yelling… GLORY!! GLORY!! And quickly on the heels of that came the word… "HALLELUJAH!! OH! OH! HALLELUJAH!!

I kept this up for I don't know how long. All I know is that it felt right and it felt wonderful. I did not stop until a sound came breaking through into my consciousness. It was the sound of someone stomping their foot on the floor above me. It was then that I could also hear that, whoever was doing the stomping was also yelling something. And I began to perceive that they were yelling and stomping at me.

"Larry! LARRY! (stomp-stomp-stomp) LARRY! Are you all right?!" And I realized that it was the only sound I heard. The music was off as well as the sounds of the screaming, laughing, raucous party. The only sound to be heard was the stomping and yelling of a lone inquirer asking if I was alright.

I realized then what must have happened. The sound of my… my… what do you call it? Screaming, yelling… praising, worship? The sound of whatever it was that I was doing with God, must have gone up through the vents into the party upstairs. As I kept it up someone must have heard it, then another and then curiosity must have overcome them all. Well… I guess I'd better let them know that I'm okay.

"YEAH… I AM JUST FINE… IN FACT I WAS NEVER

BETTER!!! I'LL BE OKAY… YOU GO AHEAD AND PARTY… I'M ALRIGHT!!"

But they didn't. The party apparently just kind of shriveled and died except for a few die-hards, but even they were greatly toned down.

***

I awoke the next morning feeling like a million dollars. I really had drunk enough to warrant some kind of repercussion—but there was nothing. Nothing but a great, good feeling and sense of total well-being. It kind of reminded me of Ebenezer Scrooge's Christmas morning. I felt like hugging the whole world. I looked around my room, and knew that what I was going to do *would* be done today.

I grabbed my leather tote bag from the closet and started stuffing my things into it. I knew I couldn't get everything and that I'd have to come back for the rest later. But that couldn't be helped. I grabbed the bare essentials and started up the stairway three steps at a time. The scene that met me was not a surprise but was still shocking all the same. The house was decimated. The party had definitely been a 'success' if this was the result. Tyrone was laying on the couch, fully dressed with his mouth wide open. Charles made it to his bedroom, not quite to his bed, but at least he was pretty well dressed for bed. As for Lyle, he was rolled up in a heap of covers on his pallet, in his usual place. He was after all—'the survivor.' I began to go through the top drawer of the bureau searching for some of my personal effects. After a while I heard a stirring and Tyrone had one eye open and was more or less staring in my general direction.

"What are you doing?" he moaned, licking his lips to no avail.

"I'm leaving."

"What?" he said and made an unsuccessful effort to sit up.

"I'm leaving Ty. I'm going away, probably for good."

"What the $%#^&$ ?" Lyle now groggily chimed in, "You're doing what? Where're you going to go?"

"Well, boys… I've given it a lot of thought, and I am going to one of three places. I'm going to go to Aspen and rent one of the cabins we've heard about, the ones with no running water or electricity… and I'm going to sit down and write my life story."

"You're *what?*" they all three exclaimed. Charles was up and leaning heavily against the door jam in his skivvies.

"Yes, I'm going to Aspen. Or… I'm going down to Guadalajara, Mexico, to sit on the white sands and write my life story. Or… I am going to college and I'm going to learn how to write."

They were all quiet, and then Lyle spoke first, "Larry… you have finally done it. You have gone over the edge and lost your mind." The funny thing was, I don't think he was kidding.

"Of course I've got to go to Pueblo first, because it's the first of the month and I've got to see my probation officer by the fifth.

Then Charles added, "Yes, Larry, it *is* the first of the month. What about your share of the rent?"

"I'll tell you what," I said, "Sell my waterbed, sell my stuff—you can even sell my vacuum." (Yes, though embarrassed to admit it, I had even purchased a Kirby. Robert Clarry sold it to me on the grounds that, I could get it cheaper, and that it would be a 'good investment.')

"Just don't sell my personal stuff… I'll be back for that. You know Charles, you might even get Lyle to pay a little rent this month. Hmm?"

"Larry…" Lyle said—no doubt to change the subject—"How are you even going to get out of town, you ain't got a car and I know Tyrone won't let you take his."

It was then that I looked at them and said, "God will provide me a ride." Though Lyle laughed and Charles snorted, Tyrone said nothing… he just stared at me. But all laughs, snorts and looks were quickly cut short when we heard a horn honking outside.

"And that boys… is my ride." At least I hoped it was. I walked quickly to the door, opened it to see Joe Arguello, sitting in his Barracuda. He smiled when he saw me and yelled, "I'm going to Pueblo… anybody want a ride?"

"Boys, I love ya, and I'll see ya later." With that I grabbed my satchel and went out the door. I was going to Pueblo to see my probation officer… then I was going on to walk with God… somewhere, someplace, somehow.

# 6
## College

Joe was not in a hurry to get to Pueblo so we decided to take the scenic route through the heart of the Rocky Mountains. Riding with Joe that morning was a guy named 'Taber.' I think Taber may have been his last name but I wasn't sure as it was difficult to get much more out of him than a grunt. My first thought was that he had a horrific hangover from New Year's Eve, but gradually came to realize it was simply his nature. Joe got more out of him than I, as Taber answered him during the next six hours with one complete sentence, one semi-complete sentence and two single words, a "yeah" and a "nah." The most I could muster out of him was the grunt business, so I gave up trying.

Taber's problem—whatever it was—might have got on my nerves had I not felt so joyous from my experience with God the night before. As it was, I really didn't mind his semi-smug silence. Joe was not a gregarious fellow himself and, all in all, the silence made for a rather enjoyable ride, as I wanted to think more than I wanted to talk anyway.

Joe, recently discharged from the army, had spent most of his stint in Vietnam as a helicopter machine gunner, picking up two purple hearts, two silver stars, an awesome car and a drug habit along the way. Because of his experiences in 'Nam, it generally took a lot to shock him. Three things that day however thoroughly 'blew' Joe's mind. The first was some pot he'd scored the night before. From his reactions, it must have been really potent stuff. The second item that numbed him was that I refused to touch any of it. The third was when I asked to be let out of the car in order to sit by the road and write some poetry.

I decided to get out when he and Taber decided to stop and knock off a bottle of wine and smoke some more pot. Being in the back seat of his two door Barracuda I couldn't just get out without being let out. When Joe asked where I was going and I told him, "To write poetry," he just stared at me. But neither he nor Taber uttered a word.

This was not the first time I'd written poetry, even at the side of the road, (I'd done it once before with Charles and Tyrone on a back road trip up to Boulder) but this was a first for Joe and it got next to him. The combination of the pot's efficiency, my refusal to try it, and my poetry writing, simply left him stunned. As for Taber, he registered nothing.

But Joe let me out and proceeded to drive on down the road saying he'd be back in about a half hour. Though I believed him, I had some trepidation that he might get too loaded to find his way back, or might even forget to come back and get me. Nevertheless, I sat on a rock with my satchel, pulled out some paper, dug around for a pencil, and began to go to work. It was the first poem I wrote after having repented and 'given my heart to God.' It was called 'Sunsay' and though it was just so much drivel… it was obvious that God was on my mind.

By and by Joe came back to pick me up. By this time he was in such bad shape that I asked to drive and he gladly assented. Joe still had the car that we'd been busted in a year ago and it really was one nice car. It had a 383-hemi engine that ran like a cheetah on meth, and a sound system that could blow your mind, if it didn't blow your eardrums first. Placed throughout the interior was a diffused lighting system that produced various colored lights to the beat and sounds of whatever music was played at the time. It was very impressive—especially if you were stoned which, up until that particular trip, I inevitably was.

We leisurely made our way through the Rockies, eventually going through Cripple Creek and driving down to highway 50 and made our way on into Pueblo.

***

Whatever it was that I'd received from God the night before,

I knew was real and I wanted more of it. I was in somewhat of a dilemma however as I didn't want to go home again—without a job and especially with no money for Buzz—and yet, I didn't want to stay with any of my friends to be continually tempted and lose what I'd received from God. Joe offered to let me stay with him but to do so would have been insane. He was the most drug-supplied guy I knew, and was 'hotter than a Saturday night special' when it came to the police. We all knew that as soon as a Pueblo policeman spotted and recognized Joe's car, we would be followed and stopped if we broke a single traffic law and probably even if we didn't.

So… where was I to go? This was the first day of the month, a Saturday, and I had until the first Thursday to see my probation officer, and had therefore five days to kill. I needed to decide not only where to go for now, but where I was going to go after that. Be it Aspen, Mexico or somehow to college, I had to do something quickly. I could never tell the probation officer about Mexico—it would be over for me—and how in the world could I go to college when I couldn't even get into the army? Should I ask Buzz for a loan? Not hardly. The more I thought about it all, the more it looked like I might be headed to Aspen. In order to do that I needed to go home, get some more clothes and hit my mom up for yet another loan on the side. I could probably get a ride to Aspen from Joe, as he was always game to try something or go somewhere new. But one thing was for sure—I didn't want Joe to start liking Aspen and move there as well. I had to get away from people like him, in spite of how much I liked and even loved them.

I finally decided to try Rocco's for a couple of days until I saw my probation officer and found out what I could actually pull off. Rocco's mother would be thrilled to hear that I was trying to live for God and would do everything she could to help me. His dad however, would be 'a little less, tender towards me, even if I had grown wings and was sporting a halo. So I had Joe let me off at Rocco's (if it didn't work I was only two blocks from my parents' home) and made my sales pitch to Ma. She readily said I could stay, but told me to 'lie low' when Rocco's father was home.

***

Rocco didn't seem to be living at home (that was the way his mother put it) so I didn't have to worry about him trying to get me stoned. I called my probation officer the next day and asked if there was any way I could come to see him since I was in town. He said that would be fine if I could be there at 2:00 that afternoon.

Roxy, Rocco's sister, gave me a ride downtown and I had her let me off at the Catholic Church on Court Street at about 1:30 p.m. I entered the church, made my way down to the front and knelt as I'd done so many times before and began to pray.

"God, it's me… Larry. I really need your help, God, and you know I've always needed it. I'm about to go see my probation officer, Mr. Gonzales, and I've got some big decisions I've got to make in my life. So, God, please help me… show me what to do. Show me where to go. Should I go to Aspen? Or Mexico? Or, God, if there's any way… please, please let me go to college. I really do want to write. God… please help me."

I rose to my feet and made my way out the door, turned to the right, crossed the street and went to see my probation officer of many years, Mr. Gonzales.

Mr. Gonzales didn't appear to be especially pleased to see me, though he would have been much more displeased *not* to see me—which had been far too often the case. He sat with his hands folded in front of him and asked what I'd been up to, if I was still in Denver and about my job situation. I told him that I'd moved back home for now but that I was thinking—with his permission of course—of moving to Aspen… to get away from my friends… which was after all, true.

He looked at me a long time as if he was debating to say something, finally gave out a sigh and said, "Larry, how would you like to go to college?"

After staring at him for almost a minute I said, "What?"

"What I said was, how would you like to go to college?"

"What… what do you mean?" I said slowly while my heart raced.

"What I mean is this… there is an individual living in this city who has contacted our office and stated that if you are willing to go to Southern Colorado State College, they will pay the bill… the *entire* bill."

Except for my jaw slowly beginning to hang I was too stunned to move. Mr. Gonzales continued, "Yes. They are willing to pay all tuition fees, book fees and if you need it, dorm fees. If you stay at the dorm they will also see to it that your cafeteria meals are paid for. They will *never* give you any cash—for obvious reasons—but will supply everything else. All you have to do is, go to school and make a decent showing on your grades. What they mean by that is, your grades must not be failing grades. If you go, you must be able to graduate."

Again I could neither move nor answer. After a while I croaked, "Who… who is doing this?"

"The individual wishes to remain anonymous."

Once more I sat trying to absorb what I'd just heard. I could feels tears beginning to well as I lowered my head and finally muttered, "Thank you. Thank you, Jesus. Thank you so much."

Mr. Gonzales slowly leaned forward in his chair and said, "What?"

What I'd meant to say to Jesus alone must have been a bolt out of the blue to Raul Gonzales who had been dealing with me off and on since I was fifteen. I looked him in the eye and said, "Oh nothing… I was… I was just thanking God for helping me that's all." These were turning into long, silent moments for both of us. He then looked at some papers on his desk and began to shuffle them while he cleared his throat and said, "Yes, well, whatever." And then, "You're going to do it then? They need to know now so that you can start this quarter. That's … next Monday."

As if in a dream, I said, "Yes… Yes, I'll do it… of course I'll do it. And please, Mr. Gonzales, please tell whoever it is that's doing this that I'm very thankful, so very, very thankful. And tell them that I'm going to work very hard. And… and, tell them that I have already quit my drinking and well, you know… everything that I've done for so long."

Raul Gonzales looked at me with a bewildered expression on his face. "Larry… do you mean what you've just said… that you've quit it all."

"Yes sir. I mean every single word of it."

He stared at me as if he were seeing an apparition, and then said, "Okay. Can you come back day after tomorrow? I'll contact the people today and try to get everything lined out by then. What about the dorms? Do you want to live there? Or do you know yet?"

The first thought that hit me was Alan's dorms in Boulder, and all that went on there. So I immediately said, "No, no I don't want to stay there. I'll probably stay with my parents."

"Well, it's up to you, but that probably is for the best."

That pretty well wrapped up our conversation and I left within minutes. I ran up the street, back into the church, all the way to the altar and fell on my knees. With my hands on the rail I looked up and said, "God! God!! I can't believe you did it! That you did it for me! I thank you so much…" and by that time I was crying. I cried like a little boy who had found something very, very precious that had been lost for a long, long time.

Roxy picked me up two hours later. As always, she was late, but I didn't care as I spent the time walking around inside the church and praying. When we got to her house, I hugged Ma, told her the good news and that I was going to go home to live. She hugged me, continued to ask me a host of questions, no doubt to make sure that I wasn't lying to her, and wished me the best in the world.

I grabbed my bag, walked the two blocks to my house, came through the front door and hugged my mother. She was genuinely shocked to see me and immediately began to pepper me with questions as to whether I was in some kind of trouble. I sat her down and knelt by her chair, and said, "Mom, I've got something very important to tell you." Her eyes grew very wide and I could tell she was afraid. I smiled at this precious woman, took her by the hand and said, "Mom, two very important things have happened. First, I am as of now… living for God." At that she raised her eyebrows, but did not return my smile. She was far too dubious of a proclamation like that to get overly excited. I continued, "And the second thing is that, as of next week, I am going to college."

At that bit of information, her eyebrows shot up.

"I just got back from seeing Mr. Gonzales, my probation officer. He told me that someone in the city is anonymously going to pay all of my expenses to go to college, that's *every bit* of them Mom. Even my food and dorm if necessary." My mothers eyes were wide open and her mouth had begun to form an 'O' but she still did not speak. "Mom, it's true... I swear to you, it's all true. If you don't believe me, call Mr. Gonzales and ask him. And listen, I can stay at the dorms, but I really don't think it's a good idea for now... because like I said, I'm trying to live for God and I don't want to get in any more trouble. If I stay at the dorms I'm afraid that's what it could lead to... you know how things can go with me."

At this she just nodded her head in agreement but had as yet not spoken a word. When I looked closely into her eyes and said, "You do believe me don't you?" she managed to croak, "Larry... I never wanted to believe anything so bad in my life."

"Well, it's true. Every word of it. And I really do want to make you proud of me. Believe me I do. And I intend to. Do you think Buzz will mind if I stay here. I promise mom, I'm going to do my very best not to get in any more trouble."

"I'll, I'll talk to him... I don't think he'll mind... but I wouldn't be surprised if he makes me call your probation officer."

After she asked me many more questions about my benefactor, to which I had no answers, I took my stuff down to my room, lay on my bed and thanked God one more time for what he'd done.

After a while I called Norma's mother to see if she was in town. I was dying to tell her about her all about it. Her mother said she was in town but that she'd not seen her for two days. She'd called home and said that she and Geri were going to see a friend in the Springs. She went on to tell me what a wonderful Christmas they'd had and how that all the girls were there and what she'd given them and received from them and how that in a few days they were probably going to go skiing, that is if the girls didn't have to rush off.

I could tell that the dear woman was wound up tighter than a fiddle string. After extensive wrangling to get loose from her I finally said good-bye and hung up the phone. I would have told her about my good fortune and my college benefactor but was not up to an hour on the phone. She was a sweetheart, and I loved her… but I just couldn't take it.

***

The following week I started classes at Southern Colorado State College. Enrollment went smoothly and I was able to get the classes I wanted: two classes on poetry, a creative writing class, Psychology 101, and piano.

It was quite an experience to go into the bookstore and be able to charge all of my books and to charge what I wanted in the cafeteria. As it turned out, my only expenses were the bus fees, which my mother was more than happy to pay.

The S.C.S.C. campus was in the far northeast part of Pueblo and I lived in the far southwest end. The bus I caught however was not far from my house, a little over a quarter of a mile, and with only one change could go directly to the main campus in Belmont. Coming home from school was just as easy. I would catch a bus that took me to the downtown campus and then after a twenty-five minute layover I'd catch another one to the same stop where I'd started in the morning. Though I missed my Triumph dreadfully, I didn't mind either the walk or the bus rides—as I now had different priorities—and no one to show off for anyway.

Word got out rather quickly that I was back in town. Friends would call to see if I wanted to go party and I always turned them down with the explanation that I was trying to live for God now and didn't want to do that stuff anymore. With the type of friends that I'd cultivated over the years, that little speech was 'nuff said' and they didn't call back.

My life therefore consisted of riding the bus, going to my classes, doing all my work… even my homework, (which was an entirely new experience) praying to God and reading my Bible.

Though I had a perfectly good Bible—my mother had purchased it for me in 1960 and it was virtually untouched—I had somehow gotten it in my brain that the 'older' and more well used a Bible was—the more 'holy' it was. I determined therefore to obtain a *really* Holy Bible. One day, after school, I got off bus in the main downtown area and went into a St. Vincent De Paul thrift store and found a Bible that was *very* holy. I bought it for a quarter and it was so holy that it was already starting to fall apart. On the way out of the thrift store my eye fell upon a little plastic cross hanging on a neck chain. I bought it for fifteen cents, put it about my neck and what with my 'Holy, Holy Bible' I looked and felt like "Johnny Christian." I caught the next bus and made my way home very pleased with myself. But it was not until I went to bed that night that I became ecstatic. When I turned off the light I found out that the little cross actually, *glowed in the dark!* I could not have been happier! I went to sleep that night, lying on my back praying, the cross in my right hand, the old Bible in my left, and both hands crossed over my chest.

When I awoke in the morning, the Bible was pretty well scattered and it took me a while to find the cross. I put the Bible back together—though I had no idea what order it was supposed to be in—and put a rubber band around it to hold it together. The cross went back around my neck while I grabbed Bible, books, and a bacon and egg sandwich my mother handed me and made a beeline for the bus. These were becoming halcyon days, that I never thought I could know again. I loved my classes, I loved being sober… and I loved God.

***

It was an unusual thing for me to be able to take both of my poetry classes at the same time as they were at different academic levels. I actually had to talk the Dean of Admissions into letting me do it. He had called me in, pointed out my less than stellar performance in high school and said I couldn't possibly 'jump ahead' like that. I told him that, if he was not already aware of it, my tuition was being paid anonymously and I couldn't therefore be *positive* just how long I would be in school. I emphasized the fact that I wanted to become a writer and that if nothing else this 'crash course' would help prepare me for that goal, especially as I had R.P. Dickey for my professor. At the mentioned of Mr.

Dickey, the Dean smiled slightly and looked at the papers in his hands. We eventually came to an agreement that we'd see how I did this quarter and take it from there, the implication being pretty plain that if I couldn't cut it—it was back to square one.

Of all my classes I especially enjoyed poetry and creative writing, though in truth, I could barely stand the professor I had for those classes. R.P. Dickey was a big man of about 6' 2" who was probably at least 280 lbs. of mostly muscle. He looked about 45 to 50 years old, had long, wild, flaming red hair with a slightly graying red beard to match. His eyes were a piercing blue that could turn to fire at the drop of a syllable and could bore a hole right through you. But a dirty look from R.P. Dickey was nothing compared to one of his dirty, soul-searing tirades.

A poet of some renown, he was an utterly brilliant man… but, he knew it. Had I not been trying to live for God, I believe I could have easily gotten into a physical brawl with him, though he undoubtedly would have beaten me to a pulp. He possessed about him an untamed animal magnetism, with a certain fierceness of temper that would brook no folly or weakness or anything he perceived to be so. Though I was with him for only a three-month period of my life, I believe he grew to sincerely hate me, and the feeling was almost mutual.

There were two reasons I could not hate the man. The first was that I'd read somewhere in the Bible that I wasn't supposed to, and the other was—I couldn't help but admire him.

As it ended up, R.P. Dickey probably helped me more than any man in my entire life to understand the power of … *words*. As a result of this, he helped me to understand the power and depths of the Bible, though he personally seemed to have little use for it. I also found out under his tutelage that the poet who said, "Home is the place that, when you have to go there, they have to take you in," was—Robert Frost.

We got along well enough in the beginning, because R.P. apparently had a habit of finding out as early as possible what everyone in the class was made out of. He then, either nurtured—if he liked what he perceived—or crushed, if he didn't. He admired a sharp mind and a bold spirit but despised stupidity and timidity.

As he was a bold and audacious man, he had neither time nor use for meekness, which he perceived as weakness.

It took the Professor a wee bit longer than usual to figure me out. By my attire, hair length and vocabulary I was of the 60's druggy genre. But, as I was trying to please God, I did not cuss in class, use cursing in my poetry, or get into off-color discussions—three things of which R.P. was a master. He had probably written me off as some kind of a 'mellow-head' until one day in the intermediate poetry class, I intervened for a woman that he was browbeating to death for her interpretation of a certain stanza of a poem. Though what she was expounding did seem pretty lame, what Mr. Dickey swore vehemently the poet meant, was simply not found in the text either—at least not to me. He was in the process of steamrolling her under when the woman—a kind of an avant-guard, middle-class, social-butterfly wanna-be—started shaking and began to cry. We all supposed that surely the Professor would let up on the poor woman… but he didn't. He just kept boring in until it became obvious that he wasn't going to stop unless the woman broke, entirely acknowledged her ignorance and swore allegiance to Professor Dickey's insightful brilliance and interpretations. Finally I could take no more and spoke up.

"With all due respect Professor Dickey, while the good lady's insight into the meaning of the stanza is, granted, somewhat on the weak side—sir, yours is no better." You could have literally heard a pin drop. Even the wanna-be butterfly took a deep breath.

R.P. Dickey's attention began to tear away from the woman and slowly become riveted on me—three seats down in the round table type format. Once his attention was fully there, he never moved a muscle, not even a twitch. He stared at me with a pair of the calmest blue eyes that I'd ever met and inspected me as if I were an apparition that had appeared from another world. He said nothing for quite a while; he just scrutinized me, no doubt 'taking my measure.' By and by he actually smiled at me—though I could tell it was not from his heart. As he still kept silent, I picked up my book, and pretended to calmly read the poem—which was bye the way, 'Mending Wall' by Robert Frost.

Then he spoke. "And let's see... I believe the name is Booker... Mr. Booker. And pray tell, Mr. Larry Booker, what is *your* perception of the line?"

"Me?" I answered, "I have no opinion, that is none to speak of. That's why I'm in this class... to learn. But concerning what I've heard so far today, I have thus far learned a lot about Miss... Miss...?"

"Sparcer," the woman said very quietly.

"Yes, well, I've heard her perception, and no offense," I said looking her way, then back at Mr. Dickey, "I cannot see that she actually substantiated the reason for her view... but from you, Professor, I have not learned anything—concerning this stanza—except that you do not like Miss Sparcer's analysis. You express your own but cannot demonstrate to us why *yours* is the correct one any better then she has... except you are a *much more forceful personality* than this *little woman*."

At this, R.P. Dickey's face grew as red as his hair and he proceeded with ice cold, measured words to once more give us his interpretation, never once taking his now blazing eyes off me. When he'd finished I said, "Prove it, Professor. Again, I see *what* you are saying but not *why* you are saying it. The text itself lends no credence to your statement. And until you can show me *why* you are saying what you're saying... Miss..."

"It's actually Mrs.," she quietly interjected.

"...*Mrs*. Sparcer's reasoning is as logical as yours."

At that I actually heard some of the other students gasp and several more shifted in their chairs. Professor R.P. Dickey looked at me for a long, long time, and I thought, "Boy, this is really it... you're about to be cremated." Then Professor R.P. Dickey smiled at me. It was almost a genuine smile. His anger seemingly disappeared and at that moment the class bells rang and he simply said, "Class dismissed."

We all got up from our seats, and no one spoke. Mrs. Sparcer gave me a look that more than paid for any of my nervousness, which I most assuredly was. In regards to nerves however, I have always been fortunate. When nervous, I am most of the time like a duck in the water—paddling like crazy underneath but having the appearance of being very calm on the surface.

I gathered my books and left the classroom not looking back to see if I was being beckoned by R.P. I made my way down the hall and was down the first flight of stairs when a very strong hand gripped my arm and continued to propel me down. It was R.P. Dickey.

"Larry, do you see these stairs?" Not waiting for me to give the obvious answer he continued, "You know you really don't *see* them, unless you're on acid… and then… and then, you don't just pass by them, and over them, as if they're not really there… but you *experience them*. You *know them*, you become *one with them*, you *feel* and *understand* them… like a man *knows* a woman. Larry," he was still walking me with an exceedingly firm grip on my arm and seemingly not about to stop, "If you'll stick with me, I'll teach you… I'll make you so brilliant and insightful that you will never be able to hang around your old buddies again, which are all probably just a bunch of ignorant nobodies anyway. You'll see things you never saw, and go places in your mind, your soul and body you've never imagined. Just stick with me… and let me teach you."

With that we had reached the bottom of the stairs—one flight lower than I wanted to go—and he let go of my arm and walked away, never looking back. I stood there, rubbing the circulation back into my elbow and watched the back of this strange, marvelous, intriguing man walk away. Then I turned and went back up one flight of stairs towards my psychology class, hoping that maybe it would help me to figure out the mind of R.P. Dickey.

***

That evening after finishing what homework I had, I opened my old Holy Bible to a book called "The Acts of the Apostles." It was not the first time that I'd read out of this book, but as I read it on this occasion I kept noticing the oft repeated phrase; the "Holy Ghost" and began to wonder what it meant and what they were talking about. After reading several chapters and pondering over it, I decided to call Eddie Weder to see what he knew about it. Eddie seemed to know somewhat more about the Bible than the rest of us—maybe that was due to his preacher grandfather—and I thought, surely it can't hurt to ask. I went upstairs to the wall phone that was around the corner of the stairwell, dialed his number and sat down on the steps. His grandmother answered and I asked if Eddie was there. She seemed to grow suspicious and asked who it was that wanted him, so I identified myself. She sounded relieved to hear that it was me and called Eddie to the phone. When he came to the phone I told him that I was surprised that he was actually home,

"Aw man, I'm working now. I gotta get home early and get some sleep or I can't make it." I told him I understood only too well and we began the process of trading information on what each other had been up to. I noticed that Eddie's speech was somewhat on the 'tipsy' side, but made no mention of it, as that was nothing new. He let me know that he'd heard I was a 'college bound Jesus freak' but that personally, he was happy for me.

Now that we were on the subject of my conversion, I asked Eddie, "Do you know anything about this 'Holy Ghost' that I keep reading about in the Bible? I'm studying the Acts of the Apostles and it seems like it's everywhere."

"Oh yeah man! The Holy Ghost… it's really neat!" he exclaimed.

"You… you really *know* about the Holy Ghost, Eddie?" I questioned more than a little surprised.

"Oh yeah man, it's awesome!"

"How do you know about it? Do you have it?" I asked him, very much in doubt of receiving an affirmative answer.

"Yeah I've got it! Of course I've got it!" I was incredulous and said, "Eddie… how do you know you have the Holy Ghost?"

"Cause I feel great man!"

"Because you *feel* great? Are you serious?"

"Of course I'm serious. Man, I'm telling you, Larry, it's awesome!" I was very taken aback at this and asked, "Eddie, how long have you had the Holy Ghost?"

"Oh, man, I've had it for years!"

"For years?" I said, "What years?"

"All these years man!"

"When and where did you get it?"

"I dunno… I just got it… it's… it's with me."

I asked him a few more pointed but fruitless questions and finally said, "Eddie… have you been drinking?"

"Oh, I've had a few. Why?"

I worked my way out of the conversation and off of the phone, and sat back down on the steps thinking. I knew that I *felt good* when I took a shower… but that didn't mean I had the Holy Ghost. I also knew then that whatever Eddie Weder *had* was *not* what the people in the Bible had. As I sat there, with my arms resting on my knees, I bent over and put my face in my hands and began to pray, "God, please listen to me, I've been reading about this 'Holy Ghost'… and, God, whatever it is, I want it… I really do. And, God, give me exactly what they had in the Bible. After all, God, I'm only going through life one time. Please, let me have it all." With that said, I got up and went down the stairs to my room to read and pray some more.

After a while I walked into the little area in my basement where my mother kept a T.V. so she could watch the soap operas while she washed the clothes. We actually had six televisions in the house and a couple more in the garage for spares. I turned the T.V. on and sat down to watch a program called "The Wild Wild West." While it progressed, the hero, a man called James West proceeded to grab a foe by the hair and beat his head on a hitching post and then throw him into a watering trough. My heart smote me as if I'd been shot as a small voice said "Larry, that is *not* the Christian thing to do."

In the past I would have thought Mr. West's actions pretty neat, and would no doubt have repeated them myself if I'd ever had an enemy around a hitching post, by a watering trough. But on this occasion, it was like an arrow had pierced my soul. I immediately moved to the edge of my chair, leaned forward and changed the channel. What was showing there was not 'Christian' either, nor the next channel, nor the next. I realized with blinding clarity that everything on television was contrary to what I had been reading in my Bible and feeling in my soul. After a time of searching my heart, I told God that I never intended to watch it again... and shut it off.

***

The next morning as I walked to the bus stop I was feeling exceptionally happy. I awoke early, felt very rested, put my Holy, Holy Bible back together, read some of it, prayed a while, put my cross that glowed in the dark around my neck, ate one of my mother's famous breakfasts, grabbed my books and my completed homework, and headed out the door—all with *no hangover!* It was wonderful.

I made my way to the bus stop telling God how much I loved Him and would do anything for Him, even coming to the place that I said, "God… I love you so much that if you wanted me to… I'd get down on my knees right here on this sidewalk and lift my hands to you and scream out that I loved you!" As I walked on, I thought to myself; "Well that's nice… but would you really do it?" This sparked an ongoing conversation with myself as to how serious I was and was it really in me to do something like that. Part of me said, "Of course I'd do it!" while another part said, "Larry, you're too chicken to ever do anything like that. What about these people driving up and down the road?" This internal debate went on until I finally set my books on the sidewalk, got down on both knees, lifted my hands and face straight up into the air and at the top of my lungs screamed, "***Jesus, I love you… God, I love you with all of my heart! I really, really do!!"*** Then I quickly arose and scurried down the street to the bus stop making it a point not to look at any of the passing cars. Presently I boarded the bus and was on my way to another day in college.

That day I had no verbal exchanges with Professor Dickey but he did manage to launch a few pointed insults my direction. Mrs. Sparcer made it a point to sit as close to me as she could in class—an action not lost on R.P. If she thought however that sitting by me would offer her protection from the professor's sharp tongue she was sadly mistaken. But she nevertheless continued to do so—almost—as long as I attended.

My most difficult class was Psychology 101. I was having a hard time relating 'primary motivational desires' to 'secondary motivational desires' when it came to explaining why I wanted a ham sandwich instead of bologna. My object was to live and 'keep on truckin' without a lot of introspection. My thinking was that I'd done enough introspection during my years in hallucinogenic drugs. But, after inspecting my feelings about the class a little more thoroughly I came to the conclusion that… I just didn't care for my psychology professor. He was, in a word, boring. The longer he talked, the more I felt like a stone slowly sinking to the bottom of the ocean.

That was one thing I had to hand in spades to R.P Dickey—nobody ever slept through one of his classes, and you were never bored. You might be scared half to death, but never bored. And again, he was teaching me to fall in love with words and their power. He drove it home again and again, that when it comes to life, the great majority of it hinges on the power of communication—and that through *words*. R.P. was fond of Mark Twain's observation that, "The difference between a *word* and the *right word* is the difference between *lightning* and the *lightning bug*." He also helped me learn to love poetry and to fathom it—well some of it.

The most important thing that college and reading my Bible did was… it let me see how utterly ignorant I was. I cringed when I thought of the years I had literally *thrown away* in junior and senior high. What a fool I'd been to have had so many teachers, so willing to invest in me—if I would have just let them. I grew ill at the thought of how much I'd slept through and what I'd squandered. But I could do nothing about the past. I could only start over from this point forward. This I did with a vengeance, and began by asking God to please help me make up for lost time.

***

One night, after another wonderful dinner, I finished my homework, read my Bible and prayed. I was headed upstairs and was just outside my room when I felt a great urge to pray some more. I knelt where I had been standing and as I prayed a strange little poem came to me 'out of the blue.' I leaned over while still on me knees, grabbed a piece of scrap paper and wrote it down exactly as it came to me, title and all. It was as follows:

**I AM**

I am q
Without U
Lord Jesus.

*The Beginning*

As I received it and wrote it, I felt the presence of God fill the room. I felt Him to the point that I literally began to tremble. As for the poem itself, I had no knowledge or recollection that 'I AM' was one of the primary names of God, and would not know it until several months later.

As to the *meaning* of the poem... the letter 'q' is virtually useless without a 'u' behind it. There are only two words in language that I know of that use a 'q' without a 'u' following. One is the name of an Arabian gulf; Aqaba, and the other is the scientific term; qat.

As the letter "q" is virtually useless without the "U" behind it, so it is with mankind in general and me in particular. Without Jesus... we are all but totally worthless. It is Jesus only that gives life meaning and lasting expression. Without Him, all we do is exist.

Then instead of ending the poem with '*The End*' I ended it with '*The Beginning*' implying that finding Jesus is the *beginning* of life, and of that life there is no *end*.

I stayed on my knees a long time both staring at the poem and praying to God that He would give my life meaning and help me find a reason for existing. A few hours later, before I went to bed, I prayed again. This time, I found myself lifting my hands into the air as I'd done on New Year's Eve and as I'd done on the sidewalk a few days before. I had never seen this done before and it was not so much that I consciously chose to, as it just felt so natural. I also began to pray out loud to God as I'd done in Denver on New Year's Eve, and again, it felt wonderful to do so. I told God how much I loved Him and wanted to serve Him and thanked Him profusely for His Goodness to me.

I talked to Him, and referred to Him using the terms "God" and "Father" and "Lord" etc. However, when I prayed saying, "*Jesus*, I love you," I felt as though a current of spiritual electricity shot through me. So, I said it again and felt it again, but I felt it a little stronger. I went back to calling on "God" and "my Father" but when I said the name *Jesus* once more I felt the 'jolt'.

I had of course prayed using the name "Jesus" before, but this time it was very different. I decided right then and there to 'check this out.' I lifted my voice somewhat louder and said "God… I love you. Father… I worship you and want to serve you. *Jesus*…" As soon as I uttered that name I felt the definite and immediate touch of the Spirit come upon me. I went back to saying "Oh, God, you are everything… My Father, I love you… precious Holy Ghost you're my friend… Jesus… Jesus… *Jesus*…

*JESUS*…***JESUS*… *JESUS*… *JESUS!*** …"

The next thing I knew I was shaking all over and starting to… well… stutter. My jaw was shaking and my whole being seemed engulfed by His Presence. My mouth and tongue in particular was… *going all over the place*, and to be honest—I got scared. I'd never had anything like this happen before and it really shook me. I loved what I was feeling and knew it was from God, but it was *so* overwhelming that I felt like I was losing control. While I'd 'lost control' for the devil thousands of times and in appalling ways, I'd never experienced anything as wonderful and splendid as this. But it seemed to be *too much*, and I didn't have any idea what was happening. So… I grabbed my Holy, Holy Bible and my cross that glowed in the dark, crawled under the covers, pulled them up close about my face, turned out the light and snuggled under the covers in effort to hide. After a while I quit shaking, and then I whispered to God, "God…uhh… Jesus… I don't know what you're doing… but what do you say we do it some other time… okay?"

I lay there thinking and prayed in tiny segments, so as not to 'stir God up again' until I finally went to sleep. The night this took place was January 10, 1972. I know this for sure as I wrote the date down on the paper after I wrote the poem, "I am q without U, Lord Jesus."

I awoke the next morning, put my Bible back together, found my cross, put it about my neck and went to school.

***

A week later, as I caught the bus from Belmont to the downtown campus, I was captivated by a stunningly beautiful sunset. The bus ride the next evening was more striking yet. Having been raised in Colorado, I was used to seeing beautiful sunsets but these were especially spectacular. Maybe my appreciation of them had to do with so many of my thoughts being upon God and His creation and with Professor Dickey making my world come alive poetically, but nevertheless I was captivated by these sunsets. When they were finally over each night I felt both sad and exhilarated. I also looked forward to seeing what tomorrow evening would hold.

I caught the bus that third afternoon, January 20th, 1972. At that moment however I had Professor Dickey on my mind rather than any sunset. It had not been a particularly great day in his classes. R.P. had been in top form and his caustic but efficient tongue had slashed about to painful effect in several directions. It was a good thing that I was trying to emulate Jesus, because if I hadn't I would no doubt have picked up greedily on his words and ways and tried them out on others. As it was, I was grieved and peeved by his aggressive, acerbic nature.

So as I carried my load of books into the bus and found a secluded seat towards the back my mind was definitely not on the afternoon sun and or the clouds.

I arrived at the downtown campus and went into the canteen to get a coke, candy bar and to watch the guys play 'foosball.' I usually had about a twenty to twenty-five minute layover before I had to go out and catch the bus that would take me to within a few blocks of my home. The foosball players were quite good and I was amazed at their skill. Whatever condition their grades were in, their games skills had been honed to perfection.

I looked at the clock on the wall and decided to go outside and wait for the bus. I approached the corner, and standing there was an acquaintance from high school. His name was Eric Craney, who had never been a particularly close friend, but he'd certainly never been an enemy either. He said he was catching the bus that day as his car was in the shop and that it was quite a shock to see me. I affirmed the same to him and we then began to trade information as to what had been going on in each other's life. As we talked I was not in the least surprised to find that he was going to college, as he was a natural to be doing something good with his life. I could tell that he was astonished to hear that I was attempting to turn my life around and attending college to boot (though he didn't say it, we both knew that he thought that I'd end up in prison or something).

He seemed genuinely glad when I told him that my way was being paid by an unknown benefactor, though at first his jaw came down and his eyes opened wide. As soon as I'd mentioned it, I wished I hadn't as I wasn't sure how Eric was making his way through school. Eric's father had passed away a few years before from a heart attack.

His dad had been a popular teacher and coach at Pitts Junior High and his death hit everyone very hard. I couldn't even imagine how it must have affected Eric let alone his family finances. Hopefully there had been some insurance or something laid up, but I didn't know how that could be on a teacher's salary. I changed the subject pretty quick by asking him about his older brother.

As we were talking, I remembered the sunsets and turned to see if today was again going to be a stunner. I was disappointed to see that everything was pretty well overcast and gray. But as I looked up through an opening in the branches of the trees I was surprised to see something I'd never seen before: in the southwest sky at about 'ten o'clock,' was a huge, perfectly oval hole set upright in the clouds. Within the oval hole were two colors that entirely filled each half. The left half was purple while the right half was green. I stood staring at the sight and finally asked

Eric to look and see if he saw the same thing. He came over the few feet, looked up through the trees to where I was pointing and said, "Wow." Apparently he did. I coaxed him to give a description until I knew that we were seeing the same thing. We both affirmed that it was unique and that we'd never seen it on that wise.

In a few minutes the bus came and we boarded it. It was pretty full so we had to split up and I found a seat next to a little old lady. After a few stops Eric got off the bus and we waved good-bye to each other. Eric really was a very nice guy that I never saw again as he was killed in a car wreck within a relatively short time.

As we rode the bus I perused my way through a stack of poems that my fellow classmates had written. After a while the elderly lady next to me said, "My, my… isn't that an odd, sunset." When I bent over a little and looked out over her head—I felt my heart stop within me. I literally felt that I could not breath. It was not fear that gripped me, it was awe. An awe that I didn't know existed. In a daze I felt my right arm going up and pulling on the cord to alert the driver that I wanted off at the next corner. I pulled it three times to make sure he understood. He did and I arose from my seat in a stunned condition and somehow walked down the back steps of the bus to the sidewalk… where I stood a long, long time looking at the sunset. My hands were at my side, barely holding my books, while tears welled up and began to run down my cheeks. Only the sound of my books hitting the ground broke my reverie—and that just for a moment. I looked at them, lying there on the ground as if they were something from another world. I finally stooped, picked them up and stood looking once again at the sunset… and the vision that would change my life forever.

Where the 'hole' in the clouds had been, there was now a large, yea giant, perfectly shaped capitol **U**… made from the clouds, and perfectly black as if it had been typed by a typewriter as big as the world. Sticking out of the lower right hand side of the cloud was the slash/mark such as you see coming out of a capitol **Q**. Inside the **U**, on the left half was the color of purple… while the right half of the inside of the letter was green. Surrounding the black letter cloud were streaking clouds of various hews of gold coming from every direction and pointing directly at it. In between the streaks of gold and surrounding them on all sides were various shades of sky that were from royal blue to azure in color. The instant I saw this on the bus I knew what it was all about… that I was receiving an unbelievable visitation from God. What I was seeing was the culmination and answer and revelation of the poem that I now knew for certain, God gave me.

I Am q
Without **U**
Lord Jesus.

The q and the U were *together!*

I began to walk and sometimes stumble down the street, never for a second taking my eyes off of the clouds, and crying every step of the way. It was at that moment I began to understand how much God desired to come into my life. When He did, he would change the 'q' of my insignificance into a capitol 'U' of His absolute significance and He would receive the glory. The 'U' would be Him, and the little slash of the capitol 'q' would be my flesh and what only He could do with it.

I somehow made my way home, totally oblivious of my surroundings, seeing only what was so powerfully emblazoned in the sky. I believed with all my heart what I was seeing, feeling and experiencing… and yet I was dumbfounded that it was happening to *me*. During all this time the black cloud of combined **U** and **Q** stayed exactly as it was while the surrounding clouds that were pointing to it, shifted slightly as if to accentuate it from different angles.

I finally made my way up Lancaster Street, turned on to Hollybrook, and walked to the house where I lived. Everything within me yearned to show my parents the sight, but when I got home, they were gone. My Dad's truck was not in the driveway, which was not unusual for that time of day, but my mother was not there either, which was unusual. When I ran back outside… the cloud, or vision or whatever it was, had vanished.

I sat down on the front steps, again as in a daze, and could not fathom what had actually happened. But it *had* taken place. And I will never forget it as long as I live.

***

Days passed, and in spite of the vision, and the prayer meetings, and the presence of God, I would at times become very lonely. I had seen virtually nothing of my old friends and no one called anymore. Word was definitely out that I was a "Jesus Freak" and no one wanted to be put into the uncomfortable position of having to talk to me about Him.

Normally, it didn't bother me to be alone with my books, my Holy, Holy Bible and pray to God. But on this particular night, I was lonely for human companionship. I visited but little with my parents, having no desire to watch television and, sad to say, that's about all they did. But, for whatever reason, this night I was so lonely, that had they been home, I might well have succumbed to the T.V. just to be with someone. Alas, they were not... and I refused to turn on the television... so there I sat, all alone.

After a while (at this very genuine, pity party) I began to cry. Larry Booker, the party animal, the life of any get-together, the gregarious rogue, was very lonely, very sad, very much had the blues, and was crying over it. Had there been a church family in my life I would have made a bee-line for it.

After a while, in the midst of a sob, I suddenly felt the presence of the Lord and innately knew that I was supposed to immediately stop crying. I tried to shed a couple more tears just for the enjoyment of it, but couldn't. Somehow I knew that my crying jag was finished and that I was to wipe my eyes and that *something* was about to happen, but I didn't know what.

I wiped my eyes, sniffled a little and began looking around the room for whatever it was that was about to take place. Then I heard it.

I heard a horn, honking! I actually heard the old familiar sound of a horn honking out in front of my house! I jumped up from the chair, ran to the door, opened it and looked outside. There sitting in his car with the window down was an old friend, Preston Ward. He yelled to me, "Hey, Larry, you old slime, c'mon let's go!"

I couldn't believe it! I ran to the car, never so glad to see another human in my life. "Get in!" Preston said. I started opening the door, then stopped, shut it and leaned in the window. "Prez buddy… I've got to tell you… I'm not drinking or drugging anymore."

"Yeah, I heard that. But it's okay… as long as you don't mind me drinking a beer or two." With that he lifted up a can of Coors as if to show me, somewhat apologetically, that that was all he had.

"Yeah, Prez, that's okay… it's just that I'm not drinking." With that, I jumped in the car and away we drove in fine Preston style, that is to say—fast. Except for the omnipresent radio which blared and the sound of the roaring engine, we traveled in silence. After a while Preston turned down the radio somewhat and said, "Larry, tell me… what's happened to you. I really want to know."

With that I proceeded to tell my old friend what little I knew about God, not even dreaming how little that really was. But tell him I did. As we talked and I 'warmed up to the subject' the words began to flow and I grew excited and animated. Preston listened closely, only interrupting occasionally with a question or two, which I either tried to answer or told him that I simply didn't know, which was more often the case. My inability to answer these questions troubled me immensely. Here was an old friend who took the time to break away from the crowd, seek me out, ask me about the God I was supposed to know—and I could barely help him. While I felt a rush of excitement over sharing the few wonderful things I did know, I was sickened by my ignorance.

We rode around for probably two hours before Preston took me home. He never offered me a drink, and only occasionally brought up 'old times.' He was genuinely interested in what God had done in my life, never laughed at me and was very respectful. It touched me more than words could tell, and I did my best to express my feelings. We then said good-bye and I went into the house.

When I got inside I could see the look of anxiety on my mother's face. She was filled with dread that I had gone somewhere and 'fallen off the wagon.' I hugged her close, so she could get a good smell, and told her that I was okay and headed to my room.

I lay on my bed and thought about the evening and about how lonely I had been. That God had interrupted my sorrow to let me know that he cared about me—and was going to do something about it, filled me with thankful wonder. What a God!

I also thought about how completely content I felt when talking to Preston about God. It was a beautiful feeling to share the knowledge of Jesus with him (precious little though it was). It made me feel *so* good and *so right* that at that moment I thought, "I wish I could do that the rest of my life."

The next moment I thought about Preston's questions that I couldn't answer and it about killed me. "Oh God," I prayed, "Please, please let me know you, and your word and have some answers... this world is so sad and sick and lost... please God help me to learn everything I'm supposed to learn and everything I need to learn."

I knelt by my bed and began to pray more earnestly and again, as I began to purposely call on the name of Jesus, I began the shaking, trembling process. I grew frightened once more and crawled under the covers with my Holy, Holy Bible and cross that glowed in the dark and once more told God that, I didn't know what was going on, but that somewhere down the road, not right now, I'd appreciate it if he'd tell me.

***

I continued my classes and loved *almost* every minute of it. The only minutes that were not enjoyable were the ones when I "slowly sank to the bottom of the ocean" in Psychology 101 and when Professor Dickey skewered someone.

It wasn't that Professor Dickey did it *all* the time, because he really didn't, it was only when some 'fool' didn't pick up on his wit, insight and understanding of poetry as fast as he was accustomed to. R.P. didn't suffer fools gladly. Still, I couldn't help but admire his wit, insight and understanding, though his arrogance infuriated me.

One day he and a fellow English professor performed the play, Beckett. It was about the Archbishop of Canterbury, (Thomas A. Becket) and King Henry II. During the entire play the two professors never left the two chairs in which they were seated back-to-back. When it was time to begin, a spotlight shown upon them and they turned in their chairs to face the audience. They then dialogued, using only their voice inflections to carry the day. There were no other gestures displayed and when that particular act was finished they again turned their backs to each other and the spotlight went out. The next act would begin with the light coming back on and the professors would face the audience once again and resume the dialogue.

Professor Dickey played the rough, rude, crude, passionate and ruthlessly brilliant Henry II (perfectly I might add), while the English professor portrayed the former drinking, womanizing companion of the King but who was now appointed by him to be the Archbishop of the Church. The problem arose between the two when the new Archbishop took his job seriously—hence the trauma and eventual murder of the Archbishop.

R.P. Dickey was mesmerizing. The pathos and tragedy of friendship, dreams and life gone bad, poured out of him with eloquence and power. It was a commanding performance that caught me by the throat, tore out my heart, and left me drained. I had no idea that a single performance, with one's soul poured into it, could be so effective. My 'awe'—if that's what it was—for the Professor reached new heights, but so did my curiosity about what it was that made this man tick. It would be but a few more days before I would see just how brutal and cold he could be.

***

One night I began to think about Norma, her world and what was becoming of it. She was still going to college in Grand Junction but I heard through a mutual friend that she wasn't doing very well. The drugs and drink were beginning to take their toll, and she wasn't happy to be there to begin with. Only pressure from her father kept her there but that certainly wasn't enough to make her do right while she was there. One of my deepest desires was for Norma to know and live for God. I had spoken to her about my change, but could see her eyes glaze over as I tried to explain it. I decided that night to pray yet once again for her. As I did I began to enter into very earnest, very intense prayer. I began to ask God to talk to her—to speak out loud to her—in unmistakable terms, that she would know that there was indeed a God. I kept praying, more and more intently, and soon found that whatever kind of prayer this was, it was taking a lot of energy and was actually straining me until my stomach muscles were hurting. After a while I felt the burden to pray so hard lessen and then finally lift completely. As I finished I somehow intuitively knew that God was going to do something for Norma.

Three days later I called a girl named Debbie that was a close friend to both Norma and I and asked her how Norma was doing. Debbie grew excited and said, "Ya know Larry, Norma told me the strangest thing yesterday, and I really don't know what to think about it. She said that she was in one of her classes and that she began to 'lose it,' you know, kind of 'crack up' and she started crying and couldn't stop. She said it was like her whole world was caving in on her and she just couldn't take it. She finally got up and left the class, leaving her books and everything. She went outside the school building and saw a big bush by the door and all but dived in behind it and hid there between the bush and the wall of the school. She lay there for a long time crying and shaking, and suddenly she heard a voice speak out loud to her from somewhere."

My heart was in my throat, and had stopped beating altogether. I couldn't believe what I was hearing, or feeling, but knew that God had heard and answered my prayer. I shakily said, "Debbie, what did the voice tell her?"

"Well, *she* said that all *it* said was, 'Norma… Norma… I've never seen you like this before.' But she also said that as soon as she heard it, she stopped shaking and crying and that a beautiful peace came all over her."

I proceeded to tell Debbie exactly how I had prayed, and could immediately tell that all of this was just a little too much for her. She mumbled a few things about all of the stuff in life that we would never understand and quickly excused herself off the phone. The quick exit didn't bother me, as more than anything else I wanted to get to my knees and tell God how very wonderful He was to hear and answer the prayers of somebody like me.

After a while, I thought of my old friend Joe Arguello and what his life was becoming. Since he'd been back from Vietnam, he was truly going downhill. He was either stoned, drunk or shooting up something all the time.

I had called him a few days before to try to talk some sense into him but he cut me off pretty quickly with a "Look, Larry, when I want the Jesus business I'll ask for it. Till then, I don't want you—of all people—preaching to me." While that pretty well shut me up, I did manage to tell him that the only reason I'd called was because I cared about what happened to him. His answer to that was, "Well, that's nice. I'll keep it in mind." Then he softened a bit and said, "Look, Larry… just pray for me."

"So," I thought, after telling God thanks for answering my prayer for Norma, "I will pray for Joe. I have met a God that will answer prayer."

I then began to pray that God would "Wake Joe up," and, "Shake him till his teeth rattled, and cause Joe to see that there really is a God that wants to save him and help him." Though I could not somehow pray with the same earnestness that I had for Norma, I had a very real confidence that God was going to do something to "wake Joe up."

Three days later, Joe and another hot-rodder were drag racing on the Beulah Highway (Hwy 78) that comes into Pueblo from the mountains. They started the race at La Vista Hills Road and ended up heading into Pueblo going 130 m.p.h.

There were certain times of the day when that portion of road was not all that busy and sometimes guys would go there to get into some mean racing. Joe was in a first class race in his Barracuda and was paying far too much attention to the car next to him. When he looked up, in front of him there was a Volkswagen beetle, poking along at about 50 m.p.h. Joe slammed on his brakes, but knew that there was no way he was going to be able to keep from putting the beetle owner's rear bumper through his teeth, so he swerved to the right and into a long string of guard rail. He was going so fast that when he hit the railing it shot him almost straight up into the air into a power transformer on the top of a telephone pole, with both the transformer and his car exploding. What was left of the car came down on the other side of what was left of the pole and hit nose first into the ground.

The only thing salvageable from Joe's Barracuda was the car stereo and the bucket seat that he was sitting in. And my friend Joe… *did not get one broken bone*. Our buddy Edmund had been in the car, but before the race started Joe told him, "Get out and wait by the road. I don't want any dead weight in the car."

I called Joe to tell him how sorry I was to hear about his car, and that I certainly knew how what it felt like to lose one that you loved. I went on to tell him the main reason for my call—exactly how I had been praying for him—and reminded him that he told me to pray for him. When I finished, Joe was quiet for a long time. When he finally spoke he said, "Larry, the reason that I'm still alive is not because of God. My father died a few years ago and he is still watching over me."

I was stunned. I tried to talk to him some more but he was *not* interested. I ended the conversation with the fact that I cared for him, appreciated our friendship and was glad he was still alive.

I mourned deeply and could not help but think of that conversation when Joe died in a motorcycle wreck a few years later.

***

School was over for the day and I caught the bus to the downtown campus. To kill the time I began watching the foosball fiends play. They were ferociously intent upon their game when a rather small fellow came and stood at the far end of the table. He watched them for about a half a minute, and then said in a solemn voice, "I want you to know that Jesus Christ is soon to come back to earth again." He did not speak *real* loud but he did make sure that everyone at the table heard him. The foosball fiends were thrown completely off stride and the players on the field reacted accordingly, becoming very clumsy while the ball more or less went where it wanted to. The competitor's eyes riveted upon the intruder but came back to the game in short order as they resumed their play. I took note that one of the boys was back to top form almost immediately but that the other three had as yet to regain complete composure.

The young man who had wreaked this havoc looked at each of us one by one and receiving no reaction other than the momentary confusion in the game turned and walked towards another group of students that were sitting in the lounge area. I watched him go and was intrigued by his audacity as well as his message, and thought to myself, "I'd like to talk to that guy."

At that moment I heard a voice speak out loud to me very clearly; "***Go to the restroom, you will meet him there***." I was astounded. I literally could not have heard the voice any clearer if I'd had a set of headphones on my head and someone had spoken a message into it through a microphone hook-up. I knew that God had just spoken to me. I was in a state of astonishment.

I picked my books up from off the nearby table where I'd left them and headed straight for the men's restroom. I walked in, looked around and saw no one, placed my books on one of the sinks and walked to the far back of the restroom. I leaned against the wall, folded my arms over my chest and watched the door. Within three seconds time the young man came walking in. Our eyes immediately locked as I unfolded my arms and stood there with what was probably a very stupid look on my face. After a few seconds, I cleared my throat and said, "I… I really appreciate what you said out there… about… about Jesus coming back. I'm a Christian and I believe that also... I mean the part about Jesus coming back." He stared at me, walked over and looked up into my face. (He had no choice but to look up as I am six-foot-six, and he was probably about five-foot-two or three.) He gazed into my eyes as if he were looking for something and then said, "Have you received the Holy Ghost since you believed?" I looked down at him not sure exactly what it was that I'd just heard.

"What?" was about all I could come up with by way of an answer.

"I said, have you received the Holy Ghost since you believed… you know, since you became a Christian?"

Though I'd been wondering the same thing myself, I managed to stammer, "I, I think so... I know that I really feel good."

"Have you spoken with other tongues?"

"Have I what?" I said.

"Have you spoken in other tongues… in another language?" he answered, just a wee bit impatient—no doubt at my ignorance.

Not being certain what he was talking about, and desiring not appear as ignorant as I knew I was, I said, "Well… I took Spanish in the seventh grade."

Though his eyes grew very wide at that, he didn't seem to be impressed. Then he said, "No… No not that… have you spoken in other tongues as the Spirit gives the utterance?"

Now I definitely didn't know what he was talking about, except that I knew I'd read these words somewhere in the Bible, probably in the part called the Acts of the Apostles. So, I honestly, and firmly said… "No. I don't think I've ever had any of that stuff happen to me."

"Unto what then were ye baptized?" he shot back.

"Unto what what?" I answered.

"How were you baptized? Was it in Jesus' Name or in the titles 'Father, Son and Holy Ghost'?"

I stared at the young man for at least half a minute and finally said, "You know… I've never been baptized... in any name."

"Then you need to be baptized in the Name of Jesus Christ for the remission of your sins."

"For the what of my sins?"

"For the remission… the forgiveness… the complete washing away of your sins. You know… so your record is completely cleared and clean."

"Now that," I said, "would be a big job… but a very nice thing."

At that moment the restroom door opened and two more young men entered into the room. One was a tall, thin young man, almost as tall as me, while the other was about maybe five foot eight inches or so. Their buddy—who had been moving in closer to me with every question he asked—now turned, saw them and said, "Samuel, Richard, this fellow has never been baptized in Jesus Name and doesn't have the Holy Ghost, but seems like he might be somewhat hungry for truth."

The two young men quickly surrounded me and began firing a host of questions at me. I stared open mouthed from one to the other and tried to give something of an answer when I could. I even tried to answer when I only halfway understood what they were talking about. Then I remembered the bus I had to catch, shot a glance at the clock on the wall and knew I just barely had time to catch it. I quickly excused myself, and tried to tear myself away, but the little guy must have felt like I was just too big a fish to let go of that easy. He was right along side of me, still making statements that I was not really comprehending and asking questions that I couldn't catch hold of with my racing, confused and running-late mind.

Finally, as I was up the stairs and beginning to run, he grabbed my coat and said, "Hey wait… please… here take this." He was holding out to me a little white piece of paper, that I could see had a name, phone number and address typewritten on it. The name was, "The Disciples," and I could tell by the address was on the East side of town—the rough part. I shoved the paper into the pocket of my ever-present railroad coat and began to run and yell for the bus that was starting to close its doors.

That night at about 6:30 p.m. I pulled the little piece of paper out of my coat pocket and stared down at it for a long time. I began to think about the three young men that I'd met that day and whatever group or church that they were with. In the late sixties and early seventies, there were many little groups of religious people meeting throughout Pueblo, and the rest of the nation for that matter. Up to that time I had paid little, if any, attention to them. They had names like, 'House of the Broken Bread,' and 'The Alabaster Box,' and 'The Good Samaritan Inn," and *House of the Free Food*, and *House of the Bare Feet*, and *House of the Strumming Guitars*… and such like.

That night as I thought of the strange occurrence of that afternoon and my meeting of the young men, I was struck by an idea. I would do my best to get as many of these little groups together as possible and with a united effort maybe we could affect a lot of people for Jesus. We could go down to the park and sing songs and tell people about the Lord and help many souls to come to God. "And I'll start with those people I met today! They need as much help as anybody," I thought.

I grabbed my coat and began rummaging through the pockets for the piece of paper they had given me. I had been somewhat rattled by them and had almost thrown the paper away, but was now very glad that I hadn't. I drew it out and read it again. I bounded up the stairs, went around the corner and began dialing the number. Almost immediately the phone was answered by what sounded like a young woman with a "Praise the Lord!"

"Well," I thought, "That's different." I cleared my voice and said, "Uh, yes... well listen... I met some young men today at Colorado State this afternoon and they gave me this paper with your phone number on it. And well, I was wondering when you meet... you know for like, church and stuff?"

"We are right now meeting every night. Would you like to come to service?"

"Uh, yes, yes I would. But I don't have a car right now..."

"Oh that's no problem! Just tell us where you are and we would be thrilled to give you a ride."

I gave her my address and the directions. We talked a little more and then said good-bye. It was already 6:30 and she told me that their services started at 7:00.

I went upstairs and washed my face, combed my long hair, and made sure I had on my cross that glowed in the dark. Just for good measure I grabbed several religious poems that I'd written, folded them and stuffed them into the back pockets of my very faded blue jeans. I guess I sub-consciously took them for my credentials, just in case they were needed.

At 7:00 p.m. I saw them pull up in a 1961 Chevy. I ran out before they had a chance to get out and come to the door, as I wasn't sure but what they might get started in on my dad. Buzz had a real hard time with religious people coming around and bugging him. My religion, he could handle as long as we only discussed it when he wanted to.

There were three guys in the car and as I opened the rear door on the driver's side, I immediately saw that it was the same ones I'd met earlier at the campus. They were grinning from ear to ear and all three gave me a hearty "Praise the Lord!" "Hi," I said, and proceeded to make myself comfortable. The driver was the first guy I'd met that day at the foosball table and then in the restroom. The little guy was like a bulldog and got started right where he'd left off.

"Now, did you say that you had received the Holy Ghost?"

"Oh boy," I thought, "Here we go again." I began slowly—with Eddie's sorry line—"What I said was, I think I do…because I've really made a change in my life and I feel wonderful…" That was as far as I got when he spun his head almost completely around (I was sitting behind him) and excitedly began telling me of the many magnificent things God had done in his life since he'd received the "baptism of the Holy Ghost and fire."

"I used to be hooked so bad on drugs, but I'm telling you… what'd you say your name was?"

"Larry… Larry Book…"

"Yeah well, let me tell you, Larry, He's wonderful! He's glorious! You just wait and see if what I'm telling you ain't so! Ain't that right, Brother Samuel?"

With that, he tossed the ball to 'Samuel' who never missed a heartbeat and ran towards the goal line for all he was worth.

"Larry, I'm telling you, when you get the Holy Ghost you're going to know it! Not only will you speak in other tongues—that means different languages—but you'll feel something so special and glorious that you'll never be the same…"

The driver at that point grabbed the ball back from Samuel and started running again with a story of how he should be dead, "But Jesus spared me, Larry, He spared ME! ME of all people! A low down wretch…"

Now with this line of reasoning I could relate, though I was beginning to wonder how much longer we were going to be spared if this enthusiast didn't get and keep his eyes on the road.

More than once the tall, quiet guy riding shotgun had to grab the wheel to keep the car from going where none of us wanted to go. He didn't say anything, or interrupt the driver; he would just every now and then... grab the wheel.

Thus we made it from the south side of Pueblo to the east side—the rough part of the east side—and by the time we'd arrived I was completely convinced that I was in the presence of animated sincerity the likes of which I'd never seen.

As we pulled into the driveway I found that we were not at a church, at least as I'd known it, but were at a house, and music was coming from the garage. They were having church in a garage of all places and I could hear the music and singing of the people before we had even pulled to a stop and turned off the engine. Though I was taken aback, the druggy, hippy world had pretty much prepared me for just about anything.

We got out of the car and the driver (I'd learned in between breaths that his name was Roscoe) literally ran for the door while the guy who'd been sitting next to me, Samuel, walked quickly, waving me onward with every step. The tall guy, who kept grabbing the wheel, seemed to be moving slower and I soon realized why. As the other two whizzed into the 'church' he took me by the elbow and stopped just outside the door. He looked me in the eyes and just barely louder than the music, said in a very serious tone, "Larry, I want to tell you something and please hear me out. My parents are wealthy people, extremely so, and to make a long story short, I have been literally almost everywhere, and seen most everything. But, Larry... when you enter into this church, it may seem strange, maybe real strange, but, please believe me... *this is where it's at.*"

With that, he let go of my arm, opened the door and showed me inside.

The one-car garage had been made into a makeshift meeting room, with a small podium at one end and a series of roughly built benches facing it. To my chagrin, the door we'd entered was just to the right of the podium and everyone's head turned to watch us come in—everyone that is but the man seated on a bench behind the podium. His eyes were closed and remained so. Their attention went quickly back, however, to their voluble singing. As the benches were pretty-well filled we made our way to a bench in the very back, a development for which I was deeply appreciative.

Hands were in the air, and many were not singing at all but were praying out loud and praising God and were especially praising Jesus. While I had to admit that I did the same thing in the privacy of my bedroom I couldn't imagine acting like this in front of other people. Then I thought of the time that I'd gotten down on my knees on the sidewalk and lifted my hands and told Jesus out loud that I loved him and thought that, well… maybe it wasn't so bad after all—but did they have to be *so* enthusiastic about it?

I guessed there to be about 30 to 40 people there and as I sat down I drew comfort from the poems I could feel in my back pockets. The young man leading the songs was very excited about his job, but I wasn't sure just what his job was as no one seemed to be paying much attention to him and most of the folks seemed to be lost in their own little private world. The rather fast song ended and a sound erupted that was even louder than the music—everybody and I mean everybody, even the kids, were now praising God out loud, yea, out very loud. Furthermore, and even more rattling to me was that several were talking in strange languages. All of this together shook me up pretty good, and I began to wonder just what kind of church this was. One thing for sure, I'd never seen anything like this in any of the churches that I'd gone to in my life.

By and by, I noticed a sign on the wall by the door that I'd just entered. It was on a piece of lightly stained plywood and was written in cursive, gold glittered lettering. The message written on it was…

> "***Then Peter said unto them, repent, and be baptized every one of you in the name of Jesus Christ for the remission of sins, and ye shall receive the gift of the Holy Ghost.***" –Acts 2:38

I gazed at the sign for a long time remembering having read it a few times in my Holy Holy Bible. At that point I realized that I'd forgotten to bring my Bible, which of course, wouldn't look good for me. After all, my main purpose in coming was to convince these people to work with me and get all the other small groups around town together to make a statement to the city. I kept reading and re-reading the sign, while the people kept singing. Every now and then I noticed that the man sitting on the bench facing us was staring at me. When our eyes met, he didn't look away—so I did.

This whole process went on for a while and then the man sitting on the bench behind the podium got up and went to it. The young man leading the songs immediately stepped down and took a seat in the front, while the man—I had guessed by this time that he was the pastor—continued the singing and worship, but only for a few moments. He brought the song to a close and the people followed suit—except for one lady who was really into what she was doing. She seemed oblivious to how things were quieting down and actually began to sing louder and then began talking in a foreign language very loud. When she stopped it was very, very quiet, like everyone was waiting for something to happen. Whatever they were waiting for didn't happen, so after awhile the man opened his Bible and said "Let's turn to…" and he at that point gave out a scripture.

For the life of me I cannot recall what scripture it was, but I vividly remember what the gist of his message was—and who it was he was preaching to. The upshot of it was, "You cannot love this world and God at the same time. Every man must somewhere, someplace, sometime must make up their mind just who it is that they are going to serve: themselves and their passions, the world and its wiles, or God and His Word." For all that this man might lack in social graces, he more than made up for in intensity and focus. He got his point across 'in spades'… which I also found out before he was through, wasn't right either.

Two things occurred to me as he poured out his heart. The first was that he was making sense out of many scriptures that I had been reading and wondering about. I knew these scriptures were calling for a life of absolute dedication, but I didn't know how they were to be applied in everyday life. One thing I knew for sure—I was very thankful that I'd quit watching television.

The second thing that kept coming to my mind was how relieved I was that I'd brought some of my poems. They were about the only thing I had on me that would prove I was as Christian as they were, especially as I'd forgot to bring my Holy, Holy Bible. Then (thank God) I remembered my cross that glowed in the dark, and from that point on kept reaching up and rubbing it whenever the preacher would hit a particularly sensitive point. I felt sure that between the glowing cross and not so glowing poems I could impress these people of my bonifides.

Finally, the man finished his comments and some of the people went up to the front and prayed. When I stayed where I was, some of the others came back to where I was to ask if I would like to pray. I told them that I'd already prayed that day and that I was sure I would do so again before I went to bed. When they began to press me on the subject, I reached into one of my back pockets and pulled out some poems. I also unbuttoned a couple of the top buttons of my shirt so they would be sure to see my cross. That must have been impressive because some of them looked quite surprised. I unfolded one of the papers and said, "Would you like to hear a poem that I wrote about Jesus?" They stared at me so I took this to mean that they were in expectation. I had begun to read the poem I'd written by the side of the road several weeks before about the sun, when the little bulldog that I'd first talked to worked his way through the gathering crowd, listened for a moment and said, "Did the Holy Ghost help you write that?"

I was rather exasperated with the fellow at that point and said a little more harshly than I meant to, "He must have, because I felt good when I wrote it… and it is awfully good," though I knew in my heart it wasn't—especially by R.P. Dickey's standards. At any rate I went back to reading it, when the tall young man, came to my side, cleared his throat and said, "Uh, Larry, let's go over to the parsonage and have some fellowship." I had no idea what he was talking about concerning the terms "parsonage" or "fellowship" either one, but was glad to oblige, simply in order to get out of the center of the ever growing crowd.

He took me by the arm and led me out of the garage and into the house. The house I gathered was the parsonage, but still didn't know what made it so, or who it housed. Anyway, in a moment or two, one of the women came approached me with a plate of what looked to be 'banana nut bread' without the banana or nuts. "Ahh," I thought, "This must be fellowship." With that I gladly took a piece—an end piece, for I love the crust—and happily placed the lion's share of it in my mouth.

It was without a doubt the driest piece of banana nut, or whatever it was, that I'd ever attempted to eat. It seemed that the more I tried to chew it, the bigger it got. In fact, I was having some difficulty getting most of it off the top of my mouth. "If this fellowship," I said to myself, "you can have it."

Presently, the little guy, Roscoe, came running up and said, "Well, tell me, tell me, what do you think?" I thought he was asking me about the 'fellowship' and said "Well… to be honest with you… it's a little dry." He actually took a step back and stared up at me in a kind of hurt astonishment. Only later did it dawn on me that he was asking me what I thought about the church service. I then asked him if I he could possibly get me a glass of water. He slowly nodded his head and proceeded to do it in a somewhat chastened manner.

As I was washing down the fellowship, he asked me yet once again if I had the Holy Ghost. I thought I'd choke and actually did start to bring back up some of the fellowship but thankfully was able to control it and get it back down. As I was clearing my throat, I stopped him from re-asking the question with a halt sign from my right hand, and finally croaked, "What I said was… yes, I do think I have the Holy Ghost as I have been feeling very good for the past six or seven weeks—since I began to live for God."

I noticed that the kitchen where we were standing was filling up quickly and that folks were sitting wherever they could, some even on the floor. Though I knew this to be an omen of… something, I was thankful that they were not all crowded right around me as they had been in the garage—I mean church. I began counting to myself and realized that there thirteen people in the rather small room, including myself. As I'd always been a little on the superstitious side I wished someone would either leave the room or come into it, as it didn't look 'lucky,' especially for me.

My momentary reverie was broke when the young man who'd been leading songs asked, "Larry, uh, that is your name isn't it?" I nodded my assent and he continued, "Larry, have you spoken in other tongues?" I decided not to bring up my seventh grade Spanish class, for I intuitively knew that we would be talking apples versus oranges. So I answered, "You know, I'm not really sure what you mean by *speaking in other tongues*." He didn't hesitate for a second before answering.

"Speaking in other tongues is simply speaking in a language you never learned before—but it's not you that is actually speaking, it is the Spirit of God. When this happens, it is the sign that He is now filling you with His Spirit." All in the room seemed pleased with his statement and began to nod their heads vigorously to show it. As for me, I didn't know what to say so I didn't say anything but simply took another drink of water hoping that I could buy some time. The water was halfway down my throat when Roscoe said, "Larry, if you'd get baptized in Jesus' name you'd get the Holy Ghost, the real Holy Ghost!"

At that, the water came back up and this time I did choke, and just barely kept from spraying it everywhere. Some of it did however come out my nose and when I instinctively reached for a handkerchief—which was stupid because I never carried one anyway—all I came up with was one of my poems. Though the poem was, admittedly, not all that great, I was not about to wipe my nose on it. I wasn't sure what to do, and was standing there looking exceedingly stupid when one of the girls handed me a dish towel, for which I was very thankful. Roscoe continued as though nothing had happened: "That is however if you repent. You surely know that you have to repent or being baptized will do you no good whatsoever. All you'll do is get wet."

Finally he had touched on something that I could speak somewhat intelligently about. I finished wiping my nose, cleared my throat and said, "I have repented… very thoroughly as a matter of fact."

"Really?" he said, but I could tell he did not believe it. "Then you ought to be thrilled about going on and getting saved by being baptized in the name of the Lord Jesus Christ for the remission of your sins and letting God fill you with the Holy Ghost, which you will know for sure you've got, because you'll speak in other tongues as the Spirit gives the utterance, not just *feel good*."

I stared at the little guy for quite a while before I answered. "What do you mean about me 'going on and getting saved'? I am saved and have been since New Years Eve when I repented and gave my heart to Jesus Christ."

With that said... we got started. Thirteen Bibles seem to appear from nowhere, and one of them was thrust into my hands. I noticed that the man that had preached was not in the kitchen, nor was he anywhere to be seen. I knew that he'd been in the house for I'd seen him come in. Now he had disappeared leaving this onerous task to his disciples—which was just fine with me.

"Larry," the leader of songs said, "Before we go to the Book of the Acts of the Apostles, which is the book that tells us exactly how the church got started, let's go to the book of Luke, chapter 24." I stumbled around a little bit, trying to find 'Luke' but finally made my way there.

He waited for me patiently, and then proceeded to say: "Now after Jesus was resurrected from the dead, He appeared unto his disciples at various times over the course of the next forty days. During that time He instructed the Apostles on what they were supposed to preach in order for His Church to be established. These instructions are referred to as 'The Great Commission.' Larry, we must pay very close attention to all of this as our salvation depends upon us being 'built upon the foundation of the apostles and prophets, Jesus Christ himself being the chief corner stone.' That's Ephesians chapter 2, verse number 20. Let's read together what Jesus said in Luke 24:44-48:

"*And he said unto them, These are the words which I spake unto you, while I was yet with you, that all things must be fulfilled, which were written in the law of* Moses, *and in the prophets, and in the psalms, concerning me. (45) Then opened he their understanding, that they might understand the scriptures, (46) And said unto them, Thus it is written, and thus it behooved Christ* **to suffer**, *and to* ***rise from the dead*** *the third day: (47) And that* ***repentance*** *and* ***remission of sins*** *should be preached* **in his name** *among all nations,* ***beginning at Jerusalem****. (48) And ye are witnesses of these things."*

After slowly reading these verses, and placing emphasis on certain portions, the song leader said, "Now, Larry, do you understand this so far?"

Not wishing to come across as being 'slow' but not wishing to miss anything either, I answered, "I think so."

"Good!" he said. "But please notice Larry, that Jesus told the Apostles that in order for '*repentance*' and '*remission*' of sins to be done correctly—it must be preached '*in His Name*' and it must begin, '*in Jerusalem.*'

So, let's read what happened in Jerusalem on the Day of Pentecost, on the day that the Church of Jesus Christ actually began." I was able to find the Book of Acts pretty quickly as I'd spent so much time there. He then led me to the second chapter where we read;

*Acts 2:1-4 And when the day of Pentecost was fully come, they were all with one accord in one place. (2) And suddenly there came a sound from heaven as of a rushing mighty wind, and it filled all the house where they were sitting. (3) And there appeared unto them* ***cloven tongues like as of fire****, and it sat upon each of them. (4) And they were all* ***filled with the Holy Ghost****, and* ***began to speak with other tongues****, as the Spirit gave them utterance.*

The song leader, Brother Tedder, (I finally asked him his name) then explained how that this phenomena of speaking in other tongues as well as the 'rushing mighty wind' had drawn a great crowd of people to where the newly Holy Ghost filled disciples were gathered. After some mocked, saying they were drunk and others sincerely wanted to know what this meant, the Apostle Peter—the man with the keys to the Kingdom—began to explain to the assembled crowd, how that Jesus had been crucified by them and that he was '*both LORD and Christ,*' that is, ***both Jehovah God as well as Messiah.*** At that point the gathered crowd was convicted and wanted to know what they needed to do.

Acts 2:37-39 *Now* ***when they heard this****, they were pricked in their heart, and said unto Peter and to the rest of the apostles,* Men *and brethren,* ***what shall we do****? (38) Then Peter said unto them,* ***Repent****, and* ***be baptized every one of you*** *in the* ***name of Jesus Christ*** *for the* ***remission of sins****, and* ***ye shall receive the gift of the Holy Ghost****.*

*(39) For the promise is unto you, and to your children, and to all that are afar off, even as many as the Lord our* God *shall call.*

This is where Brother Tedder (and most of those in the room) drove home the point to me that if the people *then and there* were baptized in Jesus name, and the people *then and there* received the gift of the Holy Ghost, evidenced by that fact that they spoke in other tongues (languages), and that I, Larry Booker, needed to obey the same Gospel and receive the same experience.

This was so because: Jesus Christ is "*The same, yesterday, and today, and for ever*" (Hebrews 13:8)

And, this gospel is an "*everlasting gospel,*" (Revelation 14:6); baptism must be done in Jesus' name because; "Neither is there salvation **in any other:** for there is **none other name under heaven** given among men, whereby **we must be saved"** (Acts 4:12); that everywhere you find anyone being saved in the first church the elements of repentance, baptism in Jesus Name and the infilling of the Holy Ghost were always the first elemental ingredients. They then took me to Acts 8:4-8 "*Therefore they that were scattered abroad went every where preaching the word. (5) Then Philip went down to the city of Samaria, and preached Christ unto them. (6) And the people with one accord gave heed unto those things which Philip spake, hearing and seeing the miracles which he did. (7) For unclean spirits, crying with loud voice, came out of many that were possessed with them: and many taken with palsies, and that were lame, were healed. (8) And there was great joy in that city.* (These verses showed the ***repentance,*** *the change of heart* of the Samaritans while the following verses reveal that they were baptized in Jesus name and received the Holy Ghost)

*(12) But* ***when they believed*** *Philip preaching the things*

*concerning the kingdom of God, and the* **name of Jesus Christ, they were baptized**, *both men and women. (13) Then Simon himself believed also: and when he was baptized, he continued with Philip, and wondered, beholding the miracles and signs which were done. (14) Now when the apostles which were at Jerusalem heard that Samaria had received the word of God, they sent unto them Peter and John: (15) Who, when they were come down, prayed for them, that they might* **receive the Holy Ghost***: (16) (For as yet he was fallen upon none of them: only* **they were baptized in the name of the Lord Jesus.)**

We then went to Acts 10:1-4

*"There was a certain man in Caesarea called Cornelius, a centurion of the band called the Italian band, (2) A devout man, and one that feared God with all his house, which gave much alms to the people, and prayed to God alway."* (This was a repented household)

*(3) "He saw in a vision evidently about the ninth hour of the day an angel of God coming in to him, and saying unto him, Cornelius. (4) And when he looked on him, he was afraid, and said, What is it, Lord? And he said unto him, Thy prayers and thine alms are come up for a memorial before God. (5) And now send men to Joppa, and call for one Simon, whose surname is Peter: (6) He lodgeth with one Simon a tanner, whose house is by the sea side: he shall tell thee what thou oughtest to do."*

In these verses I saw that Cornelius, though an already God-fearing man, received the Holy Ghost and was commanded to be baptized in the name of the Lord.

*Acts 10:44-48 "While Peter yet spake these words,* **the Holy Ghost fell** *on all them which heard the word. (45) And they of the circumcision which believed were astonished, as many as came with Peter, because that* **on the Gentiles also was poured out the gift of the Holy Ghost.** *(46)* **For they heard them speak with tongues***, and magnify God. Then answered Peter, (47) Can any man forbid water, that these should not be baptized, which have received the Holy Ghost as well as we? (48) And* **he commanded them to be baptized in the name of the Lord.** *Then prayed they him to tarry certain days."*

We then took an excursion to Acts 19:1-6 where Paul found

believers in Christ that knew not of Baptism in Jesus Name, nor of the Holy Ghost.

*"And it came to pass, that, while Apollos was at Corinth, Paul having passed through the upper coasts came to Ephesus: and finding certain* ***disciples****, (2) He said unto them,* ***Have ye received the Holy Ghost since ye believed****? And they said unto him,* ***We have not so much as heard whether there be any Holy Ghost****. (3) And he said unto them,* ***Unto what then were ye baptized****? And they said, Unto John's baptism. (4) Then said Paul, John verily baptized with the baptism of repentance, saying unto the people, that they should believe on him which should come after him, that is, on Christ Jesus. (5) When they heard this,* ***they were baptized in the name of the Lord Jesus****. (6) And when Paul had laid his hands upon them,* ***the Holy Ghost came on them****; and* ***they spake with tongues,*** *and prophesied.*

(It was at this point I realized where Roscoe picked up his opening lines to me when we'd met in the restroom; "***Have ye received the Holy Ghost since ye believed****?*")

It was pointed out to me that these people of Ephesus were like me and my experience in Christ. They, as well as I, believed, but had not yet received the Holy Ghost. Once they were baptized they received the Holy Ghost. The question was then raised if I would be big enough, willing enough to be like them and also be baptized?!

I was then shown what Ananias told Saul of Tarsus (soon to be the Apostle Paul) in Acts 22:16, after he had repented.

*"And now why tarriest thou? arise, and* ***be baptized****, and* ***wash away thy sins****, calling on* ***the name of the Lord****."*

But I, Larry Booker, was hard to convince, and took on the nature of a Sears, 'Die-Hard' battery. I argued and squirmed and twisted and turned every way possible to get out of what the Scriptures seemed to plainly declare. These that I've given were but a tiny sample of what poured forth that night. But I struggled with all of it, and one by one began to wear these dear people out. They of course did not give up on what they believed, but decided that they would pass out from exhaustion before I would 'give in.'

Finally, at about 2:00 a.m. they were all gone—but one—Wiley. Wiley was the one person who throughout the night had kept referring me back to Matt 24:35:

*"Heaven and earth shall pass away,* ***but my words shall not pass away***."

Wiley, above all others, had been exceedingly patient and kind, stopping to make sure that I understood what was being said without making me look stupid. He was a small, thin young man, maybe 5' 4" and couldn't have been over 110 lbs. soaking wet. He had blonde hair and a pleasant smile and way of expressing himself. And I, had worn out everyone else but him.

I was still making excuses for myself and the rest of 'Christendom' for not taking the Book of Acts seriously, literally and obediently, when I noticed that Wiley's face was beginning to… to shine… or glow… or something. He was sitting on the floor (why, I don't know… I guess he liked it) and I was leaning against the counter (why I wasn't sitting, I don't know… I was probably too 'wound up') when I first noticed it.

I leaned over to get a better look. Wiley's face really was beginning to glow, and was becoming brighter and brighter! His eyes were brilliant and animated, but his voice nevertheless remained very calm... and authoritative.

I didn't know what to say about this… this… phenomenon… so I didn't say anything. But I never took my eyes from off him for a second. He had been making a scriptural point when I first saw it. As I did not reply, but stared at him, he repeated the point and patiently awaited my reply. Finally, I began to answer him by way of a question, but before I was three words into it, Wiley interrupted me with the answer. I was surprised, and stared at him even closer. Then I started to say something else—got out only about two words—and he interrupted again with the answer to the unstated question. Now I was mesmerized, but nevertheless pressed on with more questions.

"But what about all the…"

"Larry, it will not matter in the end what anyone says *about* the Bible, be they a scholar, or preacher, or teacher; it only matters *what* the Bible says." He then opened his Bible (a very well used one) and after few pages of thumbing began reading to me: "*And I saw the dead, small and great, stand before God; and the books were opened: and another book was opened, which is the book of life: and the dead were judged out of those things* ***which were written in the books****, according to their works.*"

I stared at him dumbfounded. How did he know what I was going to ask? I tried again.

"But what's..."

"Going to happen to all the people that were never born again of the water and Spirit according to the New Testament experience? The same thing that's going to happen to those that *were*... they're in the hands of God... not me, and not you. Larry, the only light we have to walk by is the light of this Word, and from what Jesus said, and the Apostles taught, they are lost because they never had their sins remitted. Furthermore, how are they going to be raised in the rapture if they never received the Holy Ghost? Paul said, '*But* ***if the Spirit*** *of him that raised up Jesus from the dead* ***dwell in you****, he that raised up Christ from the dead shall also quicken your mortal bodies* ***by his Spirit that dwelleth in you****.*' Also: '*...****if any man have not the Spirit of Christ, he is none of his.***'"

"But, Wiley, they're such..."

"Good people. Yes I know. But what did Paul say about the good, religious Jewish people in Romans 10:1-3? '*Brethren,* ***my heart's desire and prayer to God for Israel is, that they might be saved.*** *For I bear them record that* ***they have a zeal of God****, but* ***not according to knowledge****. For they being* ***ignorant of God's righteousness****, and* ***going about to establish their own righteousness****, have* ***not submitted themselves unto the righteousness of God****.*' Larry, what Paul said about these 'religious' people is true of all 'religious' people. Regardless of their zeal, what's done has to be based on Truth. Otherwise people are simply trying to establish their own righteousness—like Adam and Eve's fig leaves—it's just not good enough. We must submit ourselves to God's word, God's righteousness.

Besides, Larry, none of these peoples destinations are based on me or my judgement anyway. It's not up to me, I don't even have to debate that with you… it's up to God. Even the Apostle Paul said, '*For what have* ***I to do*** *to judge them also* ***that are without****?… them that* ***are without God judgeth****…*'

I'm here to tell *you*, Larry, how to get ***within***. And, Larry, *you know* scripturally… ***you are without***… and you know what you have to do to get ***within***. The ***very same thing that they had to do to get in*** in the days of the Apostles… '*Then Peter said unto them, Repent, and be baptized every one of you in the name of Jesus Christ for the remission of sins, and ye shall receive the gift of the Holy Ghost.*'"

I thought to myself, "If I hear Acts 2:38 one more time tonight I'll…" But Wiley interrupted me yet again.

"Larry, don't ever get sick of hearing what you need to hear to be saved. If you had died in your car wreck and were in Hell right now you'd give anything in the world for a chance to be baptized in Jesus Name' and receive the Holy Ghost."

Now I was staggered. I had never said a word to Wiley or anyone else that night about my car wreck. This was entirely too much. The guy was reading my every thought, glowing like a… a… light bulb, and pinning me to the wall with his answers. I was now to the point that I was afraid to ask or *even think* anything.

"Jesus loves you, Larry… if He didn't you wouldn't be alive… and you wouldn't be here… and I wouldn't be talking to you," said one of the kindest young men I'd ever met.

"Wiley, listen… I've, I've got to pray… I really have got to pray. Can I go back into the gar… the church and pray for a while?"

"Sure. It's unlocked. You pray there and I'll be here praying for you. But Larry, listen… no matter how long or how hard you pray, you can't pray enough to change the Truth. The Bible says what it says, and when you're finished, it will still say it. Pontius Pilate couldn't have said it better, 'What I have written… I have written.'"

With that last insightful thrust, I made my way outside, looked around at the meager facilities and thought, "Surely this pitiful place can't be the hold of something this, this… profound. What about the great Cathedrals I've prayed in…" Immediately I thought of the stable that Jesus was born in, and felt ashamed. I looked up at the stars, hoping that somehow they held the answer to my dilemma. But they stared back, and kept their peace.

I went into the makeshift House of God to pray, fell to my knees, and almost immediately began to groan and weep.

It wasn't that I didn't want to be baptized in Jesus' Name—I wanted it desperately—and I wanted the Holy Ghost even more. Because of all the verses that had been shown me, I now knew what had been happening to me the several times the presence of God had come into my bedroom, when I'd been calling on the name of Jesus. I knew why I had been shaking. Had I not crawled into bed frightened, I could have already received the Holy Ghost.

But two very powerful things were at work in me that night. One was, I couldn't bring myself believe that repentance, baptism in Jesus' Name and receiving the Holy Ghost was the fulfillment of the new birth of the water and Spirit.

That the only way to fulfill the 'death, burial and resurrection of Jesus Christ,' was our death *in repentance*, our burial *in baptism in Jesus Name*, and our own personal resurrection *by receiving the same Spirit that raised Christ from the dead*.

That it really was the only way to be saved.

The second thing at work on me that night was, how could I keep going to college if I was really going to make a totally clean break with the world? How could I keep subjecting myself to Professor Dickey's filthy vocabulary in particular, and so much humanistic agnosticism in general, when I needed to be listening to God? And how could I quit college when someone believed in me enough to pay my tuition, and in quitting, snuff out the first bright ray of hope that I'd displayed to my family in many a year? My mother's heart would be broken with disappointment.

Though my feelings about school and God were based on a *misconception*, (Daniel proved that you could live for God in the middle of a Babylonian court) nevertheless, at the time it was a real issue to me. Little did I know that God would use even this *misconception* to perform His perfect will in my life.

At that moment however it was all in my face and I didn't know what to do but cry. And pray and cry and wail I did. I fell to my knees and began to cry aloud; "***Jesus... Jesus... there must be some other way... there must be other ways to be saved... this can't be the only way...***"

I looked up and through my tears saw the wall that was facing me and the sign that was upon it...

> "***Then Peter said unto them, repent, and be baptized every one of you in the name of Jesus Christ for the remission of sins, and ye shall receive the gift of the Holy Ghost.***" –Acts 2:38

I felt like I'd been shot. I buried my head between my knees and screamed, "NO! NO! NO! JESUS, IT CAN'T BE... IT CAN'T BE... THERE'S GOT TO BE OTHER WAYS TO BE SAVED!!"

I must have prayed in this horrid fashion for fifteen minutes. At the end of that time, my throat was totally thrashed, and I was physically, completely spent. I then lay down on my side in a fetal position and, unable to pray any longer, simply sobbed my heart out. After another lengthy period of time I began to straighten out at least the upper part of my body. I lay there, and after another moment or two, opened my eyes. The first thing I saw was,

> "***Then Peter said unto them, repent, and be baptized every one of you in the name of Jesus Christ for the remission of sins, and ye shall receive the gift of the Holy Ghost.***" –Acts 2:38

I closed my eyes and bent back into a curl. After a little while, I slowly straightened out, got to my knees, then to my feet, and stood there rather wobbly. I started to read the sign again, forced my eyes away and made for the door. I stopped in the doorway, raised my left hand and felt of the glittered lettering of the sign, slowly lowered my arm and went out the door.

I went to the house but was unsure as what to do. I opened the door slightly, thinking that Wiley had perhaps gone to sleep, but there he was, sitting as he had been and I could hear him praying quietly. There was now only one light on in the front room but I could make him out well enough to see that he'd been crying also. In a moment he stopped and looked up intently into my face, no doubt searching for the surrender he'd hoped I'd made.

"Wiley… I'm sorry, I really am… but I need a ride home."

"Of course. Of course, Larry… let me get my keys."

On the way to the car I saw a trash can and stopped, slowly reaching up and taking hold of the little cross that glowed in the dark. Jerking it, I broke the chain… and dropped it into the trash can. I got into Wiley's car, noted that he'd watched my every move, took note that his face was no longer glowing. It was a wordless journey, the several miles to my house.

***

I was awakened by the feeling of someone watching me and opened my eyes to see my mother. She was very close to my face and was no doubt trying to see if I smelled of liquor or marijuana. It probably confused her that I would come in so late and not reek of one or both. I hoarsely assured her that I was all right and that I'd been to a church on the East side. She looked at me dubiously, but was relieved nonetheless. I arose exhausted. I hadn't arrived home until 3:30 a.m. and didn't fall asleep until after 4:30. I gingerly dressed, forgoing a much needed shower, gathered my books and walked numbly upstairs. Mom met me with a bacon and egg sandwich wrapped in a paper towel and said, "You probably ought to take this and go right to the bus stop. Even then, you might not make it."

I kissed her on the forehead, realized that I loved this wonderful woman more than anyone else in the world, and regretted horribly having ever hurt her so much and so deeply through the years. I made my way outside and began walking towards the bus stop. Having taken a bite of the sandwich I realized I was anything but hungry, and threw the remainder of it to the dog that belonged to the folks on the corner.

"That's funny," I thought, "I should be starved." The last thing

I'd eaten was some 'fellowship' the night before.

***

Aching listlessness is the only way I can describe my next few of days at school. I rose to no occasion or challenge by R.P. or any other professor. I simply sat and stared out the windows thinking, "I don't belong here. I belong out there… learning about God, living and working for Him… enjoying the Holy Ghost." Finally, I decided to go see the Chaplain and see if he could give me some answers and alleviate my agony. I think his name was Mr. Gordon.

I entered his office and was told by the secretary that he'd be in shortly from lunch if I'd like to have a seat. My next class was piano, and I didn't care if I missed it or not. Presently the Chaplain arrived and in short order we had introduced ourselves and entered a small conference room. I asked him if he had a Bible I could use, and he quickly fetched one from off the bookshelf. I opened it to the Book of Acts, turned to chapter two and verse thirty-eight, and read it one more time to make sure it hadn't changed. *"Then Peter said unto them, Repent, and be baptized every one of you in the name of Jesus Christ for the remission of sins, and ye shall receive the gift of the Holy Ghost."* It hadn't.

I put my finger on the verse, turned the Bible towards the Chaplain and said, "Sir, could you please tell me what that verse means and what we're supposed to do with it?"

I was utterly sincere, and I'm sure he could tell it. He looked down to where my finger pointed for a long time as if lost in thought. Then he slowly pulled the Bible out from under my finger, closed it, looked at me in the eyes and said, "Larry, I know who you have been talking to. Let me tell you something, these people go around trying to turn everything and everyone upside down. What I'm about to tell you is all you'll ever need to do. Larry, all you have to do is, accept the Lord Jesus Christ as your personal Savior, and you are saved. Once you do *that*, you are totally, completely, and forever saved."

I wanted to scream that I'd done that several times in my life, once in front of my parents while kneeling at a footstool after listening to Billy Graham on television. But at this point I was grabbing at straws so I didn't say anything. I just stared at him, then at the Bible, then back to him. In a moment or two he cleared his throat and said, "Larry, would you like me to pray with you, now?"

I continued to stare at him for an embarrassingly long time then shrugged my shoulders and nodded my head in the affirmative. He smiled and said, "Let's bow our heads and pray…

"Lord Jesus, you see this young man… he is confused and in need of you this day…" Then he said, "Larry, repeat after me," and so continued, "Lord Jesus…" After realizing he was waiting for me, I said in a very weak voice, "*Lord Jesus…*"

"I ask you this moment to come into my heart…"

"*I ask you this moment to come into my heart…*"

"I accept you as my personal Savior…"

"*I accept you as my personal Savior…*"

"From hence and forevermore…"

"*From hence and forevermore…*"

"In Jesus' Name…"

"*In Jesus' Name…*"

"Amen."

"*Amen…*"

With that said, we both lifted our heads—he quickly and me slowly—he with a very gratified smile and me with what had to be a very blank expression. I didn't know what to do, or what he wanted me to do. I had hoped to at least feel *something*, but, to be honest, I felt like death, warmed-over. As he kept smiling expectantly at me, I finally offered him my best, but at best, anemic smile. He immediately took my right hand, began shaking it heartily and said, "Larry, I can tell by the look on your face that Jesus Christ has come into your heart!"

I sat, still feeling nothing but the shaking of my hand. At that instant the door opened and the associate Chaplain entered the room. The Chaplain arose from his chair so I followed suit and he immediately said, "Gary, I want you to meet, Larry… err…"

"Booker" I mumbled.

"Yes! Larry Booker. Gary, this fine young man has just received

Jesus Christ as his personal Savior."

Gary immediately began pumping my hand with the same energy and smile while saying, "Larry, I can see by the look on your face that Christ has come into your heart."

I smiled my same sickly smile—not purposely but because it was the best I could muster at the time—expressed my thanks to them and said I had to get back to class. As I looked back before closing the door they were both smiling broadly.

When I entered into the hallway I stopped and stood still to see just exactly what it was that I did feel. After a moment or two I raised my left hand to my right wrist, and pinched it as hard as I could. After a moment I said out loud, "And that, Jesus… is all that I feel."

***

A couple of days later the Chaplain caught me outside one of my classes and began telling about a trip that the College Youth Christians were about to take. It was a two night snow trip and he wondered if I'd like to go along. I assured him that I would very much like to go along and asked what I needed to do. He said for me to come to his office the next day or so and he'd have me fill out some paperwork for insurance purposes and let me know what things to bring. He also said for me not to worry about any expenses other than personal purchases I might make while there.

I was ecstatic for several reasons. One, since my trip to the little garage church, my prayer life had gone virtually down the tubes. No more were there mighty visitations of God trying to give me the Holy Ghost. For a while I would say the same things I used to say, especially focusing in on the name of Jesus… but all I could really think of was, the Acts 2:38 sign on the wall—which I was sure was still there—and I knew for positive was still in my Bible—because I tended to check on a daily basis. When I thought of that verse, and what I'd done with it, my prayers felt like spit running down my chin. Regardless, I did beg God to please not give up on me and to somehow still have His way in my life. But, due to my waning prayer life, I was becoming increasingly bored and less inclined to do my homework, read my Bible... or, as I said, pray. I had not as yet reverted back to watching television... but it was getting mighty tempting.

So the thought of getting out of my basement for two nights and three days was a Godsend. Furthermore, because it was a Christian retreat, I had high hopes that I could find answers and relief to my dilemma of disobedience to the Word of God.

On the day I was to leave I borrowed some money from the 'Bank of Booker,' that is, my mother, and packed my scanty stuff into a backpack. We were leaving from the College Campus at the end of the day and going somewhere up above Colorado Springs. In my whole life I had never been anywhere with a group of Christians so this was an entirely new experience for me. It had been years since I'd been on a school outing and this had more or less the same feel. But how did Christians, real professing Christians act anyway? Some of my buddies, like Special Ed, *said* they were Christian, but it was obvious by their lifestyle that all it meant to them was that they believed: '*Somewhere back yonder in history, Jesus really did live.*'

I climbed aboard the bus and saw that the Assistant Chaplain was coming also. I thought that I remembered his name was Gary... or maybe it was Jerry? I wasn't going to worry about it as I figured that I'd overhear someone call his name after a while anyway.

I sat towards the back of the bus, in fact, as far back as I could get. While many people thought of me as a wild extrovert, the truth of the matter was, I was actually very shy and tended to speak only when spoken to—unless I was drunk. As the bus filled up I hoped that I wouldn't have anyone sit by me.

I had my notebook in my knap-sack and was looking forward to working on a poem that had been rumbling about in my mind and scribbled on several pieces of scrap paper. I was digging through the bag trying to locate those particular scraps when presently I heard a voice ask if anyone was sitting there. I looked up into the face of a girl who was pointing to the seat next to me. She looked about my age—but then they were all somewhere around my age—was more than a little pretty, and was holding a stack of books that looked to be way too heavy.

"No… I mean yes, I mean, sure… it's empty," and scooted a little closer towards the window. I noticed as I did so that there were other seats open, some in fact that had no one on the bench. She plopped down with a sigh of relief and momentarily closed her eyes and breathed in deeply.

She had dark brown, somewhat wavy hair that reached down past her shoulders, and was probably about five foot, five inches tall (when you're as tall as I am you take notice of height). She had very large and lazy hazel eyes and a mouth that even when relaxed, as it now was, seem to be smiling. After a moment or two she let out the breath that she'd been holding and looked at me.

"Thank you," she said.

"For what?"

"For letting me sit here."

"Well, I don't exactly own the bus, and you did seem to be carrying a load."

"Yeah, too big a load," and said it like she really meant it.

"Isn't this is supposed to be some kind of a retreat?" I asked, "Why'd you bring all the books?"

"Well, I didn't really *need* to bring them, but then again, I thought if I found some time on my hands I'd wrap up some of the stuff that needs done." To that I didn't respond other than to nod of my head, and went back to finding my poem. After a while she asked, "What's that your working on?" She was staring down at my scratchings.

"Well, it's poetry… or at least I like to think it is."

"Poetry? My, my… isn't that interesting. Do you write a lot of poetry?"

"Not really… and I'm just getting started, so it's really not very well developed yet."

"Well developed? What's that mean?"

"It means it's not very good."

"You need to let someone else be the judge of that don't you?"

"Yes, and I have. His name is Professor R.P. Dickey, and he has several times assured me that it is anything but… 'developed' if you know what I mean."

"Oh I've heard about him. He's something else isn't he?"

"Yes, to put it mildly."

I didn't know her name and didn't want to ask as I was hoping the conversation would die down. I didn't much feel like talking, even to a girl as friendly and pretty as this.

"What's your name?" she asked.

"Larry. Larry Booker," I answered, not asking for hers.

"My name is Priscilla. Priscilla Colfax."

"Well it's good to meet you, Priscilla Colfax," I said with a smile and went back to what I knew was going to be a lost cause, at least for this trip. Indeed it was; before we arrived I pretty well knew the life story of Priscilla Colfax.

The bus arrived a little before sunset and we all made our way into the very nice facilities. I was given a room all to myself and couldn't have been happier. We put our belongings away and went to supper in the cafeteria. I went through the buffet line and then sat down at a table pretty much in the corner where no one else was sitting. I thought I'd managed to pull off a semi-quiet meal when Priscilla came bouncing out of the food line with four friends—two of whom were girls and two were boys. She saw me and immediately began to lead them all to my table.

"My, my, Larry, you're not going to be anti-social are you? Here, I want you to meet some friends. This here is Tony and Marie and this is Connie and Justin. This is Larry Booker and he's a poet."

I groaned inwardly, and suddenly wished that this girl and her friends would just go away. But I looked up, smiled my semi-best smile and brought another bite of chicken to my mouth. They all were seated and immediately the girls began asking me about my poetry while the guys pretty much smirked over their mashed potatoes. I couldn't really blame the guys, and I shined on the girl's questions as best as I could.

It wasn't that I didn't want to be nice to these Christians, but in truth I felt so very awkward. I was like a fish out of water. Why did I ever think that I could mix and mingle with people like this? I was only a few steps away from the heathen I'd always been, and had felt myself edging back closer to the brink ever since my experience in the east side garage-church.

We were pretty far along in the meal when one of the girls said, "Oh, we forgot to pray over the meal." I was embarrassed because the thought never, and I mean never even crossed my mind. I wasn't aware that you prayed over meals if it was not Thanksgiving or Christmas. "Tony, you pray," Priscilla said.

Tony slowly licked the gravy off of his fork, stuck it into the remaining pile of potatoes, lowered his head and said, "Rub a dub dub, thanks for the grub, Yea, God," and went back to eating. They all laughed and grabbed at their food.

I, who had never been known for being pious, was however, very taken aback at this prayer and sat back to look at this guy Tony. Tony, upon seeing me, winked and pulled a now clean chicken bone out of his mouth and wiped his lips with his sleeve. I then heard Priscilla say, "Oh Tony, you're something else," and figured that she had seen the look on my face.

That was just the beginning. As Tony warmed to his surroundings, he also warmed to his profaneness. With jokes, and jibes and jabs at everything sacred he proceeded to take my breath away. What was worse was the way everyone at the table laughed and added their own two cents worth. Finally after about ten minutes of what was sure to be a comedy hour at the expense of God, I rose to my feet—my food half finished—and turned to go.

"Larry!" I heard Priscilla exclaim, "Where are you going?"

"To my room." And with that I left. As I was walking away, I heard her remonstrating with Tony and making the case that I was after all a brand new Christian. I never heard Tony's reply but I did hear them all laugh—including Priscilla.

We gathered that night in a spacious room that held a large fireplace. The Associate Chaplain began the evening with a few remarks that seemed to be well received, though I personally didn't quite get his point. When he finished he asked each of us to please stand, state our name and tell a little bit about ourselves. He began with the first person that was sitting to his left, which meant that I had a reprieve for at least a few minutes.

Most of the young people gave only their names and where

they were from but every now and then someone would really open up. One who did so was a young man who seemed very much in earnest. He proceeded to not only give his name, but his age: 19, where he lived: Piedmont, and the fact that he'd been a Christian for the past three years. Then he actually began to talk about what it meant to him to have Christ as his personal Savior, and how that his deepest desire was to share that knowledge with everyone he could. I noticed that several of the kids were embarrassed, some faces were etched in solemnity, but a few were in agreement—at least in various stages of agreement. It made me feel a lot better to know that everyone didn't take God as lightly as Tony and company.

When I thought about Tony, I began to look around for him, and noticed that he wasn't there, nor was the other guy, Justin, that had been at the table. Nor, for that matter, was Priscilla's friend Connie. In the process of scanning the crowd I saw Priscilla, and saw that she was looking at me somewhat sheepishly.

I grew more nervous as my time to speak grew nearer. When it finally came I stood and said, "My name is Larry. Larry Booker and I'm from Pueblo. I… I've been a Christian since the first of the year, well actually, since New Year's Eve." At that, some of them giggled, and I didn't blame them. The under Chaplain, not willing to let it go said, "And while I'm thankful for Larry's resolution, he came into our offices just a few days ago and received Christ as his personal Savior." I don't know if he expected an applause or not, but when he didn't get it he moved on to the next guy.

Finally we were through identifying ourselves and we sang a couple of songs that I had never heard before. I mouthed the words as best as I could, kind of stumbling and faking my way through. When that was over, the Chaplain introduced 'Pastor McGuire' who with a set of shimmering teeth that any used car salesman would give a month's wages for, proceeded to greet us.

He started with a little light banter about what he'd had to go through to get there, but how it was worth it to be here in the beautiful Rocky Mountains with such a fine group of young Christians, who would no doubt affect their world in a wonderful way. He then told a humorous anecdote about the Chaplain and a trip they had taken together one time to Israel, and then he read his text.

I cannot recall what the verses were, but I was so unfamiliar with the Bible that it was pretty much lost on me anyway. I do recall some of the main points of his message and was deeply moved by them. One thing in particular that thoroughly gripped me was his recollection of a young man he'd met somewhere on the East Coast who had accepted Christ as his personal Savior and proceeded to sell everything he possessed, which was apparently quite a bit, and give it all to poor people. The young man thereafter possessed only a bicycle and a few clothes and spent his days going from park to park on the eastern seaboard telling people of the goodness and saving power of Christ.

I was very impressed by the story and wished that I'd known about it the night that I was nailed by Wiley and company. But upon reflection, I figured that Wiley would have an answer for that also—especially if his face was glowing.

At any rate, I was extremely impressed with Reverend McGuire by the time he'd finished. He was a powerful orator and had a lot of neat stories. The thing I appreciated the most was that when he was finished I felt much more validated in my belief (or hope) that I was indeed saved.

Upon conclusion of his talk he asked us all to bow our heads and he proceeded to pray for all of us that we would go forth into the world in the Spirit of Christ and do His will in bringing others to Him. When he finished praying I heard a few of the young people say, "Amen," so I followed suit and said it also, though when I did, mine was the only voice to be heard.

With that we were all on our feet in a matter of seconds and making our way to the game room. The pool tables were quickly taken by the guys and a few of the girls, and as I wasn't all that great at ping pong I just snagged myself a cup of hot cocoa and found a seat in the corner of the room.

After a while the evening speaker came into the room having changed out of his suit and tie into a sweatshirt and pair of blue jeans. Room was immediately made for him at one of the pool tables and he began to play with what looked to be well practiced skill. It was nothing for him to take up to six, seven or eight shots in a row with a demeanor that showed that he obviously took the game very seriously. After a while I arose from my sofa chair and made my way over to the table. The preacher was in between shots and was chalking up his pool stick when I screwed up enough courage to walk over to him and compliment him on his sermon. .

"Sir," I said, "The talk you gave tonight was really very good… and I enjoyed it immensely. I… I just thought I'd tell you." He never responded. He just looked at me, nodded his head, gave off something that amounted to a grunt, and returned to the table to take another round of shots.

I was mortified. I retraced my steps back to my chair and fell down with a plop. I rehearsed the words I'd said to the man several times to see if maybe somehow I'd offended him, and couldn't for the life of me think what I'd done wrong. Every now and then I noticed some of the guys at the pool table sneaking a glance in my direction and I began to believe that I'd committed some kind of social faux-paux of which I was totally ignorant.

By and by as I watched the man, his mannerisms, his carriage, demeanor and how he responded to the young men about him, I began to realize what the problem was; he was stuck on himself. The guy thought he was God's gift to… whatever needed a gift. Either that or he'd simply got up on the wrong side of the bed. Maybe it was both. Whatever it was I was deeply hurt and more than a little disillusioned. I finally arose and began to make my way to my room. As I went out the door of the game room the Chaplain was coming in.

"Going to bed so early, Larry?"

"I'm just going to my room. I think I'll read a while."

"Don't forget breakfast at 8:30 to 9:30, then we'll be having a chapel service at 9:45."

"Is somebody going to be speaking to us?"

"Yes. Reverend McGuire will bring us morning devotion. Wasn't he good tonight?"

I turned my head back to the pool table to take another

long look at the Reverend McGuire. After a few moments I said, "Well, he is a very good speaker, and an even better pool player… but his social skills are rather on the weak side." With that, I turned to go to my room leaving the Chaplain to stand with his mouth open. My social skills at that moment were not exactly at perfect pitch either.

As I made my way to the room I resolved to *never purposely mistreat* anyone who might someday, for some reason, have reason to look up to me for something other than my height.

I lay on the bed thinking about all these young people, the chaplain, Reverend McGuire…and the little church that I'd visited on the East Side. Eventually I turned out the light and dreamed the night away. They were not particularly enjoyable dreams as Wiley and his shining face kept working his way into them.

The next morning I ate a hardy breakfast, but not with the company that I'd kept the previous evening. The youth that gathered around my table didn't seem to have a profane character leading the way, so it was a rather pleasant meal.

I finished my breakfast and reluctantly made my way back the room with the fireplace. I made it a point to sit in an unobtrusive spot, hidden away as much as possible. As I was still smarting from the snub the night before and wasn't looking forward to hearing the Reverend McGuire. At the same time, I did decide that he'd make a rather interesting 'case study"—or at least that's what we called them in psychology class.

The group began to make their way in, and Chaplain Gary called things to order with a chorus, which everybody knew, but me. He asked for a few testimonies and presently a couple of girls said some sweet things while it took the boys a little longer to respond. I didn't move a muscle lest it be interpreted as a desire to speak and if anything seemed to shrink with each passing moment. After cajoling a couple of guys to say something, the Chaplain led us in another unknown hymn. Then it was Reverend McGuire's time to inspire once again.

He was not nearly as stimulating as he'd been the night before… must have sensed it and kept his remarks very brief. Our eyes caught once but I could tell he didn't remember me, which suited me just fine.

Before we were dismissed the chaplain stated that in the night service we would be having a talent show. All would be called upon to participate, be it with a song, a sermonette, a comedy skit, or something. Most seemed to take this news with good grace, but I was completely mortified. A *talent show?* I immediately began to think of ways to get out of it. I could feign sickness as I had a thousand times through my school years, but upon remembering that I was trying to be a Christian—at least I told myself I was—I knew that I really couldn't do that. "Well," I thought, "I'll just have to tell the Chaplain that I have absolutely no talents whatsoever and plead, yea beg, to be excused."

When I tried it, he just laughed, slapped me on the back and asked me what I was majoring in at College. I told him that I hadn't really decided yet, but that I wanted to be a writer.

"A writer of what?" he asked.

"Books... poems... stories... stuff like that."

"What have you written so far?"

"Just a little poetry," I said, and hastened to say, "And believe me its not very good."

"Well Larry," he said, putting both hands on my shoulders, "Just read us a poem." And with that said he smiled and walked off.

I went back to my room and began rummaging through my knapsack and realized that I didn't have a single poem with me—save for the scraps of what I'd brought to work on and the one in my head about the "q" and the "U." I wasn't about to bring that one out simply to be stared and laughed at.

Finally I brought out the writing tablet thinking that maybe I could put a little something together and get through this nightmare. I said a prayer that somehow God would help me, and then putting the pencil to the paper—I began to write... and the words began to flow. They came to my mind and rushed out onto the paper. I couldn't believe how easy the poem came to me and before I knew it I was finished. Not that I was looking forward to reading it—far from it. But at least it was there.

I lay down on the bed hoping to take a nap but was entirely too wound up from the poem and the exhilaration that came from writing it. After a while however sleep overtook me and I crashed.

I slept so hard that I awoke not really knowing where I was. I lay there trying to get orientated, and as it came to me I looked at my watch. Realizing that supper was being served I started to move and it was then that I remembered the talent show. I lay back down with a groan, turned my head towards the table and stared at the poem. I groaned once more and at last sat up on the edge of the bed. "Oh well," I deliberated, "It'll be over in a little while." With that, I arose, folded the poem, put it in my back pocket and went to supper with very little appetite.

The talent show was neither a smashing success nor a dismal failure. Amongst the young people gathered was the usual array of the humbly gifted, those that knew they were gifted and relished in it, the shy, the funny, the backward, the sullen, the terrified, the clueless and those that were bereft of any apparent endowments.

There were several girls with capable singing voices, a few with beautiful voices, but only one that had the ability to wrench my heart with an emotional rendition of a gospel song, which, again, I'd never heard before. A couple of the young men did Biblical skits (at least I think they were Bible—I wasn't up on it enough to know for sure) and a couple more did comedy routines. Tony and another irreverent guy did a profane Cheech & Chong skit and for a moment I thought the Chaplain might have to bring it to a halt. One girl performed a comedy stand up routine and was all in all pretty funny. She did some very good imitations of famous people from Nixon, to Ed Sullivan, Marilyn Monroe and even Elvis. Her funniest imitation was of Chaplain Gary being nervous over Tony's skit, but the very best—at least for me—was the right Reverend McGuire, preaching while he made pool shots. The girl was a hoot and my only regret was that Reverend had not yet showed up to see it. Had he been there, I would have come out of my shell, whooping and hollering and clapping just to let him know that there was more than one way to be a jerk.

But as soon as the thought ran through my mind I felt bad and knew that I was supposed to be a Christian—whatever that was. (Still… she *was* funny)

As we made our way through the talent in the room, first calling for volunteers and then relying upon the draft, I grew more and more pensive. Except for the girl who presented the emotionally moving gospel song, there was little being offered in a serious vein. I knew that my poem would be an absolute bomb simply because it was so serious—let alone not being good. I'd have given anything if the girl with the emotional song had been right before me. I was growing sicker by the minute and began to formulate a plan to slip out, hopefully unnoticed, while everybody was laughing at something.

The folks were kindly applauding a boy who had just made a donkey out of himself with a yodeling routine—he was serious for goodness sake—when I started to make my get-a-way. It was then that the Chaplain called my name. He must have witnessed my movement and thought that he'd better strike before it was too late. I fell back in my seat and stared at him like a deer caught in the headlights.

"Larry, uh… Larry… would you like to come up to the front? Larry here is a poet and he is going to, I believe, read us one of his poems."

I groaned. This was getting worse by the second and I could already see the smile beginning to appear on Tony's smart face. I shakily asked if it would be okay if I could just read it from where I was sitting, knowing that if I had to stand up in front of these people the paper would no doubt shake loose from my hand and my knees would surely buckle. Chaplain Gary consented, probably due to the nervousness he could already detect, and because he saw that I was quite pale.

I reached into my back pocket and with trembling hands unfolded the paper. I had to spread it out on my knees as hold it there as my hands were shaking and I didn't want to appear a bigger idiot than I already felt. I was already dreading when I would come to the place in the poem that I'd have to turn it over and read the other side.

I would have given anything for a glass of water as my throat felt parched—but I'd have spilt it anyway. I cleared my throat, twice, maybe even three times and began.

"The name of the poem is, 'Lost and Found." Please forgive, but it is a very rough draft and needs a lot of work. I just"—at that point I cleared my throat again—"wrote it a couple of hours ago." I looked up before I began and wished that I hadn't for I was cursed to see Tony give Priscilla a wink and a smirk, and then was cursed even worse by Reverend McGuire's entrance into the room. I took a deep breath and began,

"Wallowing, following, in sightless being
Serving one under, never quite seeing
The heads of life's coin nor joy in mere breathing,
O' one from down under you try our hearts bleeding
Out love meant for others, you've crept sweetly stealing…
Look what you've done… where lies your meaning?
Sin's muck in life you'd have us bathe,
In this you give death… in this you give shade
To hide from God's light, from the beauty we're made.
O' lost one be gone… hide in prides gaze,
Of ones you've mislead ones living though dead.
I am but one who've known you good
In blindness chopping you're vile under wood.
O' the axe truly sharp and the wood chopped good
But slowly I realized the stack ever stood."

(At about this point, I began to find my rhythm and my voice. In fact I felt as if a gust of wind had filled my sails and I was actually beginning to 'glide across the water.')

"You bellowed at sin and laughed at my toil
For wood of that cut builds fire to boil
Fools like I who've oxened your soil…
Till now.
For one day King Jesus speaking through courage,

Pronouncing through one past living in sewage,
Said unto me, "Where art thou?"
There's a line in life where good and bad touches
On one side is life, the other side clutches
Of demonry which has faith in you.
But through Jesus that grasp is quickly broken
Through love, truth and faith you'll receive God's token,
This is a promise kept on a cross,
For there Jesus died to wage war against loss
Of soul's He created to which Satan would toss
To Damnation, forever… to truth you must cross!
This I did, lost one do hear…
Your bid for my soul is leaving my ear,
For from saved day on I've taken up arms
To war against you, your evil, your harms.
My weapons are one you'll not understand
Faith in Lord Jesus… His Word, my command."

When I finished, the room was very quiet and most all eyes were upon me. Those that were not, seemed to be stuck to the floor. My heart was racing and I had no idea what they were thinking. Finally the Chaplain cleared his throat and said, "Well, Larry… that was… uh… really, uh really nice. In fact, it was uh, from the uh… heart… don't you see. Well, okay, now let's see… who's next…? How about you, Sandra? What do you have for us?"

Had there been a trap door I'd have pulled the lever in a heartbeat. I ventured a glance and saw Priscilla looking at me while Tony had now pointed his smirk in Sandra's direction. Before I lowered my head again I noticed the Reverend McGuire staring at me also.

I don't remember much about the rest of the retreat except for the fact that we did some sledding and inner tube runs down a pretty steep ski slope. Other than that, the rest was a blur and I was very glad when it was over. Nobody said anything to me about my poem except for Reverend McGuire who gave me his business card and asked me to send him a copy of it.

I never did.

***

I went back to college on Monday and sat distractedly through my classes. I saw Chaplain Gary as well as the main Chaplain in the foyer of the main entrance but I avoided them and went to class. That afternoon, as I was about to go outside to catch the bus, I felt someone pull on my coat sleeve. I turned and to my horror saw… Brother Wiley. His face was pointed up towards mine and it bore his customary kind smile. But his inquisitive eyes were locked on mine and were already searching.

"Larry, I've not seen you… where've you been hiding?" I couldn't muster any words at that moment and all I could do was avert my eyes to the ground. He just kept looking at me, smiling, and then he said, "We've been missing you and praying for you, Larry. God hasn't forgotten you and He still wants to do something in your life… something far more powerful than you can imagine."

I just nodded but said nothing. After what seemed like a large sliver of eternity he began to turn away. This time I grabbed at his sleeve and asked if we could go somewhere and talk. I began looking about for a spot and saw an empty room off the foyer. It was a conference room with a large table and several chairs and two large windows facing both the inside of the foyer and the outside where the bus pulled up. Pulling Wiley along behind me I prayed that it wouldn't be locked. It wasn't and I breathed a sigh of relief as we went inside.

We sat down and I immediately said, "Wiley, I want to talk to you some more about what it means to be saved and how you go about it." Before he could say a word I launched into another series of scenarios whereby people have given their everything for God and yet were not baptized in Jesus' Name nor had they spoken in tongues. My chief bit of ammunition was the story that Reverend McGuire told about the young man on the East Coast who ended up with nothing but a bike and a burden.

After patiently hearing me out and taking obvious pains not to interrupt me, Wiley reached into his coat pocket and brought out his Bible. Upon seeing this I winced and knew what was coming.

"Larry, have you ever played tennis?" I was startled at the question but stated that "Yes, I had played a little," and added that I'd actually taken some lessons.

"Did you ever try to play tennis on a court, where there were no lines of demarcation… no lines that showed when a ball was in bounds or when it was hit out of bounds?"

"No," I answered.

"Do you imagine that it might be pretty hard to do so? I mean how on earth could you play the game of tennis with no lines? Anyone that declared their hit was good or the other guys was bad would have the complete right to say so and who could say otherwise? Even *with* lines of demarcation people argue all the time. But at least with lines it's not *chaos*… it's a game that can be played, and judged, and won, or lost. Larry, the Bible is the only thing we've got to tell us what's *in* and what's *out*, what's *saved* or what's *lost*, who is going to *heaven* and what *isn't*. We can't afford to base eternal destinies on people's experiences. You don't examine Biblical doctrine by human experience, you must judge human experience by Biblical doctrine."

"Wiley, all you want to do is set yourself up as the judge and tell everybody they're lost!" I was very weary with all of this and was now growing very heated. What with Wiley's opinion and Gordon's and McGuire's and even Tony's, my own mind was on the verge of becoming unhinged.

But Wiley merely smiled and said, "Larry, I am not the judge nor do I want to be. But the Bible *is*, and God who gave this Bible *is*. And Larry, listen to me… I am not going to play God by telling you that you don't have to do what this Bible says. I'm not that smart or brave. *Anybody who tells you that you don't have to obey this Bible is playing God…* and they are not, I repeat, ***not your friend***! We are going to be judged in the last day by this Book. Larry, if you don't go by the Bible all you've got is man's ideas, and man's will. I'm not going to take that chance, Larry. I'd rather trust this Bible than anybody on this earth."

I started to say something but suddenly had the feeling that someone was staring a hole in the back of my head. I turned in my seat and looked up to see Professor R.P. Dickey standing with his hands in his pockets, staring at Wiley and I. He was in the foyer, one foot from the window, and he was not smiling. We looked into each other's eyes; he gave a vicious snort... and walked out of the building.

***

The next day R.P. Dickey 'took off his gloves' and came after me—and religion—with a vengeance. I'm sure the rest of my classmates didn't know exactly what was up or what to make of R.P.'s mood, but they knew that something was going on between us, and that R.P.D was not to be messed with.

"Don't give me any of this 'Pie in the sky' heaven jive! I'm not buying it! Life is here and now and you've got to take it by the throat and live it and squeeze it for every sensation that it can possibly afford. Spend your days like a starry-eyed fool if you want to... rob yourself... cheat yourself with some kind of an expectation that if you don't take it now, God is going to somehow give it to you later... because you waited, *because you waited!* You, idiot! Why in #@&!$%&! do you think you're alive now?! This is it, man! Get it now or lose it forever. This is where it's happening and it isn't going to happen anywhere else..." And with much like speech, he let me, and the entire class, know what he thought of time spent pondering over the *Bible*. R.P. couldn't even say the word 'Bible' that day without a deriding sneer.

I wanted to interrupt his tirade and ask him from where he got his authoritative information on life and how could he *assure us* that he was right, other than by sheer force of personality... but I thought better of it. After all, who was I to try to correct him? R.P. Dickey was walking according to his 'lights' as I was walking by mine—that is, without benefit of the light of the Word of God. At any rate, before the hour was over we all knew exactly how he felt about God, the Bible... and Larry Booker.

***

As I had done for many nights now, I went home with a heavy heart. No more did I read my Bible, let alone sleep with it on my chest, and my prayer life was non-existent. I still refused to watch television, but no longer had any joy or diversion in God. So, I would study my lessons—half heartedly—and muck through my days.

I was thoroughly bored, absolutely miserable, and the thought that kept going through my mind was 'Larry, you're lost anyway... just go get stoned and forget it.' But when I'd think about how good God had been to me, what with changing me so much and letting me go to college and all, I just couldn't bear the thought.

However, after many empty, useless nights—wasted, prayerless nights, I couldn't take it anymore. I picked up the phone and called Rocco.

"Rocco? ... It's me Larry," I said very quietly.

"Hey man! What's up!? Where ya been man?" I could tell that he was already six sheets to the wind and it was only 6:30.

"Hey Rocco, what have you got going tonight?"

"Hey! You coming out of your hole man? You want some action?"

"Well, I don't know... what've you got planned?"

"Not much. Me, Loren, Mac and a few guys are going to go over to Cliff's, shoot some pool and suck down some hashish. You... want Loren to pick you up?"

My heart was racing and a big part of me wanted to slam the phone down, run and hide in my room, put the Bible on my chest and cry out to God. But, from out of my mouth came the words... "Yeah, yeah, Rocco... tell him to come get me."

"Right now?"

"Yeah... right now."

I went through my pockets and found I still had a few bucks on me, so I at least wouldn't have to hit on my mother. I grabbed my railroad coat, slipped quietly out the back door and waited for Loren. I didn't want him to pull up and honk his horn and alert my parents. It's not that they would have or could have stopped me... I just didn't want to see the look on my mother's face.

Of that night I have only one recollection other than the smile on Loren's face as I got into his car. It was as we stood around Cliff's pool table. It was only 8:30 and I was already half stoned and three quarters drunk. Frank was leaning on a pool stick and he looked at me through the smoke and started laughing.

“What’s so funny?” I asked, already feeling the agony of knowing what I was doing to God and myself.

“Well Lare… it’s just that… when I heard the you had become a Jesus freak, I just laughed and said don’t worry about it, Larry’ll be back… you can’t teach an old dog new tricks.”

Everyone in the room laughed—except me. Though I managed to keep it together, just barely, and not smash Frank, or break down crying, I thought to myself, “Yes. That is probably true… but, but, if God *could have ever given that old dog a new heart, there’s no telling what he could have become.*”

With that, I took another drink and inhaled another drag of the pipe that was passed my way. I was about to take my shot, when I noticed the ball I was going for, the one I was lined up behind was… the 8 ball. I hit it with all the fury I could muster, cracked the que stick and ripped the table in the process. Larry Booker was back to being what he had always been… a loser.

***

The following couple of weeks were a blur. I continued to try to go to college but it was a major wash. I found myself once again sleeping through my classes, and homework was a thing of the past. R.P. Dickey and I had no more clashes as I had no fight left within me, and, again… what was there to fight for? Dickey could tell that something in me had died, and, since he hated losers, he ignored me. Even Mrs. Sparcer finally moved several chairs away. As for my poetry, it took on a tormented nature, which clearly depicted the distress of my psyche. Had I been an artist, I would have out van Gogh’ed… Vincent.

When I’d arrive home from school it was as if I were a caged rat. I would find myself walking incessantly throughout my basement until someone could come and pick me up and I could go get loaded and escape.

My life and actions, ever bad before, were now slipping into the realm of the bizarre. I would pick fights over absolutely nothing. One night at Pinocchio’s Bar I strode drunkenly up to the table where the two house bouncers were sitting with their wives. I stood looking down at them until one of them looked up and said, “What do you want Booker?”

"Who are these fine-looking ladies and what are they doing with the likes of you?" I said, weaving a little. With looks that could kill, they both stood and replied, "Our wives." With that, I reached down and took a beer belonging to one of the wives, said, "Then here's a toast to their stupidity," gulped it down in one swallow and slammed the glass down on the table. "Thanks," I said and patted her on the cheek.

The brawl that followed was something to behold, or at least that's what my friends told me afterwards. With the bar pretty well busted up, or at least the area where the bouncers had been sitting, somebody managed to get me into a car and out of there before the police came. One of the bouncers was in pretty bad shape but there were no charges pressed because they had decided between themselves that they were going to take care of me later and wouldn't need any help from the police. The owner hadn't been present during the fight so didn't know who the trouble maker was. And nobody was about to tell him.

So once again my world was on the slippery slope and I was losing ground fast. When I'd finally make it home from these forays, I'd lie on my bed and with no one to put on a show for, find myself sobbing until I passed out. Some nights I'd cry and pray and groan like a wounded animal begging God to somehow have mercy on my desolate soul. When memories of prayer, Bible reading and the vision of January 20th would return, I would be thrown into paroxysms of agony.

It wasn't until years later that my mom revealed that she and Buzz could hear me during these drunken, drugged, emotional meltdowns. My mom would lie in bed and ask Buzz to please go downstairs and talk to me, but his answer was… "What can I say? I don't know what to tell him." He knew better than my mother that much of my anguish had something to do with God, and after all, what could he do about that.

One Saturday, Bill, Edmund and I were riding around in the city park. I was not in very good shape and when we drove by where I'd wrecked my Triumph, I had Bill park and I walked out into the middle of the street, to the spot where I should have died. I stood while cars honked and drivers swore, and thought once again about God's mind-boggling mercy to me and uttered quietly to myself, "I should be in Hell right now. And, in a way… I am."

I got back into Bill's car and he began asking me questions about the wreck. I was starting to explain yet once again what had happened that morning when I looked to my right, and there, less than fifty feet away was Samuel, and Roscoe… and Wiley.

They were passing out religious tracts and talking about God to anybody who was willing to listen. The fear and shame that gripped me when I saw them was overpowering. I didn't want them to see me in this condition, and the thought of looking into Wiley's face was more than I could bear. I literally fell onto the floorboard of Bill's car and screamed for him to "Get out of here!" Bill and Edmund stared at me as if I'd lost my mind, and when he didn't move I shrieked out for him to "Move it! Get me out of here! Bill! I mean it! Get me out of here, now! Now!"

Bill put the car in gear and peeled out leaving rubber and smoke everywhere. After what I took to be a long enough time to clear the gate of the park I slid back up into the seat and sat, literally shaking.

"What the #%$@! was that all about?" Edmund asked. I didn't answer, for I didn't know what to say. How do you explain why 'big, tough, Larry Booker' had to run and hide from three guys who walked around the parks telling people about Jesus? Edmund asked again, and again, I was thoroughly silent. After a while, I took a deep breath and said, "I, I'm sorry. There were some guys there, in the park, that I knew when I was… when I was trying to live… different… when I was trying to live for God. I just didn't want to see them… that's all."

None of us said anything, and finally Bill went to a bar at the corner of Prairie and Thatcher called 'The Sunset Inn.' There we spent the rest of the night until I finally went home and laid down to cry some more.

One night Special Ed and I were over at Joe's, absolutely wired to the hilt. Joe's apartment was a literal drug arsenal that had a little bit of everything and a whole lot of some things. It was about

9:30 or 10:00 when Eddie thought he heard somebody beating on the door. We turned down the music and Joe weaved his way to the peephole that looked outside while at the same time yelling to whoever it was to quit beating on his *blankety-blank* door. He sobered quickly, as did we all, when he found that it was a federal drug agent as well as the same two officers that had arrested us more than a year earlier, officers Leayva and Koncilia.

The federal officer began to talk through the door, "Joe, I have a warrant for your arrest. Don't do anything stupid." As the federal officer continued to talk we realized that they were finally getting Joe for sending heroin into the U.S. when he was stationed in Vietnam. Joe was now leaning with his head against the door listening to his sentence of doom. But I had to hand it to Joe; he hadn't won his Silver Stars and Purple Hearts for nothing. He really *was* interested in rescuing his fellow men. In this case, it was me who could see my life passing before my eyes—I mean after all I *was* on probation. As for Special Ed, I thought he was about to vomit, or worse, out of sheer terror.

Joe was still leaning on the door when he called out, "I'm going to open the door, but the latch chain is still hooked, so we can talk better… and I can see the documents… okay? I won't do anything stupid, and please don't you guys do anything either."

"Yes, that's fine. You have my word Joe, we want to make this easy… and trouble free."

Joe looked at Eddie and me and whispered for us to clean up every trace of drugs we could find and start flushing it down the back bedroom toilet… as fast as we could. He told us to especially take care of the stuff in the top shelf of the closet in his room, and to also get the stuff from under his bed that was in the guitar case. "I'm going to stall them as long as I can, so you guys get with it!" As his hand was turning the knob we were racing throughout his house, grabbing stuff everywhere and running back and forth to the toilet.

While we were flushing literally thousands of dollars down the toilet, Joe was at the door pulling off one of the great coups of his life.

"Officer, there are two guys here that I swear have nothing to do with any of this. There just teens. I'd like you to let them go… no hassling."

The federal agent replied, "I've come for you, Joe, nobody else. When you let us in, they're free to go." Then he added, "I give you my word."

"Okay. Can I have five more minutes before I open the door?"

"Joe… I've got a search warrant… not that I need it. You can have three full minutes from right now, then you've got to open up or were coming in."

"It's a deal… but don't break the door, it's my mothers house. I promise I'll open up."

With that he looked at his watch and began to pull out stuff we had yet to find. I don't know what all it was, but I knew by Joe's actions, and by the fact that he was giving it 'priority flush' that it was 'hard' stuff. Now both toilets were flushing as fast and as much as they could. It had to be obvious to the officers what was going on. When time was about to run out Joe handed us the last of the pot he had and said, "Look, I'm going. Get that stuff out of here!"

We could hear him yelling that he was coming and could hear him opening and shutting the door a couple of times and the rattle of the door chain as he was no doubt fumbling around for a few extra seconds. I finally heard one of the officers yell, "Quit monkeying with us Arguello, we're coming in!" At that moment the door opened and the two local officers came running back to where I was watching the last of the pot go down the drain with me helping it along with a much needed relieving.

The officer spun me around, and was instantly sorry and furious that he did. When Officer John Koncilia saw that it was my face he was looking into he went livid with rage.

I had been called a lot of names in my life but few times, if ever, had it been done with such colorful, sober, intense vehemence. It kind of reminded me of when my cousin laid on the couch with his leg broke while I taunted him.

When officer Leayva entered the bathroom with Eddie in tow and saw me he was also beside himself. Seething, he said, "You are history, Booker, do you hear me… you are @$#%&! history. I'm calling your probation officer tonight!"

"What about?" I queried.

"Associating with known drug offenders is plenty to send you packing, you #%&!#!"

"Drug offenders? What and who are you talking about? Drugs? Joe? Joe, are you using some kind of drugs?" I said all of this while I went casually about fixing my pants and washing my hands. I really thought that at that moment, Officer Leayva—the bigger of the two—was going to take a swing at me, but at that moment the Federal man grabbed him and swung me around.

"Look punk," he said fiercely between clenched teeth, "I don't know who you are, but I made a deal with Joe… and I keep my deals… but don't push me. Get your buddy, and get your stuff and get yourself out of here, NOW!"

Koncilia and Leayva started to say something but the Fed put up his hand to silence them, "I made my deal. It's over. I've got what we came for." With that he looked back at me but I was already on my way out the door. Before I closed it, I turned and said, "Sir?" He looked my way and lifted an angry face. "Thank you sir… and… I mean it. And Joe, thank you… you're a good guy." Joe smiled at me though they were already putting the handcuffs on him and reciting to him his rights.

***

One week and a thousand stories later I heard the horn honk and I looked outside to see Joe Arguello riding shotgun in Tony Pacheco's car. "Hey! Were going to Denver… you want to go?" Joe had been released on bond within forty-eight hours and was now back on the streets doing his thing.

I stood there shaking, having not fully recovered from the previous night's revelry and thought, "Denver. Going back to Denver. Going back… broken and beaten, and… going back the same old Larry Booker that left there with dreams and hopes and a heart that I thought was full of God."

"Yeah, I'll go. Wait up." I went downstairs tremulously, got my Railroad coat and stopped by the washroom, where my mother was folding clothes to see if I could get some more money out of her.

Gone from her eyes was the joy and hope and pride she'd had for me a few weeks earlier. Now the pain was back and when on the phone she tried once more to avoid any subject that pertained to me. She never said a word to me other than for me to please be careful as she dug in her purse and gave me five dollars.

During the trip we talked more about the bust and Joe asked me one more time how come I wasn't a Jesus freak anymore. I mumbled some kind of a weedy explanation and opened another beer. We were on our way to Marcy's and Joe he said he had some 'stuff' he had to pick up at Denver University. I wasn't about to ask him what kind of 'stuff' as I in fact didn't want to know.

We got to Marcy's sometime around 7:00 p.m. and the house was already starting to get crowded with party people who'd heard we were coming. Thankfully, neither Charles, Lyle nor Tyrone were there. Apparently they had all parted company not long after I'd left and Marcy hadn't kept up with their whereabouts. That was fine with me as the last thing I wanted to do was explain my present condition… especially to the likes of Lyle.

Joe let us out and headed straight to his rendezvous. We all sat around drinking and smoking dope, and I had to answer the usual barrage of questions that pertained to the bust, college and especially the fact that I was no longer 'living for Jesus.' Though I was still enrolled in college it was obvious that when the grades came out next week I had probably failed everything. At that point, whoever was paying the bill would cease to throw their money away, and I'd be back to… where?

As for my being a 'Jesus Freak'—as my friends really enjoyed putting it—I had also failed in that, miserably. Most of them thought it was pretty funny but I could tell that it really bothered others. It was as if they had actually hoped I could make it, because if Larry Booker could change then even they might have a chance. As it was, another ray of hope had been snuffed out and once again we were all doomed to the same drugged fate.

By and by Joe came back, but when he did the party thinned out pretty quickly. Joe was 'very hot property' and we all knew that if the cops could get him again on most anything he would go up the river for sure… and nobody wanted to go with him. So folks went back to the relative safety of their homes and habits while me, Tony, Joe and Rocco sat around Marcy and Tom's and continued to obliterate ourselves.

After a while Joe went into the kitchen with Tony and Rocco. I got up to see what was going on and saw that Joe was in the process of putting a syringe into Tony's arm. He was shooting them up. In fact, before it was over, he had shot them all up, saving himself for last.

I watched them that night. I watched my friends. Friends that I'd known for many years, some since grade school. So this is what we had all come to. All of the laughs and all of the highs and all of the parties and all of the fights and all of the fun. Now we were all going to end up on the end of a needle that would probably never let go. In the corner Marcy seemed to have passed out as had Rocco and Tony and Tom. Joe alone was still sitting up but he was weaving and smiling. He'd been on it all so long that somehow his tolerance must have developed into a life of its own. They had all just done the *only* thing that I'd never done… no, not one time in my life. Shooting up was the *only unbroken promise* of a vast string of promises that I'd made to God many years before, while still in the ninth grade, downstairs, in my room, on my bed.

When I asked myself why hadn't I broken this one promise, I immediately knew the reason. It was because I truly believed that if I ever broke that one last promise, God would owe me absolutely nothing and would quite simply kill me or let me die like I should have done, oh, so many times before.

But what did it matter now? I was lost. I was going to Hell… where I belonged, and should have been for a long, long time. I knew what God wanted of me… and I didn't give it, I didn't do it… and now I was as lost, yea more lost than I'd ever been. Furthermore, I was hopeless. I would never be saved because I was too hooked and too weak and too… whatever. I just didn't have it in me, and never would. Larry Booker was a loser.

So why wait? Why continue to cause pain and sorrow? Now was the time to get it over with and just die and go to hell.

I got up from where I was sitting, picked up Joe and helped him back into the kitchen. He was in bad shape, but I knew he could get it together enough to function, more or less on me. And, after all, if he muffed it, what difference did it make?

I sat him down in the chair where he had done the others and took off my Railroad coat. I handed him his stash, that he had placed in the cuff of his boot and said, "Okay Joe… it's time now. I'm ready. Shoot me up." Joe immediately became more alert and began to smile and, had he been able to, probably would have laughed.

"Well, well, Larry" he said with a slurred voice, "I've waited a long time to do this." And he did manage a chuckle. He went through the processes of preparation, and again, for whatever else he was, Joe was a professional. As he drew the liquid into the syringe I noticed that he drew in quite a bit more than he had for the others.

"You're a big guy, Larry… it might take a little more," and he managed to get off another titter of a laugh. He had me clench my fist several times and I pulled tighter on the belt that was wrapped around my bicep. The veins stood out and with a slightly irresolute hand he found the one he wanted, thrust in the needle and with a look of real satisfaction pushed the plunger, while he whispered the words, "There you go… *Jesus Freak.*"

I sat back in the chair while Joe did the same. I closed my eyes and waited for the rush that I'd always heard about, the one that would knock me off my feet… the one that would never be matched by another no matter how bad you wanted it.

And I waited. And I waited. And…I…waited. And… nothing happened. Nothing. I kept glancing at Joe who had now sunk back into sloth lethargy, but who nevertheless would force his head up to see how I was taking it.

After about five minutes I took Joe by the shoulders and shook him a little to bring him back to alertness. He raised a frowning, groggy face as if to say, "Why don't you take your hands off me and leave me alone."

"It didn't take, Joe. Joe! Do you hear me? It didn't take, it didn't work. Something's wrong. Something is very wrong!" Now I was shaking him a little harder, and he was coming back around.

"What the #&$%! are you talking about?"

"The stuff didn't work, Joe, it didn't work." Joe was now beginning to really catch my drift and was shaking his head and starting to curse. "You're crazy… what do you mean it didn't work?"

"Just that… it didn't… and you're going to hit me again." Now he was really coming to and his eyes were definitely opening up and staring.

"Do what… what'd you say?"

"You're going to hit me, your going to shoot me up again because it didn't work… it didn't take." By that time I was pushing his stuff back in front of him and asking him what he needed me to do. Joe was now becoming alert and alarmed and began to say, "No… no! Larry, we're not going to do this… this is crazy. I may be a lot of things, but I'm not going to kill you."

"Joe… you are *not* going to kill me… but you *are* going to shoot me up again." As he continued to protest I finally took a hold of him by the collar, began to shake him and said as fiercely as I'd ever said anything in my life, "You will do it… ***do you hear me? You will do it and you will do it right now!***"

Joe was shaking now, but it was not from the drugs, nor was it from fear of me—after all he had been in the worst of Vietnam. He was beginning to shake and he was beginning to cry. He was crying because he believed he was about to kill his friend. Perhaps had he been in his right mind nothing could have induced him to shoot me up again. But then again, life had been so cheap, and the world of drugs that Joe knew had been so bizarre, that who really knew what he was thinking or why he was crying.

I watched his motions to make sure they were the same as before. He eventually drew the liquid back into the syringe—it was a 'normal' dose over which I did not quibble. I placed the belt around my arm, tightened it once again and began to flex my hand. Joe once again found the vein, quickly injected the needle, pushed the plunger… and left it hanging in my arm. He rose to his feet, looked down into my face and with tears rolling down his cheeks stumbled off into the other room.

What did it matter that the syringe was still in my arm. I was probably about to die anyway. I lowered my head to rest it on the table and wait for the… rush? Death? I really didn't know. I waited… and waited… and… and… and after all the years, and all the broken promises, and all the times my life was spared… and now… *nothing was happening*.

I felt no rush… no high. It did not affect me. I had no idea what to make of this. I entered the room where my friends were completely out of it. Even Joe now had his head lolled to the back of the sofa, which he was sharing with a comatose Neil, who I didn't even know was in the house. I walked over to the lamps, turned out the lights and sat down in one of the empty corners of the room. I looked at the clock. It was 10:45. Joe and Tony both had said that they wanted to return to Pueblo that night, but how could they? I guess after a while I could pack them up and drive Tony's car. But I really didn't care if I stayed or left. For all practical intents and purposes, my life was over. What was there left to live for… and besides my days were numbered now anyway. I closed my eyes and eventually went to sleep.

Someone was kicking me. I looked up, and it took me a moment to recall where I was. Rocco was kicking on my foot and telling me that it was time to go.

"What time is it?" I asked.

"2:15… and Tony's starting up the car."

"Can he drive?" I asked incredulously.

"Says he can. We'll see won't we?"

We made our way to the car and Joe was already in the front seat with a small pillow from Marcy's couch that he was apparently taking with him. He looked at me when I got in and asked if I was all right. I told him that I was and I heard him breathe an audible sigh of relief. Tony started the car and we pulled away. After a few minutes I heard Joe call my name.

"What?" I said.

"Larry… you are really a lucky guy. I should have never, and I mean never, did that second hit."

"Yeah, well, I'm sorry if I came on so strong."

"Larry… were you telling me the truth? Did it really not affect you?"

"No, Joe, it never did... not even the second one. Unless you call drifting off to sleeping after twenty minutes being K'O'ed."

"No, no, that's not it. You'd know if it took. I can't believe this."

We were silent for quite a while when I heard Joe call my name again. "Larry, do you know why I was crying?

"No, Joe I don't... but I'd like to know."

"It was because I had a friend in ,Nam who went down like that. On his second shot. I mean, it was his ticket... out. They sent him home in a body bag."

We were quiet for a long time. Rocco was asleep; Tony was glued to the wheel like a zombie and Joe seemed to be out again. But then I heard him call my name again. "Larry."

"Yeah," I answered.

"You know Larry... I wish you'd go back to being a Jesus freak."

Neither he nor I said anything else.

I was sitting behind Tony, resting my head on the window looking up at the moon that kept reappearing through the scattered clouds. This had to be the longest ride of my life. For the next ninety minutes I replayed every scene that had brought me to this point in my life. I knew, as sure as I knew my name that I was a walking dead man.

My only hope was to somehow get out of Pueblo and out of my world, or my life had to be over. It was simply a matter of a very short time and I knew I'd be dead... and in Hell.

Many times during that ride I felt the tears roll down my cheeks and over all my failures. I was the loser of all losers, and worst of all I'd lost God in the process. He was very best thing that had ever happened or tried to happen to me... and I'd blown it just like I'd blown every other opportunity of my life. I had never known until that moment how really low a human being could go emotionally. I wished to God that I had died in Marcy's kitchen.

Tony pulled up in front of my house and I got out without saying a word, not that anyone in the car would have noticed anyway. I walked around to the back of my house and let myself in. I looked at my watch and it was 5:00 a.m.

I began my walk down the stairs into my basement as I had done so many thousands of times before. By the time I reached my room I was crying again and when I came to my bed I fell to my knees. I began to groan and then to sob. I knew what I had to do, though I didn't for a moment think it would ever make any difference again. I buried my face in my hands and said, ***"God… if you will save me… and get me out of this city… God*** (by this time I was all but screaming) ***I will do anything in the world for you!"*** I repeated this several times to God, each time more vehemently than the last, until suddenly, I felt myself being succumbed by an overwhelming need to sleep. Sometime in the course of that sleep, I guess I got off my knees and crawled onto the covers and wrapped them about me.

Someone was shaking me. I managed to force open an eye and could see my mother bending over me. She had a hand on my shoulder and was continuing her attempt to raise me, speaking firmly but quietly.

"Larry… Larry, get up, someone wants you on the phone. I think its Larry Weder." Both eyes were immediately open, and I jumped from the bed, (scaring my mother half to death) took the basement steps two (I wasn't quite up to three) at a time and grabbed the phone.

"Hello, hello?" I blurted breathlessly.

"Larry! Larry, ole buddy, is that you man?"

"Larry… where are you?"

"I'm here, in Pueblo. I drove all night long to get here. I just pulled into town ten minutes ago. I'm at my grandmothers, and I'm looking at Eddie even as we speak."

"Larry… Larry…" I said starting to cry, "Can I go home with you?"

With a very serious voice, my old friend said to me, "That's why I came. Last night I was praying for you… and, Larry, you've got to believe me, this really did happen… as I was praying for you, asking God to save you, the Lord spoke to me… He really did… He interrupted me and said these words to me: '***Arise, go get Larry, he is ready now.***' And, buddy, that's why I'm here."

***

It was 1:00 in the morning, and I was now driving as Larry and Steve were asleep, as was Larry's brother, Special Ed, who had decided to go back to Oklahoma with us. I was smoking a cigarette, feeling like death, and I knew that I could never, ever be saved.

Larry had picked me up four hours after he'd called. His grandmother cooked him and Steve breakfast and then they slept for a few hours. Steve, a friend of Larry's that went to the same church he did, decided to come along and get me on sheer impulse.

As soon as I hung up the phone I packed two pairs of jeans, two shirts, some underclothes and socks into a leather duffle bag, along with most of my poetry. My mother fixed me a grand breakfast and slipped me fifteen dollars. I hugged her and told her that I'd probably see her in a few months—never realizing that I was finally through with Pueblo… forever.

I stalked the basement floor, up the steps, down the steps, and even kept going outside, again, liked a caged animal, till they arrived. This time, however, it was out of sheer excitement. Excitement that maybe… just maybe, there was still hope for me.

Finally they arrived. It was wonderful to see Larry and meet Steve. I hugged my mom, and even hugged Buzz. Then we left and drove back to Larry's grandmother's house to pick up Eddie.

Before we left town, I talked Larry into stopping by Joe's… so we could say goodbye.

It was a nice time of greeting old friends, and as we were about to walk out the door I took Joe aside and we went into his room where I shut the door and took off my railroad coat once more.

"Joe," I said, "I want you to shoot me up."

He looked at me as if I'd lost my mind and said, "You're insane."

"Shoot me up, Joe." And I took my belt off, sat down on the bed and began to wrap it around my arm. Totally disgusted, Joe got out his stuff, slamming things around just enough to let me know that he was thoroughly sick of me. He made a quick work of it and showed me the door. As I was about to get into the car I turned back, shrugged my shoulders, and said parting words to a friend that I would never again see in this life.

"Nothing, Joe… absolutely nothing."

At that he shrugged his shoulders, waved me away in revulsion and went into his house.

***

So here I was, ten hours later, driving Steve's car through a town I'd never heard of before with the strange name of Ponca City, Oklahoma. I knew that I had to be one of the vilest creatures that God had ever had the displeasure of dealing with. I smoked a cigarette (one of Eddie's) knowing that this entire venture was an absolute waste of time. People like me simply don't have what it takes to change.

The tears were once again streaming down my face, not out of repentance but out of shame and remorse that I had become so wicked, so vile. I began quietly muttering to myself through my tears, "I can't… I can't… I'll never be saved… it's impossible," when I distinctly heard a voice speak to me.

It was the same voice that spoke to me the day I went to the restroom to meet Roscoe. The words He spoke were short, and simple and powerful. The dearest friend that I would ever know in this world spoke to me at 1:00 in the morning, Easter Sunday, April 2nd, 1972. He spoke words of hope to a nineteen year old boy who thought he could never ever be saved. All He said was… "***Give me a chance.***"

I was stunned. After a moment or two, I stubbed the cigarette out in the ashtray, took several deep breaths and after another few moments began to pray... hoping… hoping that it could possibly be true.

Two hours later we came over the crest of a hill on Highway 60. Down below was the sleeping town of Bartlesville, Oklahoma. The mercury vapor, street lights shown like so many green stars and as we began our descent, I thought to myself, "*This is the beginning of a new life.*" Please God… please let it be.

# 7

## Bartlesville

When we arrived at Larry and Steve's apartment at about 3:30 a.m. it had started to rain. As I was grabbing my belongings out of the trunk (all it took was one hand), it turned into a deluge and we made a hasty beeline into the house. I asked the guys how we could, one moment drive through weather that didn't proffer a single drop of rain, and the next moment the bottom fall out and we were threatened with being washed away. Steve answered with a saying, oft used concerning Oklahoma weather, "If you don't like it—stick around a minute—it'll change." I must have heard and made that statement a thousand times since that night.

We made it upstairs where they led me to a mattress in the corner. Larry gave me a pillow, a blanket and a hearty "God bless you, I'm really glad you're here." I was really glad to be there also, though I had no idea what the future held for me. I did know however that, in light of my past, I was ready for almost anything.

While I still could not believe how the rain was pouring down, it was the thunder and lightning that had become fearsome. One could obviously hear thunder in Colorado, but this brand of din and clamor was entirely something else. I got on my knees on the mattress, placed my elbows on the window sill and watched it for a long, long time. Not much could be seen due to the rain and darkness until the lightning would flash and light up the world. Then driving sheets of rain would glisten and dance in cascades that appeared more like waterfalls than raindrops. What with the lightning appearing every few seconds, it was an awesome a sight to see.

I finally lay down, not because I was tired of the spectacle, but because I was exhausted. I lay and listened to the cracking thunder and beat of the downpour upon the roof and began to wonder about Larry's church and what the day would hold. It was Easter Sunday, but due to the time we'd got in, Larry said we'd probably forego the morning church service and go in the evening. Outside of going to the Christmas Eve service where John stole the rum, and to the little garage church on the east side, I'd never been to church at night. I didn't even know people went to church at night. Nevertheless I was looking forward to it, even if I was more than a little anxious.

I had no idea what kind of church Steve and Larry attended, but I hoped that God had really meant it when He told Larry that I "was ready." Larry had been very emphatic on that point and more than a little excited. He said that it was the first time that God had ever actually spoken to him and he wasn't about to blow it by letting me stay in Pueblo.

I would have been a little dubious about God speaking to Larry (or anybody else for that matter) had it not actually happened to me. I knew therefore that it could happen, and was hoping that Larry wasn't missing it somehow. I needed God and His mercy so desperately that I simply could not afford any games—especially after my last idiotic escapade at Joe's.

I'd been a stupid fool to go by Joe's in the first place. But it so blew me away that the 'shoot ups' that had been knocking everybody down the night before hadn't even affected me that I just had to see if it was a fluke or something. When I wasn't even fazed when he did it again the next day, I didn't know what to think—except of course that I was a hopeless, despicable wretch.

But, here I was. On a mattress, on the floor of an upstairs rental apartment, in a far off place I'd never heard of called Bartlesville, Oklahoma. I was nineteen; going on forty, and my life was an unqualified wreck. As I lay there, I whispered out loud, "Jesus, is there… is there really *any way* that you can save me?"

As soon as those words crossed my lips the loudest explosion

I'd ever heard in my entire life detonated in my ears. It sounded as if someone had just placed gigantic hands in the heavens and had literally ripped the universe in two and I jumped up from the bed screaming like a little girl. "Dear God! Dear God!" I kept screaming, "What was that?!"

I thought Larry and Steve would die laughing. Though one of them had been able to turn on the lights, they were literally in hysterics. For the life of me, I saw nothing funny—nor did Special Ed who was as white as a ghost, sitting wide-eyed, petrified, shivering, and squeezing a pillow for all he was worth.

"It's thunder man… it's ***thunder***!" Larry said with tears of laughter rolling down his cheeks.

Larry went on to explain, between giggles, that the thunder we'd just experienced was probably that loudest he'd ever heard as well, but that, "Here in the south man…it's just that way."

As I lay back down, my heart was still beating rapidly. I knew why I had been so absolutely aghast when the lightning hit. It was because of the question that had just passed my lips about Jesus and his ability to save the likes of someone like me. To this day, I am totally convinced that it was not a matter of coincidentally profound timing. I *know* beyond doubt that Jesus was letting me know that, "Yes… He had the power to save… even the likes of Larry Booker." I will die with that conviction, as surely as I almost died of fright.

Never in my life had I heard thunder like that, nor was I in any hurry to ever hear it again. Little did I know that in the near future I would see it, hear it and experience it on a greater, more frightening, and even more precisely perfect scale.

***

We left for church late, I don't remember the reason why, and didn't get there till about ten after seven. Larry explained as we drove rather furiously that, though service started at 7:00 p.m., there was a prayer meeting that began at 6:30.

I thought that the church must be a long ways off due to the speed we were traveling but quickly found that we were less than ten minutes away. We got out of the car and (as it had been with the 'east-side garage church') I could already hear the people singing.

I stood on the sidewalk and looked at the small building that we were about to enter. "Well... at least its not a garage," I muttered, but it was only a step or two above that. From where I stood, I saw that the building was narrow, maybe thirty feet across, and painted white. In the front on the right hand side of the building was a set of short steps that went up to a small landing where there was a single wood door. Above the door was a small white plaque with words written in black paint (but neatly done) that stated; "*Hear O' Israel, the Lord our God, the Lord is one.*" Below these words and to the right was the scripture text; *Deuteronomy 6:4.*

I wasn't sure what the significance of the verse was, but it looked nice nonetheless. Another sign out front gave the name of the church, as well as the name of the Pastor and the times of service. It was an approximately 4 foot square piece of plywood painted on both sides with the same information.

| | |
|---|---|
| Sunday School | 10:00 a.m. |
| Sunday Morning Worship | 11:00 a.m. |
| Sunday Evening Worship | 7:00 p.m. |
| Tuesday Bible Study | 7:30 p.m. |
| Thursday Evening Worship | 7:30 p.m. |

I stared at the sign for quite a while before saying to Eddie, "Man, Special... that's a lot a church services!" He didn't reply, he just stared and began nodding his ascent. I then noted that the name of the Pastor was, Roy L. Moss, while the name of the church was 'Truth Tabernacle.' I thought as I looked at the names, "I'm not even sure what Truth is at this particular time of my life—and I have *no idea* what 'Tabernacle' is." At least I did know what, 'Pastor' meant, so I said to Eddie, "Well, Special, let's go meet Pastor Moss."

I walked in and saw approximately 18-20 people seated, facing the rostrum where a tall, thin man was leading songs. Though they were all singing robustly and seemed to be paying attention to the song leader, they nevertheless did turn around to get a glimpse of who it was that just came in. When they saw me, most of them took two or three more good looks to be sure of what it was they saw, and I noticed that two of the families with children proceeded to scoot them in a little closer.

I must admit that I couldn't blame them, as my appearance was quite a sight. Here was a beanpole of a guy; 6 foot, 6 inches tall, weighing less than 190 pounds, with blonde hair that fell down to his chest and was parted in the middle. He also wore a pair of gold, wire rimmed, octagon shaped glasses, a shirt that was mostly unbuttoned, with tails hanging out, and pants that were nothing but a conglomeration of patches that had been sewn together. I know I didn't have socks on (as I hardly *ever* wore them) and I seriously doubt I had shoes on. I was told later that I possibly had on sandals. This was possible because I did slip a pair into my bag at the last minute before I left my parents' house, as well as a pair of my ever faithful boots that I threw in Steve's trunk. Much of the time I went shoeless or at best wore low-top tennis shoes that had several holes worn throughout (even in winter).

At any rate, I *was* quite a shock to the system, and… it was only natural for them to protect their young. I thought it humorous, however, to watch the kids incessantly turn in their seats to sneak a glance of the 'hippy' in the back row—who would every now and then give them a small wave.

Throughout the service I couldn't help but compare this church to the east-side garage church. The singing here was almost exactly the same, even to the point of singing one of the same songs that they had that night in Pueblo. It had something to do with a 'roll being called up yonder.' Everyone here put their hands in the air just like they did there, and the women seemed to all wear dresses and, as far as I could tell, had very long hair (which didn't bother me even a little bit). Most importantly, both places had the same feeling of expectancy, like something significant was about to happen but you didn't know what it was, and certainly didn't want to miss it.

After a while the songs were finished, and the song leader proceeded to ask if anyone had a prayer request. A couple of hands were raised, and he acknowledged the people by name, referring to them as 'sister' so and so, or 'brother' so and so. I had noticed this 'brother' and 'sister' stuff at the east side church, and even when I attended the Baptist youth retreat—though not nearly as often.

The song leader seemed about finished taking these requests, when on an impulse I shot my hand into the air. He looked at me a moment and said, "Yes?"

"Yessir… I have a request." He paused, waited, then decided to coax me on a little; "And what would that be?"

"I would like to be baptized!" He stared at me, as did everyone else, and then simply said, "Yes, well… we'll see about that a little later," and proceeded to have us all stand and pray.

It was at that point that I realized that the song leader must also be the pastor. This kind of took me by surprise because he seemed too young to be a pastor. He couldn't have been over thirty, and I was pretty much used to priests and preachers and chaplains being old guys. The next thought concerning him that hit me hard was; "Man… he really has a short haircut."

After a few more items of business, like the offering and an announcement about a 'fellowship meeting' that was coming up, it was time for the preaching. Pastor Moss asked us to stand and as we did I leaned over to Larry and whispered, "What's 'fellowship'?"

"What's *what?*" he whispered back looking perplexed.

"*Fellowship*… what is *fel-low-ship?*"

Larry looked intently at me—I think to see if I was pulling his leg—and said at last, "It's what Christians have when they get together for a good time," then began thumbing through his Bible looking for the text that the Pastor had announced. I nodded my head in understanding and wondered if their's would be as dry as the east side's.

While he preached I also picked up on another strong similarity between this Church and the one on the east side in Pueblo—both of the pastors spoke with great authority, and what's more, *you could understand what they were saying!* These aspects alone made a great impression on me, because I never remembered feeling this in any church I'd ever visited. I never before understood what was being said, or felt that the preacher really believed what he was saying, and he certainly didn't seem excited about what he said.

Pastor Moss apparently believed a great deal in what he was saying. His heart was in it, and what's more—so was mine. I do not remember the exact subject Pastor Moss preached on that night, except that, once again, I knew I was the object of most of it. The longer he talked the heavier my heart became and at one point I felt like crying out… right there in front of God and everybody. When he finished and had everyone stand, he began to ask if anyone wanted to come to the altar and pray. I definitely wanted to pray, but I wasn't sure what an altar was, or where it was. About this time Larry leaned over and said, "Do you want to go pray?"

"Where?" I asked, almost ready to cry.

"Down there at those benches, in front of the pulpit. That's where you pray when you want to repent."

I never said another word to him, I just stepped out and made my way down to the front. I knelt at the little bench and said these words, "God…I'm sorry, I'm so very sorry..." and instantly let out a sob that racked my body.

Though I did not yet know what the term "fountains of the deep" referred to, God did, and that night the fountains of the great deep were broken up inside Larry Booker. Some of the people who were there have since told me that they never, ever heard anyone repent like I did that fateful night. I screamed, I cried, I wept, and I sobbed. I asked God to forgive me of every single thing I'd ever done to hurt Him—and there was plenty. I would lift my head and wail, "God… God… God… forgive me for being a drunkard! Forgive me for my drugs! Forgive me for my fighting and stealing and lying and cussing… and…" And on, and on, and on, and on. Then I would bury my face back into the bench and sob great, racking, heaving sobs, till I thought I would die. And I did die. I died out to my sins… and my sorry ways… and my wretched life… and my emptiness… and I did it for over one and a half hours.

Finally I quit. I quit simply because I couldn't cry anymore, could barely talk, was completely spent, and had not an ounce of strength left. The sad and frightening thing was that—in my soul… I felt no relief.

It was at that point that Pastor Roy Moss came over to me, put his hand on my shoulder, and said, "Son… how do you feel?"

"I, I don't know..." I managed to croak, with my eyes so puffy I could hardly see, and my nose so congested that I couldn't breath. Then my pastor said to me words that changed my life. He said, "Larry, are you sure God hasn't already forgiven you… but that maybe, you haven't forgiven yourself?"

I didn't answer for a long time. When I did I said, "I don't know… I really don't know," and lowered my head and began to somehow cry once more. But this time, as I wept, I felt something begin to lift. It was as if an entire, sopping wet, heavy canvas tarp, that was wrapped over and around me… began to lift… lift off my mind… off of my heart… my spirit… yea, even my body.

After a while, Pastor Moss came back and said, "How do you feel now?"

It was then that a nineteen year old boy,
with hair down to the middle of his chest,
and loved having it so,
who cried when it got cut for senior high football,
who knew nothing about the Bible,
especially Corinthians,
looked up into the face of his new found pastor,
pulled the long wet hair out of his face,
and said…
"I think I need a haircut."
The surprised pastor said,
"And I think we have somebody who's ready to be baptized."
The truly amazing miracle about the whole entire episode;
from Larry Weder driving out to get me,
to my agonizing repentance,
to the forgiveness I felt,
to the drive to the cow pond
(where the church did their baptizing), was that…
*through it all,*

*till the moment it happened,*
*I never realized that I was about to be baptized...*
in the Name of Jesus Christ for the remission of my sins!
The Church that I ran from...
was the church that I ran into.
I ran right into their wonderful waiting arms.

***

I did not receive the Holy Ghost that night, though God knows He wanted to give it to me. As we were pulling up to Sister Loudermilk's cow pond, where all the baptisms took place, Larry was telling me how wonderful it was going to be when I came out of the water and began to speak in tongues. I looked at him and said, "Larry, I doubt very seriously that I will receive the Holy Ghost tonight."

"Why not?" he asked looking surprised.

"Because... because... I have been way too bad for God to do something that good for me." And, guess what? I did not receive the Holy Ghost that night!

Brother Moss leaned me back and put me under the water, invoking "the Name of the Lord Jesus Christ" for the remission of my sins. I saw—while under the water—a very bright light. As soon as I came up out of the water and began to praise God—the first thought I remembered was that, "I was way too bad for Him to do something that good for me..." Subsequently, I didn't receive the Holy Ghost. Still, the feeling I received at baptism was a truly wonderful feeling, and I literally felt like I was hundreds of pounds lighter.

The load of sin is truly a horrible burden to bear.

That was how I spent, Easter Sunday, April 2, 1972. The following Tuesday we had church and I went to the altar and 'sought' for the Holy Ghost, and did the same on Thursday night. I wasn't discouraged, however, because everyone kept encouraging and assuring me that I would indeed receive it soon, because it was a promise from God. Their words were a tremendous comfort.

On Friday night our church was hosting the 'fellowship

meeting' for the churches of our 'section.' I wasn't sure what a 'section' was, but learned from Larry that it was mainly made up of the Tulsa area churches and some of the outlying small town churches who believed in obeying Acts 2:38.

I was still in shock that of all places on earth for me to land—it was in a church that believed what Brother Wiley had worked so hard to convince me of. All I could keep saying over and over was, "What a good God, what a *good, good* God!"

At the meeting I again sat on the back row with Larry while the church filled up with visiting 'saints' (I found out that's what Christians are called—even when they're alive) and I was excited about seeing and meeting all these wonderful people.

Not all of the saints were quite as excited to see me, because of my long hair, even though I had went out and got a haircut. Now, instead of my hair being to the middle of my chest, it was only down to the bottom of my chin. I thought that it was a great step forward while my pastor said that, "Any step forward is great—however small." I wasn't sure what all he meant by that, but I took it as a compliment.

Anyway, the saints gathered, and sang, and worshipped and I felt as if I belonged. It is a truly *wonderful* thing to feel that you belong to something clean and holy, that won't get you thrown in jail or leave you with a hangover! I was finally a part of a church! Well, almost—I did know that I still needed the Holy Ghost.

Some lady named 'Sister Johns' played the piano and sang a song all by herself without everybody else singing along. That was the first time in my very short church life that I'd seen that, but I thought it was really very nice... *and* I absolutely fell in love with the song. I didn't know the name of it, but the words were forever etched in my mind. They were;

> *"Jesus... Jesus... Jesus,*
> *There is something about that name...*
> *Master, Savior, Jesus,*
> *Like the fragrance after the rain...*
> *Kings and Kingdoms, they'll all pass away...*
> *but there's something... about... that name..."*

I wept like a baby when I heard her sing and could hardly stand it when she stopped.

A man named Brother Bass was leading the service and in the course of it kept making reference to our church being 'Home Missions.' Like many of the words used in these peoples' vocabulary, I had no idea what 'Home Missions' meant. When I asked Larry he said it meant 'small.' That didn't sound quite right to me and I determined to ask Brother Moss what was really intended by the phrase.

We came to a place in the service when Brother Bass had one of the preachers take up the offering. Larry told me that this preachers name was Bryant. He thought that his first name was Obid or Orville or something. I was running very low on money, as I had spent almost everything my mother had given me, and I didn't have a job (though Brother Moss highly recommended that I get one—soon). He said it would help me to stay out of trouble.

As the collection plate went by, I put in a quarter, which left me with a dollar to my name. It was at the point that Larry began to tell me what a *really neat* church this was, and that when it came to the offering—and I quote—"It's really neat, if you have money, you put it in—if you need money, you take it out." I thought that was indeed a *very* neat thing—but when I tried it a few months later, the results were far less than desirable, even though I tried to be subtle about it.

After the offering was over, it was time for preaching! Though I'd only been in three services in our church, I already was in love with the preaching part. It was an absolutely, fabulous way to learn so much, so fast, and so easy! I couldn't believe my eyes when, the night before I had actually seen a man sleeping during the preaching and told Steve that I thought he was dead. *I truly thought the man was dead.* Steve told me that he was dead 'after a fashion' but that he wasn't ready for morgue quite yet. When he woke up, and I realized he had been asleep, I was stunned. How could anyone sleep through this kind of preaching! It still amazes me how ignorant I was in those days.

The man who preached that Friday night was named Brother

Hobbs. He was an elderly man, probably in his fifties… maybe even early sixties, (I really was ignorant) and I will never forget what he preached that night. His message was on 'Jesus, the Rock of our Salvation.'

If anyone on earth needed to hear about "THE ROCK," it was me. As he preached I finally comprehended that night, for the first time, that I would never ever make on my own strength or resolve. The only way possible to make it from here to Glory was through the power of Jesus Christ and His Spirit in our lives. We must have the Rock! It was like music to my ears. Failures like me always need to know there is hope… and that night I saw it clearly; Jesus and *His strength* were my *only hope*.

When Brother Hobbs concluded his message, I looked at Larry, Steve and Eddie and said, "I am going down to the altar… and I *am going* to receive the Holy Ghost."

And I did.

After praying but a few minutes with my hands lifted and worshipping, I began to feel Him just exactly like I did so many times in my bedroom in Pueblo. My mouth began to quiver and my tongue began to start losing control… and I'd stop… and make myself say clearly; "Thank… you… Jesus. I… thank… you… Jesus." Then, after a little bit, I'd start stammering some more…till I'd stop and get it back under control.

Finally, a small man that attended our church by the name of Danny, said into my ear, "Larry, let go! That's God trying to give you the Holy Ghost! Don't stop Him… let it go, don't keep it straight… let it go, that's Him… trust Him, He wants to give you the Holy Ghost!"

The next time He began to 'take over' I let Him finish. I began speaking in other tongues powerfully… wonderfully… beautifully! It literally was like a river of living water flowing up and out of my innermost being, and words cannot express how much I loved it! After all this time, and all the experiences I'd had… I had finally received the priceless gift of the Holy Ghost.

The **q** and the **U** had finally come together.

***

A few weeks after receiving the Holy Ghost, we experienced

another gully-washer of a rain storm. We had by this time moved into a much larger house on Maple Street, one with a covered porch with a swing on it. More importantly, it was much closer to church. It was late afternoon when I heard the rain begin to fall and I went out to sit in the swing and watch it. In very short order it became every bit as fierce a storm as the one I'd experienced that first night in town—lightning, thunder and all.

Presently, I decided that this was too good to miss, and, as you only live once anyway, sat down on the steps leading to the sidewalk and proceeded to get soaked to the bone. I was loving every minute of it and presently began to worship God while I sat soaking in the torrent. As the lightning and thunder appeared more frequently and in greater volume so my excitement and praise increased accordingly. The more its ferocity continued, the more I was swept up in worshipping God and in enjoying the grandeur of the storm.

Then a flash of lightning appeared that was instantly followed by a powerful crack of thunder—but it was different—very different—more different than I'd ever experienced in my life. The difference was that the lightning was not 'white' in color… it was red. ***Red*** mind you! Then another stroke of lightning… and it was *blue*… another… *green*… another… white… then *green*… then *red*… then *red* again… then *blue*… then *green*… *then* white.

By that time I was screaming, not out of fear, but because I was about to explode with excitement. "Larry!" Larry!" I shouted at the top of my lungs, "Larry come here!"

Larry came sauntering out, in his slow, almost lazy way, with a book hanging in one hand and working a toothpick with the other, and said, "Whassup?" Before I had a chance to answer, another flash of *blue* lightning hit. I hoped with all my heart that Larry would see the phenomena that he might at least confirm that I wasn't losing my mind. He did and I wasn't.

Immediately Larry's book and toothpick hit the porch as his eyes and mouth shot wide open. I began laughing out of pure joy. Then came another bolt—and it was green, then another…red… another… white… and on and on and on.

Larry walked slowly down the steps as if in a dream and out onto the grass lifting his hands into the air and praising God. As I was already soaked to the bone, I joined him in the middle of the front yard and we began to carry on like drunk men in the middle of the unbelievable light show and downpour.

Little did we know that we were providing entertainment for a family across the street. A forty-year-old father of four, Larry Edwards had approached his living room picture window to watch the downpour when he spotted, first Larry and then me as we made our way into the front yard. He couldn't believe what he saw and began calling for the family to come and "Get a load o' this… there are two lunatics out there in the rain, jumpin' up and down screamin!"

Mr. Edward's house was across the street from us and two houses down so he really did have an almost 'front row seat' to our carryings on. Had we known they were looking—it would have made no difference in the least—we were lost to the event. Between the lightning, the rain, and the presence of God we were oblivious to the world.

One of Mr. Edward's daughters, Nancy, was effected in a manner different than was the rest of her family. Nancy had been home for a week from the Eastern State Hospital—mental ward, in Vinita, Oklahoma. She was a patient there and would have to go back in another week. Only sixteen, Nancy had already developed an addiction for speed that had left her life a wreck. Between bouts of drug binges, depression, nerves, and paranoia that would leave her incapacitated, she had come to the place that she'd had to be committed. She had been released for a two week leave to be with her family, but had already decided that maybe she, ought to go back early… "like maybe tomorrow."

As she stood there that day watching two crazies worship God in the middle of a storm, she became entranced. She intuitively knew somehow that, "Whatever they're doing out there… God has something to do with it."

There we were, laughing, screaming, worshipping, clapping our hands in applause at the wonderful works of God, soaking wet and loving every minute of it. The word *ecstasy* cannot begin to convey the glory and joy we were feeling.

Then Larry lifted his voice, called my name and yelled, "***Just think, Jesus is the most powerful name in the universe***!"

Exactly as it was my first night—and storm in Bartlesville—at that split-second, a streak of lightning shot down in front of us. Halfway down its run, it ***exploded*** in a huge ball of light that looked as if it had been shot straight at us—and then continued its run. Though all of this took place in a literal 'flash' of time, we saw it nonetheless.

But that alone was *not the impressive thing*—it was the unmitigated ***sound of the explosion***—louder, yea even louder than what I'd heard on my first night in town, and all of this together was entirely too much. In total fear and awe, I fell on my face in the muddy lawn like a dead man. I have never been so frightened in my entire life and thought that the end of the world had come. I kept my face buried in the mud and refused to look up, grabbing handfuls of grass and mire with both hands. Larry—while not going all the way to his face—was rocked to the soul and frightened to his toenails.

Across the street (according to Nancy) Mr. Edwards and his family were howling at the two crazies that had moved into the neighborhood. That is, they all were but for Nancy. As for her, she had tears streaming down her cheeks and silently prayed; "God… Oh God… if what those boys have is real… please God, please give it to me also."

The next morning I heard I knock at our door. I opened it to find a small teenage girl with black hair, wire rimmed glasses and big cheeks standing with a very nervous smile on her face. I said "Hello," and she did the same, but then said nothing more.

I finally asked, "Can I help you?"

"I think so."

"Uhh…yes, and how is that?"

"Do… do you go to church?" My eyes opened wide, my head jerked back, and I said, "Why yes… yes! I sure do!"

"Where is it… the, the church that you go to?"

"It's down this street two blocks, then you go left two streets, turn right and it's on the right... second building on the right... right next to the house on the corner.

"Would it be okay if I went to church with you?"

Nancy came to church with Larry and I the next morning and received the gift of the Holy Ghost and was Baptized in the Name of Jesus Christ for the remission on her sins. When she went back to the State Hospital the following Saturday the faculty there immediately noticed a change in her, analyzed and sent her home the next day with the statement that she was in a better state emotionally than most of the staff that watched over her. And then, much later, her little Sister Cheryl followed her steps and also found God.

*"Just think, Jesus is the most powerful name in the universe!"*

***

In the days and months following, our church began to experience a real growth of young people coming in. One of the girls that came in was named Pam. She was a rather small girl, about my age, with light brown hair to her shoulders—which made it a little longer than mine. That is until my second and third, yea even fourth haircut. [Brother Moss said I reminded him of the man that owned a dog with an infected tail that needed to be removed. Rather than put him through any unnecessary pain—he cut it off a little bit at a time.]

At any rate, Pam was a feisty character who showed up one night with a friend named Karen. They both received the Holy Ghost and were baptized in the cow pond and were coming on like gang busters for Jesus—especially Pam.

One night after church, we were all sitting around eating chips, swigging Pepsi and talking about the goodness of the Lord, when the thought kept ragging at my mind that I'd known Pam or seen her somewhere before. Finally I said to her, "Pam, you look familiar... have we ever met somewhere before, you know, before we got in church?"

"Ya know Larry, I've been wondering the same thing. Were you raised here in Bartlesville?"

"No, I was born and raised in Colorado."

"Colorado!" she exclaimed, "I used to live in Colorado! I lived in Boulder during the summer of 71."

Instantly we both jumped up from where we were sitting and I began to scream

"YOU SPIT ON ME!" Whereupon she screamed back, "YOU DESERVED IT YOU JERK!'

Pam was the girl on The Hill, in Boulder, Colorado, that was pan-handling for money… the one that I told to "Get a job," which provoked her to say some not so nice things about my geneology, and who, when I turned away lest I slug her, proceeded to spit on me.

Now here we were, hundreds of miles away from Bolder physically and thousands of miles away spiritually, both baptized in Jesus Name and filled with the Holy Ghost. All we could say from that point on was;

"What a good God… what a *good, good* God!"

Indeed, I was learning everyday that He was not only *good*, He was amazing.

After that we all laughed, prayed, and worshipped. After a while Larry looked at me and said, "You know Larry, we made a pledge to each other years ago that if one of us ever became rich, we'd find the other and support him. Well, I became rich first… and here we are."

*"What a good God… what a good, good God!"*

***

I wish I could tell you that after I received the Holy Ghost, *everyday* was pure victory, and that *no days* offered up trials and disappointments, but that would not be factual, nor would it be spiritually realistic. Jesus said, *"In the world ye shall have tribulation, but be of good cheer, I have overcome the world."* And, regardless of any trial, I knew that my very worst day with Jesus was a thousand times better than my best days in the world without Him. It was on one of these 'not so great days' that Jesus gave me one of the most powerful epiphanies of direction for my life.

I went to church one Thursday night very, very low. I entertained no thoughts whatsoever of leaving God, but as to who I was, and what I was supposed to become, I had few ideas and no clues.

That night my pastor preached on the revelation of God in Christ. I had heard variations of this beautiful doctrine before that night and absolutely loved it—"*To whit that* ***God was in Christ*** *reconciling the world* ***unto himself***." It was during this sermon, that my Friend, that sticks closer than a brother, visited me.

My Bible was spread out on my lap as I tried hard to follow Brother Moss' message as close as possible. Still unfamiliar with the location of most of its books I fell behind pretty quickly. Most services, I'd carry a 'Big Chief' tablet to church and write down every verse that was mentioned. Then I'd go home, look them all up, and make notes or write down questions to plague my poor pastor with. This night however, I hadn't brought my tablet, and having barely made it myself, fought hard to force my mind not to dwell on my doubts and fears.

About half way through the message I looked down at my Bible and a most precious thing happened—I absolutely, unequivocally, and forever—fell in love with it. I actually felt as if I was falling into its pages as one would fall into a giant pool of warm, inviting, crystal-clear water. I started weeping as I stared down at the pages of that wonderful Book and knew then and there what my life's work would be.

I knew it would be spent... preaching this glorious gospel.

***

I got a job! I had been doing a lot of small spot jobs in order to make ends meet, but I finally found a permanent job! It was helping to hang drywall for a man in his late twenties by the name of Gene. I had never hung drywall before, but got the job based on the fact that I'd been a carpenter's helper in Pueblo—for angry Jack. [I still wondered from time to time whatever happened when they turned the water on.]

I more or less liked my boss, even though he could be as mean as a snake. Even at that, I could see the providence of God in my working for him. Gene taught me patience like few people have ever taught me patience—and I desperately needed the lessons.

My boss, as it turned out, did not like Christianity or Christians, and when he found out I was one—life took a new turn. There were days, when he was in an exceptionally foul mood, that he would lean up against the wall and curse me, *profoundly*, for forty-five minutes at a stretch. He would curse my drywalling abilities (which, granted, were meager) as well as the fact that I was wasting his time (I guess while he wasted his time cursing me). Had Gene done this to me before I'd received the Holy Ghost, I have not a shred of doubt that I would have used my hammer to beat him half to death. As it was... I was now a Christian... and had to;

"*Bless them* (Gene) *that curse you* (me), *and pray for them* (Gene) *which despitefully use you* (me)."

"*And unto him that smiteth thee on the one cheek offer also the other...*"

*(Luke 6:28-29)*

Believe me it was not easy. But God knew what Larry Booker needed, and what he would face in the future. I now look back to those days and say;

"What a *good* God, what a *good, good* God!"

One morning, well before daylight. Gene picked me up to work a house in Dearing, Kansas. I slid sleepily into the truck while Gene almost immediately put an 8-track cassette into his tape player. I no longer listened to 'worldly music,' *especially* the stuff that I used to listen to before I received the Holy Ghost. Gene knew this and loved to torment me with it.

I did not give up my old music because of anything I'd heard preached, but rather because of an experience that I had one afternoon in our apartment about two weeks after I'd received the Holy Ghost. I lay down on the bed and closed my eyes to try to take a short nap. Eddie was nearby, sitting in a chair with his feet propped up on a table reading, when I began to hear a song produced by the rock group, Grand Funk Railroad. I knew the song very well and it was one of the bands few 'mellow' songs. I heard it completely, every single note and word from start to finish. When it was over I said to Eddie, "Man, wasn't the pretty?"

"Wasn't what pretty?"

"The song."

"What song?"

"The song Eddie… the song by Grand Funk."

"Larry, I don't know what you're talking about."

With that, I opened my eyes and realized that the radio was not playing. I had taken it for granted that Eddie had turned on the radio. I quickly sat up and began looking around somewhat alarmed. "Eddie, tell me, you didn't hear anything? No music at all?"

"No… not at all," answered Eddie, eyeing me closely.

*In that instant, I realized that the rock music world was a far more 'spiritual' world than I'd given it credit for. But it was a dark spiritual world that was from that moment eradicated from my world.*

My boss Gene, well aware of how I felt about that kind of music—could care less. In fact, he would do his best to taunt me with it. On this particular morning he put in a tape that he said was new to him. It was 'Paul McCartney and Wings,' which thankfully, was not quite as 'funky' as some others he had.

As we drove down the road headed for Dearing that morning, my thoughts were on God and how very good and unbelievably merciful He had been to me. I thought about how many times I should have been killed, but He had spared me. I thought about all the drugs, the booze, the fights, and all of the wickedness that I'd committed… and yet… here I was, baptized in His name and filled with His wonderful Spirit.

As I thought on these things, I began to feel Him. I began to feel His presence come into the truck in a marked way. I was feeling Him wonderfully, and sweetly, and beautifully. I looked to see if Gene was aware of His presence but he was oblivious and simply drove on, beating time on the steering wheel and swinging his head to the music. "How could he not feel what was happening?" I wondered. Then I felt Him in even greater power. Joy was now *flooding* my soul, my mind, my heart and spirit. And it kept getting richer and more powerful by the second. I finally told God, "If this keeps up I am going to have a shouting fit right here in this truck—in front of Gene no less!" I then felt His glorious presence sweep in more powerfully still. It was absolutely, unmitigated joy. In fact it was ecstasy.

It was then that I heard the music playing... exactly the same... I felt His Glorious presence... exactly the same... and I turned my head.

I was now looking out of a truck window seeing a sight that I had seen one year before, while on opium, in Alan's dorm in Boulder. I now saw the *large, beautiful green meadow with gold flowers scattered about. At the back of the meadow were huge clusters of trees with a gorgeous array of branches and foliage. Coming up over the tops of the trees was the sun in all of its glory. The music was playing in my ears but was incidental to the monumental overwhelming emotion of rapturous delight... the likes of which I had never known before.*

At that instant, I began to cry... not out of sorrow, but out of thankfulness of heart that I never knew could exist. At that moment, looking at that meadow, God let me know that what I was looking for in my summer of 1971, on The Hill, in Boulder Colorado, while on opium, in Alan's Dorm... was not ever going to be found in drugs, or in anything else this world had to offer. What I had been looking for all of my life**...** *I had finally found in Jesus Christ and in His love for me.*

That He would stop, reach, and save the likes of someone like me—a messed up boy with a messed up life—is truly something beautiful to behold...

***and worth telling.***
***It was, after all, The Journey of a Lifetime!***

The song says it best;

*"Something beautiful... something good...*
*All my confusion... Jesus understood...*
*All I had to offer Him... was brokenness and strife...*
*But He made something... beautiful... out of my life..."*

The Beginning...

Author's note: I finished this manuscript on Easter Sunday morning, 2002. It was not until that moment that I realized that, it was Easter Sunday, thirty years ago that I repented of my sins and was Baptized in the Name of Jesus Christ for their remission. At that point… I began to… cry.

# Epilogue

As of this writing, the events that you have just read took place over thirty years ago. The axiom, 'Time tells all,' is true. I have believed for years that had I not surrendered myself to God that I would have without question ended up in one of three places: a mental institution, a penal institution, or the grave... and hell.

As I look at my friends and what the years have wrought in their lives, I cannot but pause and say, "Thank you, God for your mercy to me." After all, I didn't have to end up a Minister of the Gospel, with a beautiful family, wonderful church, and more than heart could wish. It could have just as easily:

--Blown my mind on drugs… like ________ and ________

--Been strung out on heroin… like ________

--Been beaten to death with a baseball bat like ________

--Spent time in prison… like ________ and ________

--Died in prison from knife wounds… like _______

--Been killed in motorcycle accidents like… _______ and _______ and _______

--Died in car accidents like… _______, and ______, and _______

--Ended up an alcoholic like… ________ and ________ and _______

--Died of cirrhosis of the liver like… _____ and _______

--Been killed by the Mafia like… ________

--Been killed by the Police like… ________

--Spent my life in and out of mental institutions like… _____

--Died of an overdose like… ___________

--Have the mind of a ten year old like… ____ due to a head shot from a policeman's gun

--Died a suicide like… _____

--Been divorced several times like… ________ and ________ and______ and ______ and______ and_______ and _____ ____ and on and on and on…..

Except for three blank lines in the last sentence (divorce), every vacant space in this list can be filled in by the name of a person whom I have mentioned in this book. The *only* reason that I do not 'fill in the blanks,' is that I want my friends that are still alive to be saved—not hurt or offended. Believe me—this is not a comprehensive list.

Nor do I wish to imply that all of my friends are upon the 'trash pile of life.' Several of them, as far as this world is concerned, have 'made it.' Many eventually settled down, hold employment and became good citizens. Some are quite successful and even a few are rich. I hope however, they understand and forgive me when I say, "I am the richest of them all." By the Grace of God, I possess:

"...the peace of God, which passeth all understanding... through Christ Jesus." Philippians 4:7

***

Only eternity will reveal the true value of prayer. And certainly, only eternity will be able to tell the whole story of Steve Mooney's prayer in the summer of 1971 at William's Creek, Colorado. I do know that through the years I have met or heard of others who traversed 'The Hill' in Boulder back in those days of decadence. These also were the recipients of that prayer, as well as, God only knows, who else's. I must here speak of Donald and Rachel Crum who pastored in Boulder during those crazy years, and of the literally hundreds of troubled youth they worked with and helped. Sister Crum recently told me that those were the most fulfilling days of her life.

From public forums I have told of this portion of my life and of Steve Mooney's prayer, only to be approached afterwards and to hear, "I was there during those days of insanity! But now I'm baptized in Jesus' Name and filled with the Holy Ghost!"

I need to tell of:

Roberta Boutwell Melwood, saved in 1983 of Calgary, Alberta Canada.

Lee Smith Tucker, of Alabama, who was saved in November of 1999.

Steve French of Lees Summit, Missouri, saved in Germany in 1975.

Philip Day of Denver, Colorado, saved in 1975.

As well as others who I have as yet been unable to contact.

All whom God saw, and loved, and saved.

An intriguing event, that I learned of while in the process of compiling these names, is that in 1961, Pastor Don Haymon of Denver, took Evangelist Verbal Bean (mentioned in chapter three) and his mother Bernice up to Flagstaff, a scenic point above Boulder. As they overlooked the area and city, Bernice Bean said, "I wonder if anyone has ever wept over this city?" Then she began to weep and pray for the lost souls of Boulder and that region.

No doubt her prayer (as well as others, including Steve Mooney's) were and are still being heard. One of the recipients of these prayers was John Chris Knott, who was saved in 1969. John was a hippy who had slept under a make-shift plastic tent for eight months in Boulder Canyon. Today, he lives for God and is a successful businessman in Denver.

I entitled my first book, "What a Difference a Line Can Make." Well… now I say, "What a difference the Cross can make." It is my prayer that this book will somehow make a difference in your life and that you will understand that, "If God could save and change Larry Booker… he can save and change anyone."

God Bless You is my prayer.
Larry L. Booker

# Appendix

## Chapter One—The Girl

The trip with my father took place about eight to nine months before my grandfather died. He was, as stated, convalesced at the time of our trip due to poor health and no longer lived at the "*hodge-podge, junkyard, garden, alfalfa patch and boys dream.*" My grandmother, Rena McBeth was born in 1895 and passed away in 1965. Joseph Lincoln McBeth, born in 1892, passed away during the time of my 'repentance' recorded in chapter five and six. He died on January 22, 1972, two days after I'd seen the q/U vision (depicted almost *exactly* as I saw it on the back cover of this book).

Mom, Buzz and I had gone to see my grandfather in the nursing home. The home had notified us that he would be passing very soon, he was in a comatose state, and had for days responded to nothing. When I took him by the hand and began to pray for him, he literally jerked his hand out of mine. I continued to pray however that he would "give his heart to the Lord," (which was all I knew to do at the time). We left and came back that afternoon.

After my parents left the room, I took my grandfather's hand and prayed once more. This time, rather than pull away, he squeezed my hand and held on to it. Again, it was the only movement he'd shown in days. I was the last one to see him alive as shortly after I left the room he passed away. In his own way my Grandpa showed me that I was at least headed in the right direction. He was a tough, neat man—and I loved him.

"Arvie" is not *quite* my "Aunt Arvella's" real name… but very close. I just felt like using the name Arvie. She is a neat lady, a wonderful aunt and has been good to me all of my life. I hope I didn't hurt anyone's feelings when discussing 'Roger'—not *his* real name… but we just didn't jive real well when we were young. Her daughter Carol, not mentioned in the book, but her real name nonetheless—was for years my best friend on earth when we were little.

'Molly Mae' was *not* the name of *the girl* I met that day. I refrained from giving her real name for several reasons. First, she is still alive, and married with children. For over thirty years I was under the impression, left by my Aunt Arvie, that Molly was mentally—six' years old. It was not until I began writing this book that (out of curiosity) I found out that she was 'twelve' years of age mentally (still is). However she was eventually able to 'graduate' from high school as well as get married.

Also, much of this chapter's dialogue—as well as all others—has of necessity been reconstructed due to a thirty-two year time lapse. I obviously was not into 'taking notes' or compiling a diary of my daily dealings. Any errors in reconstruction, are just that, errors. These are largely due to the lengthy time lapse, and in greater part to my almost constant condition of being drunk or stoned. Truly, one of the great miracles that God performed was in keeping my mind intact. Before I began taking drugs I had an almost perfect memory, and though it is not as sharp as it was—He has had tremendous mercy on me in that regard.

As for the actual details of the car accident that caused Molly's 'handicap,' I do *not* know them, nor did my family. To avoid any unnecessary pain to 'Molly' by 'digging about,' I created the flow and pathos of the narrative, including her sister and her death. Again, though I do not have the details, it was *indeed,* a car accident that left her impaired.

Aunt Arvie's news of Molly's malady affected me as deeply as portrayed. I was truly desperate for innocence, simplicity and purity. In other words, I was truly sick of myself, wanted to change, and seriously thought that perhaps this girl's innocence could help me get my life on track. That it could never be, that I *thought* her trapped in a six year old mentality, tore my emotions to pieces. I now wonder—so deep was my desire to change—what I would have done had I *known* she was 'twelve' mentally. For sure, God knew best, and knew how to use my 'misinformation' to eventually accomplish His will.

Though I 'recovered' *through partying*, I never forgot her, nor her effect on me. In fact, several years ago I told Rev. Murrell Ewing—pastor, singer and songwriter—the story of 'Molly' thinking that he and his wife Joan might even write a song about it. (They both being *lovers of stories and of emotions of the heart.*) Smile.

Throughout the book I have used, the actual names of my friends. In only a few cases have I included their last names, or in some cases, changed their last names slightly. In those few cases where I have used different names, or changed a name slightly—I have very good reasons for doing so. This, after all, is my story and is not meant to expose or hurt others. If the characters presented ever read this narrative, rest assured they will recognize themselves. I sincerely pray they do. May they all rest assured—I love them dearly.

Also, 'Scotty' was not the name of Molly's dog. I cannot remember the dog's name as I had no interest in *him*. But my brother Phil and I used to have an Alaskan malamute named Scotty, when "*we were little, and lived in Canon City*," who was one of the best dogs a pair of boys could ever have. I named Molly's dog in his honor.

## Chapter Two—The Journey

My 1957 Plymouth was ever bit as bad a car as described. Rocco, did not actually fall out of the car on *this journey*. He performed that feat earlier at the Grub Steak one night. It was far too funny a scene to leave out, and was easy to slip in at that juncture, but was not funny enough to devote a whole section to.

The day after I traded the Plymouth for the opium, I saw the hippy with whom I'd made the trade. He was not a 'happy camper,' and felt that I'd ripped him off. All things considered—I still think it was a pretty fair transaction—and, after all, both items were 'outlawed currency' spent by outlaws.

The 1956 station wagon that we drove to Pierre, South Dakota belonged to one of Tyrone's and JoJo's friend from the orphanage who actually came with us. The problem is (like a few other people in the book) I could not remember his name. Rather than invent a name for him, as I have done in other similar incidents, I just left him out. One such case where I had to invent the name is, "Taber," Joe's friend of chapter six. In 'Taber's' case however, he was so 'close mouthed' that I might have never known his name to begin with. And, whatever name he may have used, there's a good chance it wasn't his real name anyway. A large number of people I met back then used nicknames or assumed identities.

## Chapter Three—Boulder

The dialogue of the Mooney family was reconstructed after discussions with Steve and his mother and father. All pertinent points happened as told, and this narrative and dialogue was approved by Steve before publishing.

Steve and I did not meet until a few years ago in Hurst, Texas. His mother and father had earlier heard a portion of my testimony in a message that I preached at the Texas Camp Meeting entitled, "You Just Never Know," and had taken a copy of the tape to Steve.

Steve listened to the tape while lying on his bed in what was a very sad time of his life. When he heard me telling about Boulder, Colorado and 'The Hill,' Steve jumped from his bed and began to worship and praise God. Finally, after all these years, he understood the Spirit of travail that came upon him that morning at Williams Creek. Shouting his thankfulness to God, he kept repeating, "Larry Booker was saved as a result of that prayer!"

Little did he know (or do we yet know) how many others would also be saved.

In fact, it is his and the author's desire to know ***of any others*** *who are today saved who lived a hippy existence in Boulder during that approximate time*. If you do know of anyone, could you please contact me at the address, or E-mail given in the front of this book.

Neither Steve nor I realized till after I'd written this chapter that the family vacation that took them through Boulder actually took place in the summer of 1970. I did not change the chapter as this poses no real problem. Prayers never die, and they *were* and are *still* being answered. Also, I had been up to 'The Hill' several times during those years to get drugs, and was there at least twice in the summer of 1970. I just did not 'move there' till 1971.

The story of "Birdie" is actually a compilation of two characters that I used to hang around with. Birdie, was a boy in our class who had a twin brother named "Peepie," who both looked just as I described him. He was entirely 'capable' of the incident, and 'guilty' of much more. I really just wanted to include his name somewhere. He moved from South Hugh School, went to Central High and became a nemesis.

The perpetrator of the 'tire slashing' was a guy nicknamed "Petrol head" (for all the inhalants he used to whiff). He actually went to East High School, his real name was Cecil—I cannot reveal his last name, and you'll soon see why—and was two years older than myself.

Some time after I was saved, Cecil sold almost all his parent's household furniture while they were out of town on vacation—for drug money. When his father challenged him, he beat his father to the point of hospitalization, and carnally attacked his own mother.

A drug-wrecked life can become a most heartbreaking, tragic and sordid affair.

## Chapter Four—Pueblo

'Jack' is not the real name of the General Contractor. My understanding is that through the years he 'mellowed' quite a bit, became quite successful in construction and was actually a nice man who became a good friend of my brother Phil. [I still have a morbid curiosity about what happened when they turned the water on in the apartment complex.]

The downtown area of Pueblo has changed markedly since I lived there. Due to street renovations young people can no more 'Drag Main' (even if they wanted to). The Union Street area where we used to drink with the winos has also been renovated into a much nicer commercial area with a river walk.

As an interesting note, my brother Phil drove me downtown a few years ago and as we passed by the corner on Union, where we used to get drunk with the winos, I asked him to pull over. I got out, sat down on the curb and let my mind roam back over the past and God's mercy to me. As I started to rise, I looked down, and there between my feet—was a cork to a bottle of cheap wine. It reinforced one more time… God has truly had mercy on Larry Booker.

'Pete' is not the real name of the friend who stole my father's soldering bits. Again, as my intention is *not* to hurt, I modify the names of some of the people.

## Chapter Five—Denver

I never told the Howsing Enterprizes (not the real name of the company) that I was officially quitting, nor that I was leaving Denver, as to be honest—I couldn't face 'Mrs. Howsing.'

'Robert Clarry' was more real than I've portrayed him, but again, it is not his real name.

The 'church service' morning orientations were every bit, if not more 'churchy' than depicted. It really was a hoot!

I have met individuals that, in days gone by, used to sell Kirby Vacuum's that remember using the 'Kirby Songbooks.' Please, if anyone knows where I could possibly buy or get one—I would

***love*** to possess one. Also, the 'Kirby lyrics' were the best I could come up with—but the actual lyrics were little better.

All statements made to Tyrone, Lyle and Charles on the morning of my repentance are almost exact quotes. I was indeed, "*...going to Aspen, to write my life story. Or... down to Guadalajara, Mexico, to sit on the white sands and write my life story. Or... going to college and I'm going to learn how to write.*" That it would take me thirty years to do so is shocking. It is shocking that it took so long... and it is equally shocking that I did it at all.

After entering the ministry, this project virtually became a lost cause through the decades. In fact, I almost stumbled into it. When I wrote originally wrote Chapter One, The Girl, it was going to be a story within itself and end there. When I'd finished, and read it a few times, I decided to go on and finish the entire story of how I came to God—or rather how God brought me to Him. Believe me, the journey still amazes me.

I eventually (after I got in church) did pay my father for both the Spitfire, the insurance and a good sum of accumulated interest and inflation. Thank God! Buzz, in his exceeding kindness and thankfulness for the change in my life, insisted that I not pay him back—but I was very relieved and happy to be able to do so. And really... so was he.

P.S. After all these years, I still miss that car.

## Chapter Six—College

Mr. Gonzales, is not the real name of my probation officer. The reason I do not use his name here is that I really did like the man, he was basically good at his job, but was eventually fired. It seems that his 'credentials' has been faked and was not legally qualified for the position though he'd held it for many years. I liked him and thought the whole thing a real sad affair. The probation officer that I liked best of all however was an older man named Rusty. I cannot recall his last name, but he was a great guy and somewhat of a 'fixture' in Pueblo.

It was a couple of years after coming to Bartlesville that I found out that Norma's father was paying my way through college. The sad part is, I put off thanking him until I felt that I could do it in 'grand style,' and had really 'made something' of myself. When he passed away of a sudden heart attack, I felt terrible and immediately called his wife to express to her my condolences and to thank her from the depths of my heart for being so good and kind to me. They were truly wonderful people and were genuinely thankful for the change in my life. They loved me and I loved them—I just wish I could have shown them how much.

R.P. Dickey was more real than I've depicted him. He was one of the most powerful personalities, with one of the most powerful intellects that I've ever met. He did in fact cause me to fall in love with words and their power. When I received the Holy Ghost, and the Bible came *alive* to me, I could not but help but inspect its *words* and try to fathom the reason that God (or even the translators) put that particular *word* on that particular spot. Again, R.P. Dickey helped me tremendously. I couldn't help but respect him, though I didn't care for some of his ways. The sad thing is… I really wish we could have been friends.

The 'garage church' on the east side of Pueblo was as I described it, but "The Disciples" was not what they went by. Actually, I don't think I ever knew what their church name was.

The scriptural dialogue between them and I was obviously reconstructed as best as I could remember, but the salient points were made very clear to me that night.

The Scripture of Romans 10:1-3, were not however pointed out to me that night by Brother Wiley. Almost twenty years after that night, while pasturing in Arroyo Grande, California, and in prayer one night, the presence of God swept into the church auditorium in an astonishing way. In the midst of this presence I asked God what ***He wanted me to say*** to people that asked me about various denominational people who are not baptized in Jesus' name, nor have received the Holy Ghost. He immediately spoke to me those verses. I picked up my Bible to read what they said, and as I opened it, immediately, they were there before me: "*Brethren, my heart's desire and prayer to God for Israel is, that they might be saved. (2) For I bear them record that they have a zeal of God, but not according to knowledge. (3) For they being ignorant of God's righteousness, and going about to establish their own righteousness, have not submitted themselves unto the righteousness of God.*"

I placed these scriptures in Brother Wiley's mouth—because they were so fitting. While he did not officially say them that night, he showed me many other scriptures which I have *not* included. And, these, as well as they, are all—very true!

The leader of this group, was, sad to say, a somewhat arrogant fellow, that I really didn't feel good about, even then. They held some beliefs back then that were... different, and their leader eventually led these sweet people off into the "Yahweh" movement. My understanding is that they have since disbanded.

Brother Wiley treated me as portrayed, and I done my best to treat others the same ever since. I deeply appreciated his kindness, his wisdom, and his forthrightness with the Truth. I was obviously impressed when he began to 'glow,'—which I know now was the *shikinah* presence of God. I have since witnessed this presence several other times, and once saw it on another man while he received the Holy Ghost and spoke in other tongues as the Spirit gave the utterance until five in the morning—whereupon he went home to do it some more.

I wish I knew Wiley's last name. I would love to meet him again. I do know that not too long after he talked to me, (within a year) he left that church. My hope is that he did so in order to retain Truth. God used these dear people, and without them, I wonder if I'd be saved today. However, words cannot express my thankfulness, that in the 'wisdom of God,' I was led into the arms of the church in Bartlesville.

## Chapter Seven—Bartlesville

Some of the best advice Pastor Moss ever gave me concerning

my ministry, had to do with my 'hippy' past. I was young, felt my call to the ministry, was zealous, and hungry to 'go places' in God and in the Kingdom. He sat me down and said, "Son, you are an ex-hippy. If you want to build your ministry upon your testimony and on where you came from, you can. There are people who will use you right now, and take you to 'the top'—wherever that is. Or you can take your time, get your nose in the Bible, pray, and hew you out a ministry in the Word and in the Spirit. If you do that, I think you'll be shocked at how far it will take you, and your ministry will last much longer. There are men who will take you to the top but will drop you like a hot potato as soon as they're through with you."

This was one of the single greatest pieces of advice that I ever received, and I did my best to follow it.

This is one reason why, when I evangelized, I would not give my testimony—if I gave it at all—until I'd been at a church for at least two weeks. I wanted the people to know that my priority was God and His word—not my past. My son Phillip, told me that he never knew why I didn't give my testimony more until he'd read of Pastor Moss' advice. This is also *one* of the reasons that I produced the theological work, "What a Difference a Line Can Make," *before* I wrote this autobiographical sketch of my early life and God's saving power.

The song "Jesus, There's Something About That Name," that was sung the night I received the Holy Ghost was of course written by Bill Gaither, as was the song, "Something Beautiful." To this day, they are both, two of my absolute favorites.

Never did I dream that Orville Bryant, the pastor who took up the offering the night I received the Holy Ghost, would within a year become my uncle by marriage. I married his niece, Brenda Faye Lang, on January 20th, 1973—one year from the day that I saw the **q/U** vision. We chose the date of our wedding for that reason.

How I met Brenda and we came to marry is another fascinating story within itself. But that must be for another time—or perhaps, another book. Suffice it to say that God used Brenda to help remove from me the last remaining vestiges of 'hippydom' as much as He used anything or anyone. This faithful woman and I have now been married for almost thirty years. We have three beautiful sons that love and live for God. Joel Matthew Booker, Larry Andrew Booker, Phillip Wayne Booker and his beautiful wife Katie (who came up with the name for this book) and an adorable grandson, Logan Chase. We also have a beautiful 'adopted' daughter, Andrea, her great husband Robert Carpenter and lovely baby, Hannah Marie.

"What a *good* God, what a *good, good* God!"

*Fishing with a friend on the banks of the Arkansas River (appox. 1957-58)*

*Upon the shoulder of my cousin Bobby Masteller (1960)*

*My brother Phillip Booker on the far left with two friends, I'm on the far right soon after moving to Pueblo from Rye, CO. (1963)*

*Taken during my Senior year at about the time I met 'Molly' (1971)*

*Graduation photo (1971)*

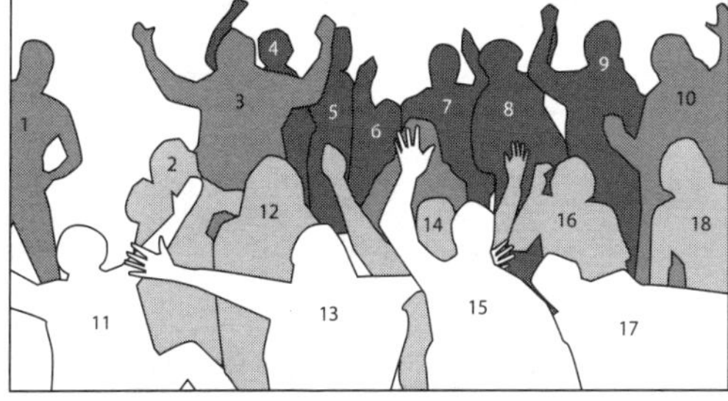


*Taken in the middle of Prarie Avenue.*

| | | |
|---|---|---|
| *1. Edmund "Hair"* | *2. Dennis* | *3. Ambrose Esquibal* |
| *4. Winkleman* | *5. Cliff* | *6. Rick "Z-man" Thomas* |
| *7. Bill* | *8. Frankie* | *9. Frank* |
| *10. John Garza* | *11. Artie* | *12. Alan* |
| *13.* **Larry Booker** | *14. Mike* | *15. Rocky* |
| *16. Bob "Mac"* | *17. Joe Arguello* | *18. Loren Oliver* |

*(Those with last names included are now deceased.)*

*Soon after entering college (January, 1972)*

*My first photo after having received the Holy Ghost in Bartlesville, OK (also after my first haircut) (April, 1972)*

*In Bartlesville, OK after my 4th haircut (June, 1972)*

*One of my earliest discussions of the scriptures (October, 1972)*

*My wife, Brenda and I with Pastor Roy Moss and his wife Barbara (Shortly after our Wedding on January 20, 1973)*

*Rev. Larry Booker delivering the precious Word of God.*

*The beautiful congregation of Inland Lighthouse Church.*

*The Family (left top to right bottom) Sons: Joel, Larry Andrew and Phillip Daughter-in-law: Katie (Phillip's wife) Wife: Brenda, and Larry (taken in 2000).*

# About The Author

Noted evangelist, pastor, Bible teacher and conference speaker, Larry L. Booker came to God in 1972 at the age of 19 in Bartlesville Oklahoma. Though a former slave to drugs and alcohol, he went on to become assistant pastor to Rev. Roy L. Moss. In 1977 he, his wife Brenda, and infant son Joel evangelized until assuming the pastorate of the First United Pentecostal Church in Miami, Oklahoma.

Returning to the evangelistic field in 1981, his family, with two more sons, Phillip and Larry Andrew, spent the majority of the next 3 years in California. In 1984 he became pastor of Gospel Lighthouse Church of Arroyo Grande, California where he served for the next 12 years. During those years, the congregation grew and new facilities were added, including a five story Lighthouse office structure, the only one of its kind in the United States.

He served for several years as the Home Missions Director of the Western District for the United Pentecostal Church International, and is in great demand as a speaker. In 1996 Reverend Booker felt the call to the Inland Lighthouse Church of Rialto, California. Since arriving, the church has grown steadily from under fifty into the hundreds. Pastor Booker has now turned his capable hand to the written word, including the story of his life and deliverance from drugs.